The Hide

MM Gibbons is an English playwright, poet, critic, broadcaster and novelist. His research for The Hide included a calendar year living rough in a Fenland swamp.

Follow his exploits at:

www.mmbooks.net
www.facebook.com/gibbonsmm/

Books by the Same Author

Sonnets to Gertie

Three Days in a Tree

One's Inner Idiot - Biography of FR Spoon

The Shed

The Pavilion

The Ski Lodge

Pandora's Inner Goddess

The Laboratory

MM Gibbons

The Hide

A Comedy of Birders

Press

The Hide

Published by MMX Press, 2017
Copyright © MMX Press, 2017

MM Gibbons has asserted his right under the Copyright, Designs and Patents Act (1988) to be identified as the author of this work.

Most characters appearing in this work are fictitious; any resemblance to real persons, living or dead, is purely coincidental. However, some characters appear as themselves, either by their permission or in some cases, not. The author trusts that these persons will be flattered and amused by their fictional and imagined participation in this comedy.

This book is sold subject to the condition that it shall not, by way of trade or otherwise, be lent, resold, hired out, or otherwise circulated without the publisher's prior consent in any form of binding or cover or electronic format other than that in which it is published and without a similar condition, including this condition, being imposed on the subsequent publisher.

First published in Great Britain and on-line by MMX Press

A subsidiary of MMX Global Ltd
Registered Address:
15 High Street, Brackley
Northamptonshire, NN13 7DH

www.mmbooks.net
www.facebook.com/GibbonsMM/
www.twitter.com/MMGibbons1966

Published by MMX Global Ltd. Reg. No. 10057740
ISBN 978-0-9546514-7-3

Book design by PT Digital www.ptdigitalagency.co.uk
Cover illustration Kit Summerfield © 2017

The Hide
A Comedy of Birders

By MM Gibbons

Illustrated by Kit Summerfield & James Ross-White

"Everyone likes birds. What wild creature is more accessible to our eyes and ears, as close to us and everyone in the world, as universal as a bird?"

David Attenborough
(1926 -)

"Bird-watchers are tense, competitive, selfish, shifty, dishonest, distrusting, boorish, pedantic, unsentimental, arrogant and - above all - envious."

Bill Oddie
(1941 -)

The Cast of Characters

Mr Ron Bullock	Sextenarian retired loafer
Mr Tom De'Ath	Sextenarian retired loafer
Mrs Bella Bullock	Wife to Mr Ron Bullock
Mrs Dot De'Ath	Wife to Mr Tom De'Ath
Basker	The Bullock's bloodhound
Mr Colin Dredge	Bird watcher and twitcher
Professor John Ball	Retired Professor of Chemistry
Sir Humphrey Hedgehog	Mischievous glove-puppet of Prof John Ball
Ms Vera Clapp	Receptionist, Oldshire Wildlife Trust
Mr Aldous Stern, MBE	Chairman of Clarendon Marsh Volunteers
Mr Jack Ward	The Birdman of Clarendon
Mr Arthur Lostweathiel	Proprietor of 'Boptics' and fiddle player of 'The Hurdy-Grinders'
Mr Leonard Bristow	Taxidermist
Ms Bet Flinch	Insouciant waitress
Mr David Smith	Benefactor to Clarendon Marsh
Mr Nigel Shiltberry	Moth expert and hang-glider
Miss Amber Mudd	A beautician
Mr Paul Gascoigne	Retired footballer
Ms Temperance Pychley	Small hotelier and cat fancier
Mr Seaton Pychley	Brother to Ms Temperance Pychley
Puffin Billy	Captain of 'The Glad Tidings'
Mr Fred Hopple	Northumbrian artist
The Parchment Family	Annoying tourists

A Young Couple from Hartlepool	Vapists
The Icelanders	Foreign tourists
Miss Charlotte Bird, MSc.	Farne Islands tour guide and puffin expert
Mr Chris Packman	Naturalist and TV celebrity
Mr Olly Nice	Bird ringer
Mr Bill Oddie, OBE	Writer, composer, musician, artist, ornithologist, television presenter and actor
Miss Clarissa Foxman-Hunt	Fundraiser, Bewick Swan adventure project
Malcolm	Osprey Volunteer
Colonel Sykes CBE	Retired soldier and game shooting enthusiast
The General	Colonel Sykes' Labrador retriever
Mr Maurice Brown	Neighbour to The Bullocks
Sherry	Maurice's border terrier
Mr Sellars	Neighbour to The Bullocks
Mr Cyril Cobbles	A Lancastrian
Master Jocky Flintoff	A mischievous schoolboy
Mr. Fortbrough	School teacher
Mr 'Sonny' Robards	Professional twitcher
Mr David Lindo	Professional birder and writer
Mrs. Winterbottom	Blackpool landlady
Mr Alan Allen	Semi-professional actor and proprietor of 'Make Mine a Murderer Theatre Company'
Sir Ian Botham, OBE	Retired cricketer and game shooting enthusiast
Mr Henry Blacklock	Gamekeeper
Mr Terry Sneddick	Game shooting enthusiast and Ron Bullock doppelgänger

THE HIDE

Mr Hugh Barley-Waters	*Game shooting enthusiast and wine merchant*
Mr George 'One-eyed' Pogson	*Reluctant game shooter*
Joseph	*West Indian butler and chef*
Mr Bill Bailey	*Entertainer and birdwatcher*
Naughty Boy	*Music producer, DJ and amateur golfer*
Master Tanaga Waradi	*Grandson to The Bullocks*
The Hedgepug	*A school bully*
Mr Andi Fox	*An ornithologist and musician*
Miss Lorna Coop	*Playmate to Mr Andi Fox*

THE HIDE

- CHAPTER ONE -

The Observer's Book of Birds

Wherein Messrs. Bullock and De'Ath discover there is more to the thrush than suspected, begin to study garden avi-fauna and to inspect The Observer's Book of Birds. There is a walk on Oldside Common. Professor Ball introduces Clarendon Marsh and Dirty Colin. Birdwatching commences in a hide wherein there is an extraordinary and spectacular accident. They make the acquaintance of The Birdman of Clarendon.

After the disaster and disgrace of The Laboratory, Ron Bullock and Tommy De'Ath were in pursuit of a hobby less ambitious than applied chemistry, and one which would get them "out of the house". Bullock's wife Bella had less than wryly observed that their last indoor hobby had resulted in the near combustion of the De'Ath's house and home, and firmly instructed them both to "get out from under her feet".

A mild spring day found the conspirators in Bullock's lounge, the French windows open to the wan sun of a fresh morning and a dewy lawn, two huge steaming mugs of milky coffee on the low table in front of them, which was asprawl with various hobbyist and sports magazines. The men crouched forward, in postures of concentrated study.

"Pass us a HobNob will yer, lad?" Bullock was thumbing rapidly through the *Practical Photography Magazine* wondering what had become of his Kodak Instamatic and Zenit SLR camera - probably in a box in the loft, he thought.

By way of response, De'Ath distractedly riffled his hand about under a pile of magazines and newspapers concerned with trainspotting and war gaming, attempting to locate the plate of biscuits they had been dunking into their coffee mugs. However, during his careless search, he clumsily knocked the plate, which was buried under *The Angling Times,* off the table and onto the carpet. The oaty HobNobs rolled asunder, but not for long, as Basker the bloodhound, alert to his opportunity, leapt up from his apparent slumber by the hearth.

"alert to his opportunity"

Basker then wolfed up the lot apart from one, which had rolled underneath the sofa. He pawed and mewled to try to reach it.

THE HIDE

"Oh for God's sake Tom, what are you doing throwing the bikkies about, lad?" moaned Bullock. "You can't blame old Basker - 'e never teks from t'plate but if they are strewn about on the floor like that, well that's more than temptation can tek, that is!"

"I didn't throw them on the floor, Ron. Obviously I didn't. You know how partial I am to packet of McVitie's HobNobs. One nibble and you're nobbled, as they used to say. Well, not the chocolate ones, never been bothered about them."

Bullock wasn't listening as he splayed himself out on the carpet and tried to poke out the lost HobNob from beneath the sofa with a carpet slipper. Basker watched eagerly as the biscuit was slowly propelled towards his drooling mouth, but both dog and De'Ath were surprised as Bullock pounced on it first and popped the whole biscuit into his mouth, crunching avidly.

"What?" exclaimed Bullock, in response to the disapproving gazes from both. "I weren't lettin' 'im ave any mower, was I? Now bugger off in the garden Basky and work them biscuits off yer, yer fat greedy beggar!"

Basker slouched off in brooding resentment, feeling robbed and insulted.

"Do you know where the expression hob-nob comes from, Ron?" asked De'Ath, continuing his perusal of *Golfing Monthly.*

"Erm, let's think…hob-nob, well it means to be sociable in't it? Hob-nob with the gentry like - perhaps it means 'upwardly mobile' as they say these days. Prob'ly Shakespeare, I shouldn't wonder?"

"Spot on Ron!" beamed the bearded one. "Shakespeare's *Twelfth Night.* Sir Toby Belch. "Hob, nob is his word." I don't know how they made the leap to biscuits, though."

"Eh, p'raps we should go into amateur dramatics, lad!" Bullock rose from his chair, assuming *dramatis persona,* as he vanished into a draped curtain and emerged with it draped over his shoulder, like a toga.

THE HIDE

"Friends, Romans, countrymen, lend me your ears!
I come to bury Caesar, not to praise 'im.
Erm...the evil that men do lives after them;
Is...erm, summat to do wi' their bones."

"Very good, sir!" applauded De'Ath.

"School play lad, Barnsley Grammar. 1963. Amazing what you remember in't it. Yes, ah reckon ah could tread the boards again, what about thee lad?"

"Not for me I'm afraid, Ron. Apart from being a hopeless actor, I would forget my lines. I would certainly dry up on stage. Terribly embarrassing that would be. And anyway - it's hardly the great outdoors, is it? Our good ladies were very firm on that point."

"Aye, they were, weren't they..." remembered Bullock ruefully, scratching the sandpaper of his jutting miner's chin, and picking up a copy of *BBC Sky at Night Magazine*. The two men returned silently to their search, De'Ath slurping his coffee, to Bullock's mild annoyance.

Outside in the garden, Basker was mooching about in the shrubbery, still sulking about the lost HobNob gobbled up by his master. But then, he was distracted by something rustling about in the dry fallen leaves of the previous winter, and went to investigate. Often there were blackbirds hopping about in there, or sometimes he would encounter a grey squirrel or a hedgehog - and he knew better to play with one of those - squirrels tended to attack him and hedgehogs turned into a sharp ball. So carefully, as far as his huge paws would allow, he crept surreptitiously forward, and as he got closer, he could see that it was not one of those creatures. It was a small spotted bird, and it didn't try to escape - even when he got very close to it. It just looked at him, curiously. It cocked its head, blinked its black eyes and fluttered a bit.

Basker was pleased with this encounter, since most garden wildlife just ran away from him, and never wanted to play. But it seemed this young fellow might be more fun, so Basker took the fledgling bird into his soft mouth and lolloped across the lawn to show off his prize to his master.

THE HIDE

Bounding enthusiastically into the lounge, Basker tossed his prey into the air, whereupon the terrified bird tried to exercise its immature wings and half-flew, half-blithered around the room like a feathery tennis ball, rattling into the TV and then, just like the HobNob, disappeared under the sofa.

"Oh bloody Hell, Basker, what have you brought in? A little bird, oh 'eck! Yer a bloody nuisance this morning, so you are!"

The two men bent down to peer at the young bird, which was a shivering mess of unkempt feathers. Bella bustled in to see what the fuss was about.

"Get Basker out so we can rescue the little birdie, Bella. He's fetched him out of the garden."

"Naughty Basker!" Bella admonished, "what kind is it?"

"I think it's a baby thrush," ventured Tom. "You know, the ones that bash snails on rocks with their beaks. It probably fell out of its nest."

"Right Basker, I am not talking to you now. You are a bad dog. To your basket with you." Basker was hauled reluctantly away to the kitchen by his mistress, feeling rather wronged. He was only playing, after all.

"We'll never poke it out, Tom. Let's get quietly on with our reading and see if it hops out. Ah'll get some bread from t' kitchen and see if it comes out for a feed."

After about half an hour of intermittent cheeping, the bird did venture out from beneath the sofa, and noting that there was no large animal predator about, waddled about the carpet, inspecting the men with a cock of its head and large innocent eyes. It evidently had not yet fully learned the life-preserving concept of fear.

"Aye, it's a thrush alright," whispered Bullock. "But there's two kind tha' knows. Song thrush and mistle thrush. The storm cock, they call the mistle one, cos it sings in bad weather. Hold up though - baby blackbirds look a bit like thrushes, don't they?"

THE HIDE

"Search me. Sounds like you know your birds, Ron, I had no idea there were two kinds of thrush. Ooh look, it's off out."

The fluffy bird didn't have an opinion on its species or much else, and hopped and fluttered across the threshold of the doors and inspected the patio with interest, before waddling onto the lawn.

"Eh! Next door's cat'll 'ave that little feller with Basker locked up. We'd best shoo it back to its nest if we can find it. And we can 'ave a pipe smoke at t'same time."

Pipes loaded and fuming, the pair watched the fledgling blunder to the relative safety of the shrubbery. Bella was also observing its progress from the kitchen window, giving the thumbs up in a pair of pink Marigolds, as she washed up.

"Look over there, Ron," whispered the whiskered De'Ath, pointing with the stem of his briar pipe towards the rockery. "There is an adult thrush over there. Look, it's banging a snail on a rock, just like I was saying!"

"So there is! Goodness, you have sharp eyes, Tom. Or good glasses, any road. Isn't it well camouflaged against them big stones! I reckon that must be the mum. Or the dad. I don't know how to tell. Shall we creep over and see if we can see the nest?"

After much peering into various shrubs, it was Tom who located the nest, deep in a bushy, glossy-leaved laurel. Parting the leaves and branches, he could see a nest of twigs and moss. Two pairs of curious black eyes met his - identical to the ones of their itinerant sibling. De'Ath waved his mate over, whereupon they both inspected the nest, which seemed to have a smooth lining of mud and containing an unhatched turquoise egg spotted with black at the feet of the two chicks. Knowing that the parents could easily be spooked from the nest, the two slowly backed off towards the patio table.

"Eeeh fancy that, Tom!" beamed Bullock, "ah never knew we 'ad breeding thrushes in the garden! Let's stay and watch a while shall we, ah've got a pair o' binoculars 'anging up in t'shed."

THE HIDE

Bullock retrieved a dusty though serviceable pair of Kershaw army binoculars in a brown leather case, and adjusted them to focus on the laurel. He began a whispering commentary in a very bad David Attenborough accent, as if Sir David had been born and raised in Barnsley, instead of Leicester.

"And 'ere we are, observing t'rearing of young…t'parent bird returns to the nest with the snail it smashed on yonder rock. Into t'shrubbery she flies; no doubt to feed the hungry chicks, which surely are about to fledge the nest. We have observed at least two chicks and the third one is about somewhere. This is a most perilous time in a bird's life. Leaving the nest. They think they know what they are doing, but they haven't a clue, much like their human teenage counterparts. We have observed at least one egg not hatched. I wonder why. Perhaps it weren't warm enough…or summat."

De'Ath was much amused by Bullock's impression, and hooted with laughter like a wheezy owl, which set Bullock off. Pretty soon they were laughing and coughing, as they often did when together.

"Eh, haha, Tom, ah'm pretty good at this, aren't ah? They should have me on that Springwatch on the telly shoudn't theh! Them as does it ain't much good that's for sure, have you seen it?"

"Errr…no I don't think I have Ron, we don't tend to watch many nature programmes, Dot and I. I gather it is very popular though."

"Oh yes, millions watch it. But the presenters aren't any use, Packman or summat and some woman who was a dancer. Anyway, here lad, have a butchers with these binocs, 'ere shape, will yer! Put 'em round yer neck. You'll 'ave to adjust 'em for your glasses. I am off to get a reference book which will be very useful to us here. If I've still got it, that is."

Bullock was gone some time. De'Ath observed with quiet delight the adult thrushes disappearing into the laurel bush with worms, shelled snails and grubs, listening to the "chook-chook" scolds of the birds and the quarrelling cheeps of the chicks. He noticed other birds flitting around; he recognized blackbirds, blue tits and a wren and other small birds that were probably sparrows, though not house sparrows, he thought.

A beaming Bullock arrived back with a small brown and battered volume, which he opened and placed triumphantly on the patio table.

"*The Observer's Book of Birds.* Ah knew I had it somewhere, lad! It were under the bed in a box of auld books. Look, there's me name written in it. "Ronnie Bullock, Barnsley, Yorkshire, England, The World, The Solar System, The Universe." Ah must've been about ten when me dad bought me that. Do you know, me and this mate, Tich Sprat, we used to go all over the lanes on our bikes, looking for birds' nests. We used to tek the eggs and blow them, y'know, put a little hole with a needle in both ends and blow the stuff out. We 'ad a little collection in cotton wool in a shoe box, me and Tich. We used to label 'em - pigeons, robins, blackbirds, all sorts. We were quite good me and Tich. He was up them trees on me shoulders and 'e could crawl through any 'edge that lad could - even the spiny blackthorn, mark you!"

"What became of Tich then, Ron? He was quite small, I suppose, with a nickname like that?"

"Tiny little feller was Tich. But ah looked after wee Tich, nobody would dare bully 'im while auld Ronnie was about. Ah think 'e is still up in Barnsley somewhere. Who knows. 'E came to me wedding ah reckon - ah'll ask Bella, she'll know. Ne'then, page 80. The mistle thrush and the song thrush. Eeeh, that's not a very elegant Latin name is it. Turdus. *Turdus viscivorus* and *Turdus philomelos.* Ah like them scientific names, do you lad?"

"Ah yes, the Linnaean classification, Ron. Genius. Do you know that some animals, especially insects, don't even have a common name. Just the scientific one."

"Really? Well, I was reading that we are still finding new species, in the jungle and that. Even big ones like badgers. Imagine discovering a new species - I would call it after meself. *Turdus bullockus* or summat like that. Though it don't sound very nice, does it - mebbe not that, p'raps summat else. Nethen, I think that we can clearly establish that

THE HIDE

our little birdies over yonder are indeed the song thrushes. Why, you ask me? I will tell you. The mistle one is big and grey, it says here. And the eggs are whitish, not like the blue one we saw. And it seems the storm cock doesn't smash snails up like these ones do."

"There are quite a few other birds in your garden, Ron. I've been watching those little brown ones, over there - see?" De'Ath handed the binoculars over to Bullock, who adjusted them and pointed them at the privet hedge.

"Oh yeah, I see them! Like little brown mice creeping about!"

"I thought they were sparrows, but they don't have a bib on them. You don't see as many these days do you?"

"Oh no, that ain't a spadger lad. Loads o' them there were in Barnsley, commonest bird. Spadgers and starlings. They used to say even the spadgers 'ad a cough round our way - it was all them coal fires. Do you know, I don't know what these ones are. Let's look in the book, shall we. House sparrow. *Passer domesticus.* Haha, listen at this, Tom. *"Of our small British birds, perhaps this is the commonest and well-known, as it frequents the dwellings of man and even lives in the heart of great cities."* Eeh, they don't write like that anymore! And… yes, the male has a black bib…but…the female is all brown. Perhaps those there are female spadgers, Tom, but I don't reckon so. Perhaps we 'ave discovered a new species - *Turdus bullockus,* Bullock's sparrow! Eh?!"

De'Ath grinned and knocked out his pipe. "Well there is another sparrow on the next page, *Passer montanus,* the tree sparrow. This one *"avoids the dwellings of man"* though, and it has a little black bib thing as well. The cock and hen birds are alike. So I think that rules them out."

Bella joined them on the patio and lit up an Embassy.

"I 'ope you two are not spying on the neighbours with them field glasses. You know what 'er at number 42 is like. Leaving 'er curtains open all the time. Brazen woman she is."

"Love, ah'd be a sorry mess if it came to me ogling Mrs Merryman. Ah'll be ogling you though missus, in yer pinny and carpet slippers!" Bullock trained the binoculars on his cackling wife, who simply kicked him hard in the shin.

"You daft 'aport, Ron Bullock! Any'ow, did yer save the poor little birdie?"

"Aye, we did love. Do you know, there is a nest of song thrushes in yonder bush. Tom and meself 'ave been studying them. We reckon they are about to fly the nest and that one jumped too early before it could fly proper. Look, it's still mucking about - ooh, it's managed to get up on the wall, look."

"Well, we'd best keep Basker inside a bit then, you can take 'im for 'is walk, whilst I peg the washing out."

"Just look through these glasses, Bell. What do you reckon those little birds are, creeping about?"

Bella inspected the hedge, her cigarette dangling from her smudged lipstick mouth, her wiry hair wrapped tightly in giant curlers.

"Jenny wren is it? Little sparrers?"

"Theory!" announced De'Ath suddenly, carefully inspecting the *Observer's*. "Page 94. The hedge sparrow, *Prunella modularis*. *"This quiet, brown, insect-eating bird is misnamed "sparrow", as it is no relation of the house sparrow or tree sparrow, and is a most harmless and useful little bird, correctly named hedge accentor and also called dunnock. The sexes are alike. The plumage is striated brown above and sombre slate grey beneath. The bird has a quiet, mouse-like way of creeping about under bushes and herbage in search of insects.* Look at its picture, Ron. I think we have a positive ID."

Bullock grabbed the binoculars back from Bella, who slapped his bald head for his rudeness. He seemed used to violent treatment from his spouse and ignored it, as he resumed his study of the flittering birds.

"Yep," he muttered, "confirm stripy brown on the top and grey beneath. One o' them has a bug in its beak. What does it say about nesting behaviour?"

"Nest. Of moss, wool, grass and hair; in a bush or hedge, or in a brushwood or faggot pile. Haha, faggot pile. When was this published...let's see...1965. Hmm, I thought it was earlier than that."

"Well, the *Observer's* series certainly did start in the 1930's, Tom. It was a funny decade the sixties, weren't it - in many ways not much changed from the thirties. Everybody goes on about the swingin' sixties, but ah didn't do much swingin' - that were for the hippies!"

De'Ath fell silent on that point and blushed a little. The Bullocks knew that expression well enough, and teased him.

"Oooh, ah'll bet you and Dot were hippies weren't you!" cackled Bella, jabbing him with a gnarled index finger. "I can just see you!"

De'Ath grinned and nodded. "I am afraid we were a bit, Bella. Hippy clothes, beard, well - I've still got me beard obviously, Jimi Hendrix..."

"Waccy baccy, eh was it, Tom, eh? Eh?" grinned a ruddy faced Bullock. "Eh? I bit you did, I bet you did, you weirdy beardy!"

"Erm well, yes I used to imbibe a little of the mind expansive herb. Not Dot though, Bella. Me and my mates used to sit about listening to Pink Floyd and Janis Joplin and get a bit, you know, high."

"Ah that's probly what did yer mind in, Tom. I expect you thought you could fly or summat. Probly you get flashbacks still and think you are an orange. Any'ow, on t'subject of flyin' I reckon you are bang on, Tommyboy. Hedge sparrow. Or shall we call it dunnock. Or hedge accentor?"

"I have heard of dunnock I think, Ron, but I presume the accentor one must have gone out of use. Hey, you know who is good on birds, don't you. Professor Ball."

"Really? Bally? Last time I saw him was when he blew himself up at

THE HIDE

our bonfire do last year…"

Noticing a sudden malevolence in his wife's eye, Bullock quickly changed the subject from the disastrous November 5th bonfire party of the previous year.

"…er, no I must have seen him since then, probably in the butchers or summat. Well, let's give 'im a ring then shall we - he was never any trouble, old Bally, not like that prat Reakes."

"Poor Dr. Reakes. Such a shame what happened to his face."

"Shame, Bella? He is a bloody lucky man to be alive, 'e is. If not for my heroics he would've been a dead gonner. I'll be giving him a wide berth, ah can tell thee. Weirdo, that's what 'e is."

"Never mind wide berth, take your wide girth out of my way whilst I peg the washing out. Out from under my feet, that's where I want you two - just remember that. Now shoo. Take the dog out."

As arranged by telephone, Professor Ball was waiting for his friends on Oldside Common that very afternoon, and when he saw them approaching he made an odd mewling sound and greeted them with a wide few-toothed grin and a handshake each - though it was already obvious he was hiding something behind his back with his left hand.

"Good to see you, Bally!" smiled Bullock, shaking his hand heartily. "Last time ah saw you, you were being blown off yer feet by a Bullock's Banger!"

"Ah yes, I was, wasn't I! What fun that was. Well, apart from when Tom's house caught fire, obviously. But I do hope that Dr. Reakes has recovered from his near-death experience! AND….poor Buzzy!!!"

Bullock's smile was wiped instantly from his face, as Ball revealed his left hand… over which was rolled a charred sock puppet vaguely resembling a burned bee, its beady black eyes glowing mischief.

"Look, he's crawling on your head, Ron! Buzzy is thanking you for his rescue!"

"Get that ruddy thing off me 'ead, Prof! It still smells of burning napthalene, for Heaven's sake!"

De'Ath's hooting amusement at Buzzy's attack on Bullock was short lived - it attacked him as well.

"How aaaare you, Tommy!" squealed Ball, pulling De'Ath's wispy beard with the charred remains of Buzzy.

"Gaah, yes I'm fine Professor, eeaaah...hello again, erm, Buzzy."

"Oooh, do you remember when I got stuck in that elder tree over there - I was collecting elderflower for Eleanor's products, wasn't I?"

"What is a dunnock, Professor?" Bullock had quickly recovered from his sock-puppet mauling and decided to get straight to the point of their meeting.

"Ah yes, the dunnock," replied Ball, assuming a serious expression and stuffing Buzzy into his jacket pocket. "I don't know when they started calling it that, but to me it is the hedge sparrow."

"*Prunella modularis,*" added De'Ath, straightening out his beard.

"Very good, yes, Tom, *Prunella modularis.* I think what happened taxonomically is that it was never really a sparrow, in that it doesn't belong to the family *Passeridae,* like the house sparrow or tree sparrow, the seed eaters. It is a member of the family *Prunellidae,* or the accentors, which are mainly insectivorous so I reckon the 'hedge sparrow' got dropped and they call it dunnock now; personally I would prefer the hedge accentor."

"That's what they call it the t'Observer's, Prof! Look, page 94."

"Ooh, *"The Observer's Book of Birds!* Number 1 in the series that was, it looks like a 1965 edition that one. I remember collecting all the Observer's Books. *Wild Flowers* of course, number 2; *Freshwater Fishes,* number 6, I think, erm, *Ships, Sea and Seashore,* erm…*Cats,* that was another one…Number 30."

"How many did they produce in total, then?" asked De'Ath. "I remember being given the one on old English churches by an auntie of mine for my eighth birthday - and my father gave me the one on heraldry for some odd reason."

"Well, it sort of fizzled out in 1982 after number 98 in the series came out - *Opera*. But then seventeen years later," the wide few-toothed grin re-appeared, "…in 1999, they produced number 99 in the series - *The Observer's Book of Observer's Books!*"

"Ah, yer mekkin that up lad!" protested Bullock. "*The Observer's Book of Observer's Books?* Come on Prof, pull the other one, it's got bells on it! You must think me and Tom came in on the last bloody banana boat!"

"No, no!" squealed Ball, "I have a copy, I can prove it, doubting Thomas and Ronnus! It's really good, about the history, authors, and various print-runs. And then, finally, they brought out number 100 - *Wayside and Woodland* in 2003, actually in homage to the series that pre-dated the *Observer's* series, which was called the *Wayside and Woodland* series, and I *think* - that was the last one."

"Ah tell yer Prof, if these kids today had the series of 100 Observer's books instead of Smart Phones and Pokemon Ghosties, they would grow up much more interesting people. I am gonna find some of those old books for my grandson Tanaga. He could do with a bit of culture that lad, 'es gone a bit wild lately. Charging around after these Pokemons, 'e is."

"Ah now - I met your little Tanaga at the fireworks party, didn't I - he loved it when those jumping jacks attacked me, didn't he? I don't think I've ever seen a little boy laugh so much!"

Bullock and De'Ath couldn't suppress a smile at the vivid memory of

THE HIDE

Ball attempting to fend off home-made leaping pyrotechnics with a garden broom.

"There aren't many birds about on Oldside Common these days are there, Prof," remarked Bullock, surveying the various copses of gorse and hawthorn with his army binoculars.

"Well, with great respect to Mr. Basker here," replied Ball, footling the ears of the bloodhound, who was warily sniffing the sock puppet in Ball's jacket pocket, "there are too many dogs about. But if you want to see birds, I can take you to Clarendon Marsh. I am afraid Basker will have to stay in the car though, no dogs allowed."

"Isn't that the Wildlife Trust place - the disused sand and gravel quarries? I think me and Dot went for a baked potato at Brock's Tea Rooms. Very nice toasted tea cakes as well."

"Yes Tom, I volunteer there on Wednesdays, helping the planning officer. It's great fun, all the birdwatchers go there. We could go now if you want?"

"Ok, why not, let's go!" agreed Bullock. "Walk back with us Prof, and we'll drop old Basker off and go in the Rover. Bella would be pleased to see you again. Reakes got all the blame for burning Tommy's cellar down, well, Reakes and me and Tommy, of course. Come on, let's go and do a bit o' this bird watching malarkey! I'll bring me book wi' us!"

An hour later, the intrepid three were bumping down the track in Bullock's old Rover to Clarendon Marsh Visitor Centre, on the outskirts of Oldside. From the back seat, De'Ath noted in the frothing hawthorn hedges and the expanse of swaying reedbed, many birds flitting and flying, and wished that he had his own binoculars - he was catching the identification bug.

Parking the car, the ever-enthusiastic Ball led a merry way to the Visitor Centre, riffling about in his wallet for his membership card.

THE HIDE

The ancient lady at the reception desk emitted an audible groan as Ball walked through the door.

"Good morning, Vera!" beamed Ball, splatting his membership card on the desk and assiduously signing in the visitors' book.

"No need to sign in, John. We know you." She groaned again. "Are your friends members?"

"Not as yet, my dear," interjected Bullock. "How much is a day ticket?"

"Well, it's five pounds, but you can join as a member for three pounds a month and then you get all the benefits."

"What benefits?" insisted Bullock.

Vera Clapp went into her practiced sales spiel. "A Members Pack full of information about local wildlife and how YOU can get involved." She paused to point aggressively at De'Ath, who cringed, and then at Bullock, who frowned. She continued, unabashed.

"You get *Discover Wild Oldshire,* your free guidebook to local nature reserves; you get membership cards giving you free entry to over 2000 nature reserves nationwide including our flagship nature reserve and Visitor Centre – RIGHT HERE at Clarendon Marsh. You get *Wild Oldshire* Magazine three times a year edited by our Director James Bald...PLUS *Natural World Magazine* containing the latest news from Wildlife Trusts across the UK; access to local events, activities, courses and special offers run by Oldshire Wildlife Trust. AND your money goes towards protecting local nature for generations to come. What do you think about that then? Eh?"

De'Ath felt he should applaud, and unwisely did so. It was a mistake, as Vera thought he was being sarcastic, shooting him an icy Gorgon stare, which froze De'Ath in mid-clap. Professor Ball added to the tension.

"Well, I prefer to call us 'Oldnact', rather than Oldshire Wildlife Trust," he announced, rootling in his jacket pocket for an ancient

THE HIDE

baseball cap which may once have been yellow. The faded words above the peak read 'Oldside Nature Conservation Trust (OLDNACT)' - and Ball jammed it decisively on his head.

"It hasn't been OLDNACT since 1983, John," reposted Vera wearily. Bullock simply continued to frown, wondering if this was the sort of place and in the sort of company that he should wisely be.

"What is this *Adopt A Species*?" inquired De'Ath of a leaflet on the reception desk, attempting to redeem the situation a little. "That looks very interesting."

Revived, Vera sprang again into her well-rehearsed sales speech, perhaps a trifle over-effusively. "Many iconic birds and mammals are under threat and need our help MORE THAN EVER BEFORE. Our *Adopt a Species* scheme raises both awareness of the plight of local wildlife and funds for our work to protect threatened wildlife and wild places. And threatened by what? US! THE HUMANS! THE DESTROYERS OF PLANET EARTH!!!"

The intensity of Vera's furious warble increased, as she shook her bony fist, first at her target audience, and then at herself. She realized she had gone off-script somewhat, and remembered that she wasn't supposed to do that. With a deep breath, she attempted a more moderate tone, delivered though a highly unconvincing half-smile.

"The species that are currently available for adoption ARE - *Adopt a Hedgehog*, *Adopt a Badger* and *Adopt a Peregrine*. Adoption packs for both adults and children include an adoption certificate, soft toy, pin badge, factsheet and more. Each species has its own story for you to follow, the first part of which is included in the adoption pack with two further updates sent during the year. Each pack is £25 and makes a lovely gift for wildlife enthusiasts - young OR old."

Heaving a sigh of relief, she dropped like a sack to her chair, spent of energy and seemingly uninterested in whether or not she had made a Membership or *Adopt A Species* sale. She sat fuming, muttering "Earth Destroyers" repeatedly under her breath.

Bullock and De'Ath were not sure what to do or say, but Ball did. He was grinning again and rooting in his voluminous pockets. "You know which species I have adopted, don't you, Vera!"

"Oh Jesus. Not Humphrey." Ball donned a grimy spiky-haired glove puppet, which started waving ominously at her. With what appeared to be the last of her strength, Vera sank to her knees and crawled under her desk, where she hugged her knees and shut her eyes tightly, as if she were a small child pretending it could not be seen.

But Humphrey the Hedgehog needed a much bigger hint than that to be dissuaded from his mischief. Climbing on top of the desk, Ball simply lowered Humphrey into Vera's hidey-hole, and began singing Humphrey's theme tune.

"Hedgehogs are our little friends,
We like hedgehogs..."

Unscrunching her eyes to see Humphrey apparently dancing upside down in time to his theme song, a blinding red mist overtook her. Above, Ball continued the song, apparently unaware of the danger lurking below.

"Hedgehogs are our little friends,
We like ...oooow! Ow! Ow! Owwwwhhh!"

Vera had ripped her Oldside Wildlife Trust name badge from her lapel, bent the safety pin to an obtuse angle, and stabbed wildly out at Humphrey, catching him repeatedly.

"Poor Humphrey!" protested Ball, inspecting a punctured thumb, "that isn't the way to protect his species!"

A sobbing Vera crawled away on all-fours to the safety of the staff coffee room, bolting the door behind her.

De'Ath and Bullock were considering leaving what seemed to be a peculiar madhouse - although they had come to know and become fond of the Professor and his eccentricities, they weren't quite prepared for a scene which went well beyond Rod Hull and Emu on *Parkinson*.

THE HIDE

"John!" A short bulky man, munching a bacon sandwich and laden down with all manner of telescopic equipment, waddled amiably over. "What are you doing kneeling on the reception desk? Where's Vera?"

"Hello Colin! Say hello to Colin, Humphrey! He is feeling sad because Vera stabbed him."

Unlike Vera, Colin seemed much amused by the hedgehog, and shook its paw with a wide smile. "How have you been John, you daft old prannet? WOO!WOO!WOO! BELL END!" Colin slapped himself in the face and convulsed violently.

Bullock was taken aback by Colin, and said so.

"Eh, we'll be 'avin less of that language, thank you very much! There was recently a lady present 'ere!" he protested sternly.

"Oh, don't mind me," beamed Colin, extending a fat hand, "I've got Tourette's. Nice to meet you, you big fat WOOOO! FECK OFF!"

Bullock inspected his man carefully and the hand Colin extended to him. He had never actually met anyone who claimed to have Tourette's syndrome, though he had seen programmes about it on television. With his firmest possible grip, he took Colin's hand and crushed it like an empty beer can.

"YAH WOOH! WOOH! You got a strong grip boy, yowzah!! TITS!"

"Ron Bullock, Colin. Good to meet you, yer foul-mouthed ruffian!"

"Haha, yes that's it Ron, you give me as good as I give it out. BUNGHOLEBUMMER!! Oops, there it is again. Just can't help it. Done all the classes, hypnotism, the lot, no help. It's genetic. My mother swore like a trooper and was fired so many times she gave up work in the end and took in ironing. TOSSER. Who's yer..WHOA!... silly mate? BISCUIT BEARD!"

"Yeah, erm, Tom. Nice to meet you..." De'Ath proffered his clammy fish handshake, as he desperately tried to swear at Colin, in the spirit of general proceedings, "erm...dirty Colin!"

THE HIDE

"Ho ho!! I like that one. Dirty Colin! Blimey, it's like shaking hands with a bream."

The newly christened 'Dirty Colin' wiped imagined slime from his hand on his Barbour jacket, on which was pinned a multitude of badges, all seeming to relate to 'Rutland Bird Fair', dating back to the mists of time.

"What's out and about, then Colin?" grinned Ball, sucking his punctured thumb.

"Oh there'all sorts, John - spring is springing on, as it does. Hobby and water rail this morning. Loads of different warblers. Spotted flycatcher behind the Steetley Hide. DYYYYAAAAH!" Colin involuntarily convulsed and twitched as if attacked by a nest of bees.

"Wow, spotted flycatcher" exclaimed De'Ath, thumbing through *The Observer's*. "*Muscicapa striata. This quick, quiet little summer visitor is most interesting to watch. It is constantly darting out from its perch after a passing insect, twisting and turning in the air so quickly as to confuse any fly.*"

"What the actual *fuck* is that?" spat Dirty Colin. "*The Observer's Book of Birds*? What are you, twelve years old, Tom? Reckon you need to get yourself a new ID guide mate! Haha, *The Observer's Book of Birds*! What a prannet!"

Bullock's reaction was swift and aggressive. Within a moment, Dirty Colin could smell Bullock's rancid breath and felt the sandpaper of the jutting chin rasp one of the many fleshy folds of his neck.

"That's my *Observer's Book of Birds* that is, Colin. If you've got a problem with that book, you've got a problem with me. And that's something you don't want." He clenched his fists, menacingly.

Colin took a step back and raised his hands. "Nooooo problem with you or your book, Ron. Don't mind me and my Tourette's ways, I am mentally ill, I am. FAGGOT!"

"What the Devil is going on here?!" Vera had heard the commotion

THE HIDE

from her pantry and intervened, seemingly re-energised. "There's no fighting at Clarendon Marsh THANK YOU VERY MUCH. If you can't help your swearing Colin, I'll thank you to keep your potty mouth closed. And as for you, if you want to be a member here I suggest you take your fisticuffs to the cage fighters mixed up martial arts club or whatever they are called."

"F-f-f-f-f-f-f...." mouthed Dirty Colin, desperately stifling himself until his face went puce.

"I apologise on behalf of us both, my good lady. Colin was just offering to buy us all a cup of tea in Brock's...weren't you, lad?"

"F-f-f-f-f-f-f...." stammered Dirty Colin again, before being smartly led away by the arm by Bullock in the direction of the tea shop.

De'Ath's eye was taken by an open notebook on the reception desk, with four neatly ruled columns headed in Biro: 'DATE, SIGHTINGS, LOCATION, SIGNATURE'.

"11th May. Redstart. Female. New Hare Covert. DGH," he read in a murmur to himself. "Garganey. From John Baldwin Hide. J.Peters. 12th May. Montague's harrier. Near golf course. CBD."

De'Ath felt like he was reading a hidden arcane manuscript revealing wonders of the natural world. He recited the names again, relishing their strangeness. "Redstart. Garganey. Montague's harrier."

His reverie was broken by Vera tapping her broken and dirty fingernail on the page and leaning into him, stale body and mothball odour rising from her baggy fawn M & S V-neck sweater.

"Montagu's harrier. Montagu's. There's no 'e' in it. And I doubt he saw it at all." She cocked her thumb towards the tea room where Ron, Colin and Ball were sitting.

"Ah, I see CBD is Colin, is it?"

"Yes it is. Wherever you see CBD, take it with a pinch of salt. As well

THE HIDE

as his foul mouth he has a good imagination, <u>if</u> you know what I mean."

"Erm, do you mind if I take this book into the cafe to study, Vera, for a few minutes? Most fascinating, it is."

"What, the Sightings Book? Well, it shouldn't leave the desk really. Oh go on then - as long as you bring it back - and DON'T get cup rings on it!!"

The windows of Brock's tea rooms looked out onto a hedged area containing a multitude of bird feeders and tables, and swarms of tits, finches, woodpeckers and sparrows helped themselves to nuts and seeds. Bullock and De'Ath looked out with broad smiles, trying to remember what species some of them were.

Over a pot of tea at Colin's grudging expense, things became more civil, though peppered with Colin's intemperate and apparently uncontrollable language.

"No, look, no offence to *The Observer's* intended, lads, we all started there. Ooof, WANKERS! But you need something more - you need *Collins* for starters."

"What, you have authored a field guide for birds?" asked De'Ath, impressed.

"No you silly prat! Not 'Colin's'... *Collins*. There must be one in the shop somewhere, I'll go and ask Vera, er, second thoughts...*you* can ask Vera, Tom. That is, if you can find anything half-decent in there for sale these days among the plastic foreign creepy crawlies made in China - or crap cards. CRAP SHOP! BOOYAH! WOOOOF!"

"I have mine in me pocket somewhere!" announced Ball. It was a wonder how much stuff Ball could cram into his jacket and anorak, and after fussiling about in his various pockets and removing many obscure objects including a cotton reel and a fold-up beekeepers mask, he found an exceptionally battered and well-thumbed paperback copy of *Collins Bird Guide.*

"Ah well done, Bally. DYYYYAAAAH!! AYYYNUS! Tom, I see you are flipping through the Sightings Book there. Come on, read us one out at random, I will show you how to use the *Collins.*"

"Oooo- k…6th January. Bittern. Flying into Carlton reedbed. TC."

"Oh, Top Cat is a birdwatcher here, is he? Who does he go with, OD? Officer Dibble?" guffawed Bullock.

"BUMHOLE! That's Tom Clarke. Very reliable birder Tom is." Colin shook his head, turning his attention to the *Collin's Bird Guide,* putting on a pair of spectacles in order to consult the index.

"Look here, this is where you'll find your bittern, Tom - or should I say - bittern-s! See, here is your old common or garden bittern, or great bittern as some call it…"

De'Ath inspected the page carefully. *"Botaurus stellaris. L.* 69 – 81cm. That must be L for 'length'? Ooh, quite a big bird. WS? Wingspan? 100 – 130cm. *"Breeds only in extensive Phragmites reedbeds"."*

Ball slurped his tea and nodded. "Indeed, *Phragmites australis,* the common reed. Used for thatched roofs, of course. And here at Clarendon Marsh, we do have extensive *Phragmites* reedbeds, thanks to the efforts of the Oldnact Volunteer group, led by Aldous Stern. And I believe that as a result, we have had breeding bittern, is that right Colin?"

"No John, not yet anyhow. FECK, FFFFAYYYYY, FECK! We have them regular over-wintering though, I have seen plenty of the crepuscular crapsters, of course."

"What does this code mean, Colin," continued the poring De'Ath, "rB5/W4"?

"Let me show you the codes bit, Tom, it's at the front of the book. There you are rB. Resident breeding species. 5 – that means rare, less than 100 pairs. W - winter visitor, 4 - means scarce or local, more than 100 pairs. And whilst we are at it let me explain these little maps. Orange is the breeding area, which they leave in winter. So you see - the bastard bittern mainly breeds in the east of Europe in the spring and summer. Dark blue is where they are present all year including breeding, so you see AAAAAHH....OOOOFF....OOOOF....WIZZLERS! we have some spots across Spain and central Europe, and even some here as well, they will be Minsmere reserve in Suffolk and Leighton Moss in Lancashire. Light blue - the winter range, so you can see 'em farting about all over England where there's a decent reedbed, like here. Then the light brown is where you can see 'em on migration. Basically everywhere."

"Eh, this is quite technical!" grinned Bullock. "summat we can get our teeth into this is, Thomas!"

De'Ath continued reading about the bittern. "Food is mainly fish, frogs and insects. Rarely seen on the ground. When alarmed adopts camouflage posture known as "bitterning". Bitterning!"

Ball decided to do a bit of bitterning. He stood up, stuck his elbows into his waist, and stretched his wattled neck and pointed his nose high to the heavens.

"Hahaaaaaa! You bitterning old fool!" exclaimed a delighted Dirty Colin. "'ang on a minute...." He reached for an empty J2O bottle on the next table, and blew across it to emit whumping sounds.

"Ah yes, the booming of the male, Colin, excellent!" Ball added the whumping sound to his bitterning repertoire.

Bullock was still in two minds about this eccentric behaviour, but De'Ath was getting into the silly spirit, and joined Ball in a bit of bitterning.

"That's it, Tom! Haha, you are creasing me up you two pillocks are! You'll be doing the mating dance together next! Go on, give Bally a mounting, Tom - p'raps 'e'll lay an egg for us and *then* we'll have the

THE HIDE

breeding bittern alright! BITTERN BUMMERS! WOO! MONOCULARS!!"

"I see, it's a type of heron is it, the bittern?" Bullock was now studying the *Collins,* ignoring the bantering bitterners.

"That's it, Ron, you know the grey heron I am sure, see - on page 35. It's related to that. I have seen all the heron species, I have. Take this one, the night heron. That used to be quite a common visitor that did, but pretty rare now. See the code – V for Vagrant."

"Vagrant – sounds like a tramp!" remarked De'Ath, de-bitterning and returning to his seat and tea mug.

"Sort of." Ball had also de-bitterned. "It means a bird that has strayed or been blown by the wind from its usual range or migratory route. And that really is the basis for "twitching", is it not, Colin. You are a twitcher!"

De'Ath and Bullock could not fail to notice Dirty Colin's bizarre and extravagant repertoire of convulsive twitching spasms, and were surprised at the usually polite Professor Ball's sudden reference to them. But Colin didn't seem bothered. He swatted away invisible flies, rising compulsively to his feet as he did so.

"Me, I was the bloody king of the twitchers, son! Regular 300 plus on the British List. I don't do it so much now, lost one marriage over it and thought that was probably enough. And honestly, some of the tossers you bump into, time and time again, wherever you travel. Especially that Sonny Robards…SHUT THE FECK UP...BUMMARD!"

De'Ath was remembering that "twitching" was something to do with obsessive bird watching and that Ball probably wasn't being personal after all, so he felt able to join in.

"How is twitching different to bird watching then, Prof? How does a birder become a twitcher?"

"Well, I suppose the easiest way of describing it is to say that the goal

THE HIDE

of twitching is to tick off as many species as you can, there are Year Lists and Life Lists. It can get very competitive, can't it, Colin."

"Tell me about it. When I was one, I worked out I drove 70,000 miles in a year, jumped on a plane dozens of times at short notice, chartered boats, hotels - I spent a fortune. But I notched up 350 species. Not the record, but not far off. DAMN THESE FECKIN FLIES, GET OFF ME!!"

"'Ang on a minute," said Bullock, producing *The Observer's Book* again. "It says here that there are only 243 species in Britain, and I don't think that number will have gone up since 1965 when it were published!"

"Well it gets complicated, Ron. WAAY! KNICKERS, KNACKERS, NNNN... KNOCKERS! For a start off, we have climate change affecting which bird species can settle here, or just get blown off their usual course. Then we have introduced species - who would have thought that Hyde Park in London would be full of breeding Himalayan parakeets for example!"

"Yeah, I read about them. That can't be right can it, a park full o' parrots in our capital city. So how many species can these twitchermen find then, like?"

"Well some of them, and they include Ireland in the geography - are nearly at 600 species for their Life List!" responded Colin. "Though some of their claims are what you might call - decidedly dodgy. DOGGERS! DOGGER, FISHER, SOLE AND BAILEY! FECKIN FORTIES! CROMARTY IS A C..."

Colin leapt to his feet and gave the rest of the tea shop a loud and filthy rendition of the Shipping Forecast. Fortunately, everyone present seemed used to it and ignored him, as they nibbled tea cakes and watched the birds outside. Someone had apparently seen a stoat sneaking around the bird tables, and everyone was eager to catch site of it, relegating Colin's familiar performance to remote interest.

De'Ath too was already used to ignoring his tics and outbursts, and was studiously inspecting the 'Sightings Book' once more.

THE HIDE

"Well I would be delighted to see just some of these birds listed here! Goldfinch. Greenshank. Lesser whitethroat. Ruff."

"Ooooh, I can do an impression of the ruff *Philomachus pugnax*!" announced Ball, wrapping his scarf around his neck in the fashion of an Elizabethan gentleman.

"Haha, you are looking a bit 'rough' you big plonker!" laughed Dirty Colin, seated again after his wild performance. "Look, they are my initials in the book against the ruff and the greenshank. ...CBD. Colin Brian Dredge!"

"Dredge?" asked Bulloch, suspiciously. "You're not related to Cliff Dredge are you? The gardener?"

"Yes I am! Cliff is my uncle - brilliant gardener, he is. He has won a lot of prizes, he has! FILTHY WELLINGTON BOOTS...NYAAAH! WOOO!"

Bullock winked at De'Ath, who nodded back. "We know 'im, lad. We know 'im very well actually. We 'ad a go at allotment gardening a year or two back. Oh yeah, we got to know Cliff Dredge alright."

"Come on, I'll take you down the reserve, lads. I've got an hour to spare." Colin slurped up the rest of his tea and belched loudly. "No charge, I like to spread me wisdom. WAAA-RBLERS!"

Leaving the tea shop and the visitor center, the four walked down onto the reserve via sinuous footpaths, passing reedy pools, various display boards with illustrations and maps, and what appeared to be a large wind turbine revolving in the slight wind. Colin's fly-batting tic became more and more flamboyant and he started jumping up and down, issuing a torrent of profanities.

"What's that, harnessing the energy of Willy Wind," enquired De'Ath, attempting to politely ignore Colin's frantic fit. "Is it a wind turbine?"

"In fact not," replied Ball, pointing back to the direction they had walked from. "This pumps water - in a sustainable manner, not like before when we had electric pumps - to the top reedbed. Aldous managed to raise some money from the Lottery, I believe."

"It pumps watter up the hill? What fower?" Bullock looked at the tall structure, perplexed, also noting a fisherman out of the corner of his eye. "Eh look, yonder feller is fishin'! Brill!"

Colin spat in the grass. "FISHWANKERS!" he shouted.

"Erm, yes," grinned Ball. "The fishermen and bird watchers don't always see eye-to-eye. I must say it's a mystery to me why they allow fishing on a nature reserve. And they don't even eat what they catch… they just throw them back! And in answer to your first question, if we didn't pump water up the River Old valley - the top reedbed would just dry up. All the pools here are artificial, as it were - they were created when the cement company extracted the sand and gravel. The top bed is quite shallow, and it would soon scrub up and revert to woodland - Aldous and his team spend a lot of time here chopping out the willow and birch."

"Oh, I see," said De'Ath, stroking his beard. "And you don't want woods, you want reedbeds - for the booming bittern!"

"Exactly! Whump! Whump!" Ball bitterned again.

"I never realized it was so much work, this nature conservation," proffered Bullock, scratching his chin. "Any 'ow I like a fish meself, I wonder what yon mon is catching down there, I will go and see. Erm, you'd better stay 'ere Colin, eh?"

Whilst Bullock was in animated conversation with the fisherman, the other three inspected the trees and bushes with their binoculars. Dirty Colin went into a running commentary of the birds he could see. He found concentration on the birdlife helped greatly with his Tourette outbursts.

"Willow warbler, marsh tit, bullfinch, female blackbird, greenfinch, cuckoo coming into the marsh from the north…"

Even with the aid of Ball's Leica's, De'Ath swiveled around, seeing no birds at all, and mystified with Colin's rapid-fire identification. "Cuckoo? Where?"

"You great bumchum! Look over there, man!"

"You great bumchum!"

De'Ath lowered his bins and followed the line of Colin's podgy index finger. He thought he could see a moving dot on the horizon, which could have been a bird, but equally a distant aeroplane or a midge on his glasses. Locating the swift-moving object through his raised binoculars, he wasn't a lot more certain.

"How the Devil can you tell if that's a cuckoo, Colin? It must be a mile away at least."

Colin sported a knowing and rather smug smile as he followed the bird to its landing in a distant reedbed.

"Ah, that's the jizz, that is, and no - that's not one of me swear words. Ooof, GOBSHITE! That one is. It's the way a bird moves, either in flight or in its habitat. It takes practice, Tom, but after a while, even a

THE HIDE

dot on the horizon becomes recognizable. Well, to some." De'Ath rather thought he might be one of those not blessed to enter among the jizz cognoscenti.

"Perhaps one of the requirements for a good birder is keen eyesight," he ventured, forlornly. "And as you can see from my glasses, that isn't one of my strong suits. Though I did play cricket a couple of years ago and I could see the ball pretty well."

"You might be a four-eyes, Mr. Magoo, and though I must say having keen eyes is an advantage, it isn't a requirement. Start with the simple ones. Kestrel, woodpigeon, that sort of thing. Watch them and in no time, you will spot them from a distance. But I'll tell you what's more important. Ears. Listen to that..."

"Cuckoo, cuckoo, cuckoo..." went Ball, with a benign smile on his face.

"Shut up, you daft prat!" issued Dirty Colin. "Give the man a chance!"

Gradually, a smile spread over De'Ath's face as he recognized the distant call of the cuckoo bird himself. "Ah yeee-eees! I can hear it! It must be ages since I heard a cuckoo call! How marvelous!"

"Thank Christ for that! Some calls are obvious, but...listen to that one coming from those reeds...Cetti's warbler...it's like a loud liquid metal!"

"*Listen!...What's my name?...Cetti-Cetti-Cetti - that's it*!" mimicked Ball, much to Colin's amusement.

"Ha-haaaaar! You crack me up you do, you idiotic old fool! BOLLOCKS! But yeah, it does sound a bit like that, don't it! *Cetti-Cetti-Cetti - that's it*!"

De'Ath smiled as he also recognized the Cetti's call by Ball's mnemonic. "That's useful that, Prof! Are there any others that could assist me?"

"Oooh yes!" responded Ball enthusiastically. "The great tit, *Parus*

THE HIDE

major, is the "teacher bird", because it sings a *"tea-cher, tea-cher"*, listen, I can hear one!"

"You are a great tit, John, you are and no mistake! What about the 'Chiswick fly-over', the pied wagtail - because they call "chis-ick" as they fly overhead!"

"Yep, and then there's chiff-chaff chiff-chaff, hence its common name of course, or in the Latin, *Phylloscopus collybita*. Then there's kitti-wake, kitti-wake *Rissa tridactyla*. Let's think, oooh yes, here's a good one *"smidgen of wholemeal and forget the gorgonzola'* - yellowhammer, you don't see so many about now do you, thanks to agricultural improvement. Oooh, you used to see whole flocks of yellowhammer in the fields when I was growing up."

"When was that then, the 1880's?' cackled Colin. "Gorgonzola my arse! I make my own ones up I do. The blackbird - *"I'm a little wwwannker. I am a piece of shit, shit, shit.* Then there's the wood pigeon – *"fuuuuck off you, you can all fuuuuck off, fuuuuck off..."*

"Let's be 'avin' less o' that Colin, you'll never be invited as a guest on *Springwatch,* that's fer sure." Bullock jauntily returned from his conversation with the fisherman.

"There's some good carp in this lake! Yon mon's 'ad roach and tench as well. Tell me Prof, does joining OLDNACT entitle you to have a fish?"

"It doesn't I'm afraid, Ron. The fishing club is separate and I have no idea how you apply to join. I think there may be a waiting list actually. As I said, well, I am not a fisherman myself of course, but shall we say, there is some…antipathy between the birders and the fishers here."

"FISHFECKERS!" confirmed Colin.

"Well I am going to see if I can join," puffed Bullock. "You up for a fish, Tom?"

"Oooh yes, it's been years since I went fishing. I caught a burbot once in the canal. Quite rare they are now."

"The burbot - *Lota lota*! I think they are even extinct in England now! Are you sure it wasn't a gudgeon, Tom - *Gobio gobio*?"

"Quiet sure, Prof. Perhaps I caught the last one!"

"That would be a good nickname for you, Prof, Gobio gobio. On account of you never shut that sodding trap of yours. Prof Ball, the Gobby Gudgeon!"

"Well, it's better than yours - Dirty Colin. You know what they call me? Ronny the Rhino, and I will bloody well charge you the next time you are abusive. That'll cure you and no mistake."

"Haha, I like you Rhino Ron! I tell you, I wish you could cure me. It's the bane of my bloody life this condition. YRRRRRRRRR....ARRRSSSHOLES!"

The four resumed their walk, Ball twittering further bird call mnemonics and Colin swearing at him, copiously.

By and by, they arrived at a long wooden shed-like building, with a plaque above the steps to the door, reading *"The David Smith Hide"*.

"Who is David Smith?" asked De'Ath. "Is he dead - is this a memorial of some sort?"

"Oh no, Dave is very much alive and kicking," replied Ball, mounting the wooden steps and opening the door, reducing his voice to a whisper as they entered. "I think he came into some money and donated it to the Trust."

De'Ath and Bullock squinted into the interior of The Hide – it wasn't completely dark, as at the far end, light poured from a thin rectangular window framing a large reedy pool.

THE HIDE

The silhouette of a solitary birder sat hunched, his back to the door and his binoculars trained on the middle distance. The four newcomers straddled themselves over wooden benches, twisting pegs to release wooden flaps, which when lowered revealed a reed-fringed lake containing numerous islands. Bullock and De'Ath beamed at each other - they were enjoying themselves. The musty wood smell and creaking timbers reminded them of The Shed - and for that matter The Pavilion and their ski lodge *Enchantement* - they felt immediately at home. They inspected various sign boards on the walls; Bullock read out loud from a brass plaque above his seat.

"In memory of Arthur Badstone, 1922 – 2006. From this corner he spent many hours watching, recording, contributing and sharing his time with those who cared about Clarendon Marsh Reserve."

"Ooooh yes, Arthur! He actually died just there where you are sitting, Ron, everybody thought he was still observing but he'd long been dead apparently."

"Shhhhh will you!" came a hiss from the end of The Hide.
"Afternoon, Aldous. YOU BIG BENDER!" Dirty Colin greeted the incumbent birdwatcher cheerfully, who looked around with disdain. He raised his large fluffy white-haired head and with evident disgust at the intruders, shut his wooden flap, pegged it up and immediately clomped from The Hide without uttering a word.

"Rude old buzzard, ain't 'e!' smirked Colin, swinging his binoculars onto the shelf in front of him.

"Noooo!" protested Ball. "Aldous is a very nice man, well, usually he is. The Godfather of Clarendon Marsh, they call him. He has led the Volunteers for years! He usually says hello to me!"

"Godfather my farty arse!" chirped Colin. "Always making up sightings is Aldous. A right royal stringer."

"Stringer? As opposed to a twitcher is it, Colin?" enquired Bullock, who was trying to focus on a perching cormorant with his ancient field glasses.

"Yeah, a liar in other words. Blinking 'eck Ron, where did you get yer bins - Oldside Museum? Try mine mate. You might even see something resembling a bird with these. Swarovski EL Swarovision - best that money can buy. Two grand I paid for them. Put 'em round yer neck, you big fat pillock, I can't have you dropping them."

Bullock had to admit, as he focused the upmarket optics, that the difference between them and his own binoculars was astounding.

"Blimey, I can see that bird in absolute detail. Like I can reach out and touch it. Just look at the sheen on its feathers. And by gum, it's eating a little roach! I can see its red fins and even its blue eye. Just look, Tom! Here, put them round your neck, you don't want to upset that impertinent gobshite do you?" Bullock winked at Colin; he was rather enjoying the abuse he was openly allowed to confer on him.

Ball possessed a pair of small but expensive-looking field glasses, which he gave to Bullock. "Not quite as flash as Colin's but rather good! Leica 8 x 32 BA. They could do with a service really, but they've done me rather well for fifteen years."

Bullock was no less impressed with Ball's optics, though Colin was full of disparagement.

"They are alright for an amateur, I suppose. Look, I'll set up my Leica

THE HIDE

Apo-Televid 'scope. Then you'll see who the AAAAY, ARRRRSSEHOLE…professional is".

Grunting and sweating, Dirty Colin set up a telescopic tripod, and attached a green canvas-covered instrument which looked like something a professional sports photographer might use behind the goals of an international football match. He adjusted the swivel of the tripod, and the viewing lens, and then played with the focus wheels.

"I'll train it on that oyster catcher bitch over there. There - come and see it, Tom!"

Crouching to squint down the telescope, and adjusting the focus where Dirty Colin was showing him, De'Ath literally gasped, and a beam of pleasure overtook his face. "Wow! That is superb, Colin! Look at its pink legs and its red beak…how very…red it is!"

"Bill, Tom, not beak. That's what the amateurs call 'em. BEAKYBUMCHUMS!! NYAAA!"

"Ron, you have to come and look at this…what was it called Colin, oyster bitch?"

"Oyster catcher - look there's a whole flock of them…*ke-peep-peep-peep!*…noisy effers aren't they!"

Bullock handed Ball back his binoculars, and swiveling his weighty hips, rose from his wooden seat, eager to take a peek through the telescope at the oyster catchers. But in his eagerness, Bullock's legs became entrapped and entangled as he attempted to step out of the fixed bench, and he pitched suddenly sidewards, flailing his arms to try to break his fall. This caused a violent and noisy chain-reaction of unfortunate events in The Dave Smith Hide, as follows.
The flailing massive arm of Bullock caught the seated Ball on the side of his head, knocking off his OLDNACT baseball cap and propelling him into De'Ath, who was standing hunched over the bird 'scope, squinting into the eyepiece. Emitting a surprised "oooof", on the impact of Ball's head into his midriff, De'Ath's forehead fell forward onto the eyepiece, causing the large lens body to rise suddenly upwards on its tripod like the end of a see-saw with a fat child on the

bottom end. Colin, who had been trying to help De'Ath with his focusing and was bending over the end of the 'scope, received the full upward force of the large lens at the base of his jaw, which was similar to receiving an uppercut from Tyson Fury. Immediately knocked unconscious, Dirty Colin reeled backwards with his full and considerable relaxed weight, keeling over into the end panel of The Hide.

"An Extraordinary Accident"

The David Smith Hide had been constructed entirely from wood in 1979; though it was subject to regular repair, the last winter gales had strained at its rusting pins and hinges, and the spring showers had soaked its rotting posts. Its structure had further weakened with the return of the warm spring sunshine, which contracted its boards and cracked them as they dried out. Suffice to say that the structure of The Hide was not as robust as it once was – certainly not robust enough to withstand the seventeen stones of Colin, as he collapsed backwards.

With a splintering crunch, the end of The Hide simply gave way,

THE HIDE

landing with a gigantic splash onto East Marsh Pool. Colin's limp and unconscious body followed; he spread-eagled belly-up on the floating wood, which began to slowly drift away from the bank. Colin resembled a deceased yet serene Viking warrior, who had been laid to rest on his ship and then pushed from the shores to seek Valhalla.

Apart from the end panel, the rest of The Hide; roof, the other three walls and the decking, somehow remained intact, despite intense creaking. Recovering themselves, the remaining three inhabitants watched on, as Colin floated surreally away up the pool.

Ball was first to speak, choosing to state the obvious. "Ooooh! I think Colin is out cold. And all the birds have flown off!"

No longer requiring the door to exit The Hide, the three men gingerly stepped off the gaping hole and onto the marsh below, which seeped above their ankles.

"Erm, Colin seems to be floating away," noted De'Ath. "Perhaps we should do something."

Bullock, ever the man of action, and well aware that this unfortunate domino-effect of destruction was precipitated by himself, was wondering if he should wade or swim after Dirty Colin afloat on his peculiar raft, which he thought might give way at any moment and sink.

"Ow deep is yonder pool, Prof?"

"Oh, not that deep where Colin is at the moment Ron, only about four feet, but the sediment will be deep. Very sticky, I should think, and not very good to stand up in."

Just as Bullock was taking off his boots and taking stock of what to do, a whiskery fellow with a lined and tanned face, a silver hoop in his ear and amused blue eyes, arrived to take in the strange scene.

"Have you killed Colin?" he asked with seriousness, smoking the end of a roll-up cigarette. "I thought somebody probably would, one day. I've thought about it myself." He eyed up Bullock with a species of

THE HIDE

admiration.

"Hallo Jack! How are you keeping?" beamed Ball, as if nothing much unusual had happened.

"Oh it's you, Prof! I didn't recognize you without your hat!"

"Yee-ees, it got knocked off! It must be on the floor somewhere…well, Ron knocked me into Tom, and I think Tom hit Colin with the telescope?"

"Did I?" responded De'Ath. "All I remember was getting punched in the stomach and then the next thing I knew was Colin falling out of The Hide! I thought you might have belted him, Ron, he was getting on your nerves, wasn't he?"

Jack's blue eyes sparkled. "Ah, so there *has* been some fisticuffs by the sounds of things!"

"I never belted him, Tom. The telescope clocked him full in the mouth and knocked 'im cold! Look, e's comin' to! 'E is wakin' up!"

Colin had no recollection of being kaylied by his monocular, and though his mouth tasted of metal, as far as he was concerned he was waking up from a peculiar dream. It took his fuzzy consciousness quite a while to discern that he wasn't in his bed, but was floating about on a panel of wood on East Marsh Pool. Deciding it was a weird dream, he closed his eyes again, feeling his jaw throbbing and a big lump rising on the back of his head. Raising himself to an elbow, his waterlogged raft lurched to one side, the strong smell of the silty water rising to his nostrils, and a mallard with a line of chicks behind her swam anxiously by. His blurry vision slowly returned; he could see four human figures on the bank - one waving at him cheerfully. "F-f-f-f-f-f" he managed, through his swollen lower lip.

The bankside personnel were relieved to see that Colin was still alive, with the possible exception of Jack, although he was thinking that it was highly possible that Dirty Colin could still drown if nothing was done. But his better nature got the better of him.

"Oh well, I suppose I should get the boat out to him. If you come with me big feller, we should be able to tow old Colin in. I suppose."

It didn't take long for Jack and Bullock to launch a nearby punt which seemed to be used for reed cutting, and with the skilled use of a pole, Jack soon reached the drifting raft. Colin had resumed a prone position, and was staring with his eyes open into the cloudy sky.

"F-f-f-f-f-f…" he croaked again.

"Crikey, we'll be in for some language here!" Jack peered down at the floating birdwatcher, and issued instructions to Bullock. "Matey, can you tie that rope somewhere on the, erm, raft, well, the side of The Hide, whatever. Colin, you best lie absolutely still. We don't want you rolling off. I am gonna aim for the island and we can wade back from there, it's not deep."

"Alright Jack, you…good lad. I got smacked in the gob with the telescope, I think. What the f….flippin' eck am I doing 'ere? I feel all discombobulated."

"Dont worry about that just now, chap, just lie still. Well done, matey, tie the rope on firm. OK, sit back, that's it. Nice and slow we go. Jolly boating weather, la-la-la-la-la, la-laaaaa!"

Jack punted the boat towards an island which was separated from the bank only by a narrow gully. Ball and De'Ath watched on with approval, the Professor prematurely applauding and jumping up and down, as the punt and stricken raft glided slowly to land. He shouted encouragement as Bullock and Jack first hauled the punt, and then Colin and his raft, onto dry land.

Bullock rolled Colin off the raft into a great deal of greasy duck guano, moving him into the recovery position on his side and inspected the victim's head.

"Ow many fingers can yer see, Colin?"

"F-f-f-f-five."

"Yerve got a nasty lump on yer 'ead but I reckon yer jaw ain't broke. Can you sit up?"

Colin felt groggy; though his vision was returning, something felt different. He rubbed the egg on his head, and noted a few splinters in back of his hands. But he could easily sit up, and after a few minutes, could also stand, with the support of his rescuers. Quite a crowd had gathered on the bank to figure out what was going on, including the giant form of Aldous Stern, who seethed in silent fury. Plastic bottles of drinking water were thrown onto the island, allowing Colin to rinse some blood from his mouth, though he was fortunate to have suffered no more than a split lip. After a few more minutes, Colin was able with Bullock's assistance to stagger to shore, and even the end of The Hide was recovered and laid out in the sun to dry.

An ambulance had been wisely called by one of the on-lookers, though as it was unable to park very near The Hide, two stretcher-bearing ambulance men awaited the return of Colin, and checked him over. Though not needing the stretcher, he wasn't able to walk up the footpath unaided, and staggered off under the support of the medics.

"Right I want a full account of what has happened here!" boomed Aldous Stern, producing a field notebook and sharpened pencil from his Barbour jacket. "If there has been any fighting I will have the police down here as well as the ambulance service. And you will undoubtedly pay repair damages for The Hide. That's the David Smith Hide that is! He will be quite furious when he sees what you've done to it! You first, you look like a tough. Who are you and what are you doing on the Marsh - I have never seen you before? You are not a Member, are you?"

Bullock wasn't displeased to be called a "tough", though he did resent the accusation that he had simply belted Dirty Colin and knocked him clean through the end of The Hide, as might happen in a good Western saloon fight.

"I can assure you there was nothing of the sort. Just a bizarre accident. One moment Colin is showing us an oyster summat in 'is telescope, next minute 'e gets clobbered with it, fell backwards on the back of the shed, or hide, or whatever you call it. 'E's a big lad Colin, but it

THE HIDE

couldn't 'ave been in much repair to give clean away like that. Then 'e just floated off on the panel, like baby Moses on t'Nile."

"What?" frowned Aldous, shaking his head. "who co-lobbered him with a telescope then? Was it you, man? I haven't seen you before either! Speak up!"

De'Ath took up a simpering, even groveling posture, wringing his hands and looking deferentially down at Aldous's large wellington boots. He unwisely decided to introduce himself with a proferred hand.

"Tom De'Ath, sir, at your service."

"I don't want to shake your hand, Mr. Death," scolded Aldous, "I want to establish the cause of this very unfortunate incident. Obviously nobody here likes Colin and his foul mouth - which by the way I DO NOT believe is due to a medical condition - but you can't go around bashing him with a 'scope and sending him up the creek without a paddle. Your account if you please, sir!"

"Well, I, I…" stammered De'Ath.

"Come on, OUT WITH IT MAN!" bellowed Aldous, shaking the red wattles of his neck like a furious turkey.

Jack attempted to intervene. "From what I understand it was just one of those things, Aldous…"

"That's enough from you, Ward! Hardly surprising to see you associated with this bedlam is it, with your track record. Now shut up whilst Mr. Death gives his account!"

After De'Ath had unconvincingly relayed his recollection, and Professor Ball (at great length) and Jack Ward (highly succinctly) had done the same, Aldous, having completed his notes, decided to inspect the gaping hole in The Hide, and the torn panels which once constituted one wall.

"This is quite shocking," he muttered. "Well, it will have to be repaired of course, but I will have to see what Colin has made of this business. I am still not convinced there wasn't a set-to - I have never in all my eighty-six years heard of a bird 'scope accidentally knocking a man through a wall. I have your addresses. And I know where you live, Ward - unfortunately. You haven't heard the end of this, not by a long chalk, you haven't. " With this, he stormed off, two similarly clad but much shorter ancient acolytes following him up the path, both shaking their heads vigorously.

"Erm, I think I will go and have a chat with Aldous when he has calmed down a bit," grinned Ball. "He doesn't seem to believe what happened, does he? It was a freakish thing though! Aldous can be a bit severe, he was a magistrate you know, Might still be one, actually! Oooh, I'd better take Colin his telescope as well. He'll want that back! It doesn't seem to be broken, fortunately."

"Yeah, I guessed that, Bally. That man has 'magistrate' written on 'is for'ead - pompous auld bugger if you ask me. I dunno who 'e reckons 'e is. Anyway Prof, you go and 'ave a talk with 'im. Strange things do 'appen at sea! He can't allus 'ave somebody to send down! A right kangaroo court that was!"

Ball bounded off enthusiastically up the path, leaving three behind as the rest of the crowd drifted off. Ward made a roll-up, Tom and Ron stuffed their pipes. They sat smoking in silence, looking up the pool as various ducks slowly returned and the sediment settled.

Then there was a moment when they caught each other out of the corners of their eyes - it was De'Ath who started laughing his owlish hoot first.

"Eh, don't set me off lad…don't…" But it was too late. Bullock began a gravelly laugh, and that sat Jack off with a chuckling fit. Pretty soon, they were all three helpless in thigh-slapping, breath-gasping, tear-running, fits of laughter.

"Ah, ah, we shouldn't...!" gasped De'Ath.

"I 'ope Aldous don't return!" spluttered Jack Ward, "He'd lock all three of us up for insolence!"

THE HIDE

Bullock stood up with his hands on his muddy knees, purple in the face, attempted to speak, but just gave in to another wheezy fit of laughter.

As they slowly returned to a quiescent and sensible state, Jack proposed that they return to the top of the Marsh and have a little drink at "his place". This seemed like a good idea, so still giggling; they set off up the footpath.

John's "place" turned out to be a small caravan on the edge of the reserve car park.

"Come in, 'scuse the mess. I'm looking after quite a few guests at the moment." Ward bade them enter the caravan, where he lit a wood burning stove and offered them old chairs covered in gypsy fabric.

"I'm a Laphroig man meself. Will that do yer, gents?" Both nodded in approval, and soon all three were grinning and toasting again. To De'Ath's surprise, an immature jay hopped onto his shoulder from what seemed to be the recess of Ward's bed. It rooted about in De'Ath's beard for something interesting to eat or treasure.

"Evening Eric," bade Jack to the bird, which nodded back in acknowledgement. "Eric had a poorly leg, but I think it's getting better now."

Bullock was looking around, sipping his whisky when something below alarmed him. A lengthy snake slithered from under his armchair and disappeared among pots and pans on the floor. He rose in instinctive alarm, bashing his head on a lantern, which swung as if in a storm.

"Bloody Hell, Jack. I just saw a snake!"

"I wondered if he was still here! Don't worry, he's a grass snake, he don't bite."

Bullock sat back down, grateful of the whisky. Inspecting the shadows, De'Ath noted other animals skulking about. Something popped its

THE HIDE

head out from the punctures in Ward's armchair.

"Erm, is that a mouse in your chair there, Jack?"

"What…where? Oh, that's Peasel the weasel, that is! Hallo mate!"

"A weasel! I don't think I've ever seen one of those before. He is smaller than I thought." Peasel hopped onto the floor, caught a beetle and shot out of the door with the insect in his mouth.

"RRRRAK!!" A crow, perched on the curtain rail, decided to join the party and strutted about on the floor, inspecting Bullock warily.

"A right menagerie, you've got 'ere Jack. Got any other tenants we should know about? Golden eagles? Scorpions? Grizzly bears?"

"Ah well, they come and they go. Sometimes I pick up an injured bird on the reserve and take care of it. I had a barn owl last week but it had to go to the vets. I must go and see how he is getting on."

"The birdman of Alcatraz, well, Clarendon Marsh, anyway!" mused De'Ath, studying the strutting crow. You must know a lot about birds, Jack."

"Well, I wouldn't seek to be compared to Robert Stroud, Tom! I seem to recall the real Birdman of Alcatraz was a homicidal nutcase. Though there are some comparisons, I suppose. I don't live in solitary confinement, but I do live on my own in this little shack of mine. And for sure, I wouldn't mind Burt Lancaster playing me in a film!"

"Ah, Burt," purred Bullock. "My favourite, he was. Birdman. *The Swimmer. Trapeze.* There's nobody can touch old Burt. *From Here to Eternity* of course."
"*Gunfight at the O.K. Corral*" added Ward, pouring them all another whisky.

"*Apache.* He was good in a more recent one too, set in Scotland. *Local Hero,*" offered De'Ath.

The men spent some time discussing Burt Lancaster films, before

THE HIDE

Bullock looked at his watch.

"Eh, we'd better be on our way, Jack, I didn't notice the time. It's been a very interesting afternoon. I reckon we wouldn't mind 'avin' a go at this birdwatching business. But I reckon we need a bit of kit first. Some new binoculars mebbe. I reckon not one o' them lethal telescopic weapons just yet though. And why don't we join the Trust, Tom, it's not much to pay and it's a good cause. It's a decent bacon buttie at Brocks an' all, by the looks of it."

"Well, you're welcome to visit anytime lads, and if I can help you with anything just give me a shout. I can see you will cause quite a stir among the birdwatching fraternity. To be honest, it needs livening up a bit. I recommend a trip to Boptics for some bins, it's a shop down Oldside. Take the Prof with you, they know him well there."

"Boptics. Sounds good. C'mon, Tom, let's go and see if we can still join the club, p'raps we've already been blackballed by old Judge and Jury Aldous."

Back at the nearby Visitors' Centre, Vera seemed delighted that Colin had been somehow assaulted, and welcomed her new members literally with open arms. Despite Bullock's protests, she was adamant that he had in fact punched Colin's lights out.

"He's had that coming a long time, he has, him and his potty mouth! We need somebody a bit tough round here. I think Aldous is a bit cross with you, but then again…he, erm, always is. He said you'd better come and help mend The Hide. That'll put you back in his good books."

"Well, thanks Vera, tell 'im 'e can reach me on this number, we'd be delighted to 'elp. Wouldn't we, Tom."
"Yes, I would feel a bit better about things if we did that. Well, cheerio, Vera, see you soon, we hope."

"Here are your Membership Cards. The rest will be in the post. Welcome to the club!"

The two men sauntered to the car park, apparently receiving knowing

THE HIDE

and approving looks from two arriving visitors in full birder attire. Ron nodded in their direction, and waved to Jack, who was smoking in the doorway of his caravan. Back in the Rover, they bumped up the track to the main road.

"Well, Tom, that was an adventure…wait 'til Bell and Dot hear about this little lot! I reckon we should get kitted out at that, what was it called? Boptics? We have our new hobby, Thomas. Or possibly…a new obsession?"

- CHAPTER TWO -

Redemption Song

Wherein Messrs. Bullock and De'Ath repair The Hide and their relations with Dirty Colin and Aldous Stern. There is a highly rewarding visit to Boptics. Birdwatching commences in earnest matched by commensurate research studies.

"There's a call for you love. He sounds posh."

Bella handed the telephone to Bullock, who was studying the *Birdwatch* magazine he had picked up in the local newsagent, and watching the *Easybirder* DVD he found inside, on his massive TV set. He muted the sound using a remote control.

"Ron Bullock speaking?"

"Mr. Bullock, Aldous Stern here from Clarendon Marsh. Calling to say you are in the clear with this Colin Dredge business. His story corroborates yours and I am prepared to accept it, providing that you and your associate, Mr. Death, undertake to assist with repairs to the David Smith Hide. We are planning an extraordinary work party next Sunday if you can be available?"

Bullock already knew he was "in the clear" and didn't feel the need to express any relief or gratitude - but since he was now fully immersed in the business of bird watching, his response was deliberately magnanimous.

"Very good. Yes, I think me and Tom could manage that. What sort of time are you thinking?"

"I am not thinking a "sort of time" Mr. Bullock. We will all meet at The Hide at 9am sharp. After our usual dawn survey of course. David Smith will be in attendance, and I would recommend an apology. He is understandably rather upset."

"Aye," responded Bullock, scratching the bristles of his chin and rolling his eyes. "OK, we'll be there, Aldous…or should I call you Mr. Stern?"

"I don't think we are quite on first name terms as it stands, Mr. Bullock, so Mr. Stern will be better appropriate. Good day to you; we are expecting rain so do dress accordingly."

"Aye, I w….oh 'e's gone. Officious old scrote."

Bullock called De'Ath to arrange a Sunday morning pick-up and they agreed that this was a good opportunity not only to redeem themselves but to join the Clarendon birding *cognoscenti* and elite.

"We'll bloody show these people, Thomas. We'll go all kitted out with the right gear, they'll soon know who they are dealing with. Still OK for a trip to Boptics this after? Good, ah'll see you then lad. The Prof will meet us there."

Boptics turned out to be a tiny shop tucked away in an obscure alley off Oldside High Street. A torn canvas blue and white striped awning tattered about in the breeze above a faded and crooked sign which in italic red letters read "*Boptics. Look ye whilst life lasts.*" As the duo arrived, they could see Professor Ball inspecting a note stuck on the inside of the door.

"Hello friends! Erm well, the shop *should* be open. I know that it is closed on Mondays, Wednesdays, Fridays… and Sundays of course. It

THE HIDE

says here that he should be open at 2, though I make it 2.30 now, and it looks like it's all locked up and dark."

"Blimey, no wonder people shop on t'internet! Are you sure this is a good place for purchasing our birdwatching kit, Bally?"

"Ooh yes, Mr. Lostweathiel knows his optics alright. And a well-known birder. He is from Cornwall originally. He leads tours to the Isles of Scilly, I went with him once. Very good indeed, it was. I especially remember the Manx shearwaters. *Puffinus puffinus*."

"*Puffinus puffinus?* Would that not be the Latin name for the puffin, Prof?" enquired De'Ath looking even more confused than his usual default expression of mild puzzlement.

"You might think that, Tom, but in fact the puffin is *Fratercula arctica*. Fratercula means "little brother", a reference to their black and white plumage, which was thought to resemble the robes of Franciscan monks. They are part of the auk family, you see."

"Orcs? They are in the Lord of The Rings, they are. The badd'uns. They don't look owt like puffins! Well, I say that - I've never seen a puffin meself, but I've seen 'em on the telly!"

"Oooh, The Farne Islands are good for seeing puffins, Ron! And terns! It's a bit of a long way, but you should go and see them this summer. Oooooh puffins, I love puffins, I do. Now, I do have a puffin puppet somewhere..."

Just then, an ancient gentleman appeared from an arched ginnel further up the road, looking around him as though he was completely lost. He started walking away from them and his shop, and then after stopping for extensive contemplation, turned around again and ambled towards them. He stopped, looking at the trio open-mouthed.

"Hello Arthur! It's me!" grinned Professor Ball.

Arthur Lostweathiel shuffled closer to Ball, and inspected him quizzically with eyes so creased that it was impossible to distinguish the colour of the pupils. He removed a red woolen cap from his head

THE HIDE

and toyed with a tuft of the white fluff that remained of his hair. There came a guttural noise from the back of his phlegmy throat.

"Wurgle?"

"You know...John Ball! We went to The Scillies together!"

Lostweathiel turned away from Ball with a confused frown and shuffled to the shop door, where he spent an age fumbling about with a jangling bunch of keys on a key ring containing a large pendant in the shape of an anchor. After having dropped and then retrieved them from the pavement three times, he tried a number of different keys in the lock, before finally succeeding in opening the door. He shuffled in and then promptly shut and locked it again without a word or glance.

Bullock exchanged disdainful looks with De'Ath and then raised an eyebrow to Ball.

"Is this bloke all there? He wouldn't 'ave lasted long selling carpets with me and Barry, ah tell thee!"

"Ye-es, he does tend to be a little distracted at times. But he will offer you a very good deal on his optical equipment, I am sure."

"Well, does he want to make a sale, or not?" Bullock stomped impatiently around the pavement. "Is 'e opening up, or what? Tom and me 'ave done our 'omework, Prof, and we 'ave a pretty good idea of what we want. And a budget to match those requirements. We know what these things cost on the tinternet, so 'e won't be selling us up the river, ah can tell yer that!"

After a while, a gnarled and veiny nut brown hand with a blurry grey tattoo on the back of it appeared at the grimy window, and turned a hand-written sign on a square of cardboard hung by garden twine from 'Closed' to 'Open'. A sun-bleached blind was unfurled to reveal once more the creased eyes and weather-beaten face, peering out at them in bafflement. After several further minutes had passed, they heard the sound of the keys jangling again in the door, which then finally opened slightly. Lostweathiel, far from greeting his prospective customers, walked off to the other end of the shop, and took a low seat behind the

THE HIDE

counter and folded his arms.

"Erm, shall we go in?" De'Ath asked Ball, in continuing puzzlement.

"Oooh yes! I love it at Boptics!"

"Yeah, well, let me handle this," scowled Bullock. "I didn't spend a career in sales for nowt. He'll soon find I am nobody's mug!"

Entering the shop, which was dimly illuminated by a bare and dusty 40 Watt bulb dangling from a tattered wire, the trio creaked the oaken floorboard as they entered, inspecting as they did so the yellowed walls, extensively papered by posters, pictures and photographs of birds. Also mounted crookedly on the walls, or wedged precariously onto shelves or bookcases, were various taxidermy specimens of birds, some in glass cases, others simply mounted onto perches. A large crow peered at them with its glassy black eyes; a peregrine falcon, mounted as if in rapid descent, seemed to hurtle at them from above; a kingfisher, drained of all its natural colour and more or less yellow, peered miserably into a mottled mirror below its perch of willow branch. There were also birds not easily recognizable, certainly to novices like Bullock and De'Ath.

"Quite a few stuffed birds yer've collected then," noted Bullock. "I like a bit o' taxidermy, I do. I got a fish in me study, a big carp I caught decades ago. 'Ad it stuffed, I did. Me missus 'as tried to get rid of it a few times, but no, old Big Bertha is still there. Some o' these are quite old, aren't they? Look at this one, Olivaceous Warbler, 1915, it says on the label. They keep well don't they, eh?"

Lostweathiel became briefly animated, and apparently rather ruffled.

"T'aint fer sale, if that's way yer thinkin' mister! None of 'em are, so think off!" he wurgled, red-faced and wobbling his head around like a riled turkey.

Bullock shook his head and thought about leaving the shop there and then. But he settled for muttering under his breath, peering into various locked glass cases containing binoculars, bird telescopes, and other more obscure apparatus.

THE HIDE

"Rude old buzzard. He'd 'ave to pay *me* to tek one of 'is mouldy old birds!"

Lostweathie, only his head visible above the counter from his low seat, watched his visitors impassively, as another man entered the shop, in a manner best described as furtive. Lostweathiel raised one shaggy white eyebrow by way of greeting.

"Alright, Arthur?" the visitor greeted the eccentric proprietor in a whisper, looking around suspiciously at the three browsers. "See you got people in. What they 'ere for then?"

"Dunno, Leonard. What you want?"

"Well, erm, I might pop back, er, when these've gone?"

"Wont be open long. State yer business, Leonard."

The Cornishmen folded his arms and stared intently at his visitor, nodding his head and gurning his mouth into a fish-like grimace.

Leonard Bristow was a slight, nervous man who dressed and looked like he had stepped out of a Dickens novel as a clerk or tradesman, with his thin and receding grey hair oiled to his scalp, his waxy complexion, and long dark coat of ragged hem and worn elbows. He shuffled from foot to foot, his darting black eyes, which looked like they had been inserted by a taxidermist, flew around the room without gaze alighting.

"I…I…wondered…" he stammered, partially wringing his long-fingered and bony hands…"

"What you wonder at boy? Spit it out then yer pilchard!" wurgled the Cornishman.

"Well, see thing is, this year, it's 70 years since George was laid to rest, and I thought, you know, I could take one of 'is specimens to show in the shop. You know, bit of a celebration, like?"

THE HIDE

"Yer not 'avin the olivaceous!" snapped Lostweathiel, unfurling his arms and pointing his gnarled index finger at Bristow.

"No, no, not the olivaceous, Arthur. That would be too much to ask, the money you paid for it. I thought maybe the black lark...or the grey-tailed tattler? They were both great-grunpa George's, weren't they?" He pointed tremulously up at two glass cases mounted high up on the wall, one containing a bird not unlike a small starling, and in the other, which hung tenuously from one remaining hook at an angle far from horizontal, was a drab grey wader, its legs painted in bright yellow.

The Cornishman turned to inspect the cases, perhaps trying to work out how long it would be before the grey-tailed tattler lost its remaining hook and crashed onto his head.

"Alright, Leonard. You can take the tattler fer a bit, if yer want. But I see no sense in reviving the 'Hastings Rarities Affair', do you? Nothin' ever proved."

At this point, Professor Ball unwisely joined the conversation.

"Er, did I overhear you mention the 'Hastings Rarities Affair'? Interesting business that, wasn't it? Was it 1962? A case of statistically demonstrated ornithological fraud that misled the bird world for decades since the 1900's! Although... most have subsequently been re-admitted as known visitors to Britain, you know!"

"Well," breathed Bristow through a nervous smile, "I do know. Actually, I am the great grandson of George Bristow, the taxidermist at the centre of the row! And still keeping the art of taxidermy in the family!"

"Really!" responded Ball enthusiastically. "Fascinating! Of course, they used to shoot the birds back then and have 'em stuffed! Quite a market, back then...the start of the twentieth century. Well, they didn't have opticals like we do now, like you sell, Arthur, so you couldn't see them in any detail. You can understand it, really. Though we don't shoot them nowadays of course, hee, hee!"

THE HIDE

On this point, Bristow looked furtive, and his beady eyes scanned the floor.

"They was ALL GEN-UI-INE!" suddenly barked Lostweathiel, rising to his feet, and raising both arms high in the air. "Them chum-buckets what doubted – Witherby, Nicholson – both armchair dogfish with them bloomin' mathematicals! Them specimens wot 'is great granpa stuffed – some o' which I done collected as you see on my walls - They was ALL GEN-UI-INE! All shot 'ere – in England, and thereby - GEN-UI-INE visitors!"

"Well, Arthur, p'rhaps not all," the taxidermist smiled nervously. "The white-winged snowfinch has never been seen 'ere again. Nor the moustached warbler. It was always rumoured in the family that mebbe great-grunpa perhaps 'turned a blind eye'. Prob'ly Michael Nicoll was the bloke who shot 'em abroad and brought 'em back like they was all shot 'ere."

"You spiny gurnard, Leonard! Don't be daft, boy! All your great granpa's' stuffing - all shot 'ere - in Engy-land, and thereby - GEN-UI-INE visitors! An' collector's items, ter boot! Right, you can come an' fetch tattler ter-morrow. But take my advice, boy, don't' be revivin' the 'Hastings Rarities Affair' in yer little exhy-bishun. Nothin' ever proved, neither wun way nor t'other! An' I say… GEN-UI-INE!!"

"I know you do, Arthur! Anyway thanks, I'll come back in the morning. Good day to you, sir…"

"Ooooh yes, nice to meet you! I didn't know there was still a taxidermist in these parts!" grinned Ball.

"Oh yes, we've had a little shop on the edge of town for years. Here's my card, Leonard Bristow. If you ever want anything stuffed and mounted, you gentlemen just let me know!"

"If I ever catch a bigger carp than Big Bertha, I will let you know, son!" blustered Bullock from a dusty corner of the shop.

"Right you are, sir! Bye, Arthur!" Bristow sidled out of the shop,

THE HIDE

wedging a flat cap on his head as he left, wrapping about him a muffler scarf and pulling on fingerless gloves. He looked like the kind of man who was always cold, even in mid-summer or if sat before a blazing fire.

The groaning and concave bookshelves heaved with an extensive array of books on birds and birdwatching and many racks of outdoor clothing and hats made it difficult to negotiate the shop interior without bumping into things.

"Bloody Hell," muttered Bullock under his breath to De'Ath, "this bloke has no idea about shop layout, has 'e! Or perhaps 'is plan is we break summat so as we 'ave to pay, like them souvenir shops at t'seaside!"

Right on cue, De'Ath blundered into an ancient mannequin dressed eccentrically in a bobble hat with an embroidered herring gull; a scarf decorated by partridge in flight; a tartan shirt topped by a camouflage gillet with dozens of pockets, each of which contained something presumably essential to outdoor craft, including a compass, a Swiss Army knife, and less explicably, a *Mars Bar;* a pair of shapeless brown corduroys tucked into thick woolen socks with a duck on each ankle, above sturdy waxed walking boots, and draped in an enormous floor-length Barbour coat which looked more like cape than coat. Someone had rather half-heartedly drawn a moustache on the mannequin's faded yellow face with a marker pen, and pair of round glasses without lenses in them perched on its tiny snub nose. It looked like a photo in a newspaper that a bored schoolboy had decided to deface. De'Ath's attempts to grab and stabilize the swaying explorer failed, and it crashed to the floor, taking with it the dusty stuffed crow, which lost its beak on impact, and the decapitated head of the mannequin rolled away under the counter.

"Oh bugger, I am most dreadfully sorry!" exclaimed De'Ath, "have I broken anything?"

"That's just what 'e wants yer to say, Tom!" boomed an exasperated Bullock. "'Ow the 'eck are we supposed to get around this shop, wi'out bumpin' into owt – it's not humanly possible!"

THE HIDE

But Lostweathiel didn't seem much concerned. "Allus 'appens," he grunted, rising to haul the mannequin upright again. "Where's 'is 'ead gorn, then?"

"Erm, it's just under that chair, shall I get it?" offered Ball, scrambling about on the floor. "Oh dear, his glasses are a bit broken, look."

"No matter, I got a stickin' plaster as will repair them. Stick 'is 'ead back on. Oh, old Joe Crow lost 'is bill. Again. Gotta bit o' blutack for that somewhere." The old Cornishman shuffled about his repairs and it didn't take long before he was back seated again with his arms folded, though his display mannequin looked as though it had been roughed up in the alley by a gang of thugs and then had a long night on the cider. The semi-repaired crow didn't look much better, its beak now stuck back on at a jaunty and improbable angle to its head.

Boptics

THE HIDE

Bullock had been expecting the shopkeeper to craftily issue a bill of repair to De'Ath, but no sign of such thing came. In any case, Bullock was rapidly losing his patience.

"Sir, I won't muck about." Bullock placed his meaty hands on the thick glass counter and peered down at the vendor below him, attempting transactional eye contact. But the Cornishman was more interested in watching De'Ath peer myopically at a case containing Zeiss binoculars.

"Ahem, as I was saying, I won't muck about, Mr...?" continued Bullock.

"Lostweathiel!" called Ball, helpfully, examining the bookshelves with much interest.

"Yeah, OK, Mr. Lostweasel, look, you've been recommended to us… for some Godforsaken reason," he muttered under his breath, "to sell us some stuff we need. My friend Tom and me are taking up birdwatching and we need decent bins for a start. As you know, Professor Ball is an expert and is here to ensure we get a good deal. We know the prices, having done very considerable and exhaustive research. I expect it's cheaper on the tinternet, but we like to support the local high street where possible, don't we, Tom?"

"We certainly do. Vegetables, flowers, fish, meat, we buy them all from the market or high street shops, my wife Dot and I."

Lostweathiel hauled himself up, and attempted to find his keys again.

"What'd I do with me blummin' keys, then?" he asked himself and ignoring Bullock. Eventually, he located them in his coat pocket and shuffled over to the cabinet that De'Ath was inspecting. After trying many keys, he opened the glass door, and took out a pair of exceptionally expensive looking binoculars.

"Troi 'em. Be best wi yoor gal-asses, boy."

De'Ath remembered to put the strap around his neck, then attempted to squint through the lenses to the roof of the building opposite, through the dusty shop window.

"Tek lens caps off," instructed the vendor, impassively.

"Ah, haha, yes, of course," flustered a blushing De'Ath.

Bullock, bunching his fists in fury, muttered under his breath again. "Well done, Tom, that shows us up as right bunglers. That'll raise the price, without doubt."

"Oh, I say, these are crystal sharp! Wow, I can see the moss on the roof!"

"Probably *Brachythecium rutabulum*, Tom," called Ball helpfully. "Ooh yes, very nice those, Arthur. Zeiss Victory 10x42 SF. Lovely engineering, ooh yes."

"They'll do yer." The Cornishman turned his expressionless gaze to an increasingly exasperated Bullock, and having inspected him for some time, shuffled off to another cabinet, this time branded 'Leica'. After further key fumblings, he opened the door and lifted out a pair of binoculars with a red spot on the moulding, cleaned the lenses with a cloth from his pocket and handed them to Bullock.

"Troi 'em. Be suitin' you best, boy." Then Lostweathiel shuffled back to his seat behind the counter, sat down and went immediately to sleep.

Bullock peremptorily tried out the binoculars, played with the focus and then put them down on the counter.

"All very well 'im trying to sell off old stock on us novices, but ah'll be damned if ah don't try out every pair of binoculars in the shop before ah part wi' a grand n 'alf! Bella took some convincing, ah tell yer! She'll be wanting 'olidays on a cruise ship in return for this considerable expenditure!" Bullock helped himself to all the other binoculars in the cabinet, muttering over each one as if he knew what he was talking about. "And much 'elp old Lostweasel is - 'e is fast asleep and there aren't even any prices on these bloody things!"

"Wurgle." Lostweathiel awoke from his apparent slumber - one

THE HIDE

crinkly elephantine eye opened to reveal at last a beady bright blue pupil. "Them Zeiss for 'im an' them Leica for you. Two ton each."

"Two…two…" spluttered Bullock in self-righteous indignation. "Two grand! Yer little robber - that's an inflated price and you know it! And you aren't even giving us a choice! Do you think we came in off the last banana boat, lad?"

Lostweathiel rose from his low seat and folded his arms. He leaned forward and scrunched one eye closed completely, as if he was dealing with an idiot of foreign origin.

"Oi sayed two ton not two grand, you pilchard."

Bullock was confused. He looked at the binoculars that the Cornishmen had recommended – they looked brand new rather than second hand. He went into a hissing huddle with De'Ath and Ball.

"Two hundred? Is he serious? Are these knock-offs? Or is there summat wrong wi' em?"

Ball inspected both the recommended items, squinting with them into the middle distance and wrinkling his nose.

"Oh no. They are superb. But I told you he would offer you a good deal! I think his prices got stuck about 1971."

Bullock looked over his shoulder at the ancient vendor, who stood muted and regarding them with folded arms. Bullock was an honourable man, and though he was keen on a sharp deal, he wasn't about to be cheating an old salt.

"Erm, are you sure that these bins you recommended are suitable for us? Do they come with a guarantee, lad?"

"Them be roight. Guaranteed for loife. 'Course I'll 'ave to give 'em a service now and agin. BUT THAT'LL BE A FIVER, MIND!" Lostweathiel wagged his finger in warning of this extravagant extra.

"Five..five 'undred?" wondered Bullock, aloud.

"I think he means five pounds, Ron," suggested Ball. "Actually I think I will bring mine in. I bought them here, you know. For two hundred pounds as well - though that was fifteen years ago…"

"Ahem, let's be clear, Mr. Lostweasel. You propose to sell us these brand new, top of the range binoculars – for two hundred pounds each. With an occasional service for five pounds. Am I understanding you correctly?"

"Aye. CASH MOIND!"

De'Ath looked out of the window, feeling a bit embarrassed. He knew the instrument in his hand was worth well over a thousand pounds, as did Bullock, who tried a little upward negotiation.

"Look old feller, we know our budgets. Let us give you five 'undred for each, at least, it's…"

"Don't be buggering me about, boy! Tek it or leave it. Final offer."

"Right…" Bullock looked at the old man with something approaching pity. "Well, we'll go to the cashpoint and get some dosh then…I suppose. But I insist on paying the right price for some clothing items – and some of them books as well."

"Right you are. Wurgle." The Cornishman sat down again and apparently went back to sleep.

The trio quietly exited the shop and walked back onto the High Street.

"This is ridiculous, Prof!" blustered Bullock. "'ow can 'e possibly mek money? Is 'e one'o them secret millionaires in disguise?"

"I don't think so," mused Ball. "But he certainly gives his customers a good deal, does he not."

"Good deal? I don't know what his accountant must say. Perhaps it's a tax write-off for smuggling barrels of rum or something. I am not buyin' from a criminal – even at them prices!"

THE HIDE

"Oooh, I don't think so, Ron. He is a celebrated birder, Arthur is."

"Perhaps he discounts his binoculars and makes a premium on the other stuff, Ron. Let's get five hundred out each and see if we can pay him back a bit, as it were. I am very happy with his recommendation, I must say, I think our bins are better than Dirty Colin's!"

"Oh aye, me too, lad! I dunno why 'e thought I was a Leica man and you a Zeiss. I don't think 'e sells Swarowskis does 'e? We could ask. P'raps you get a free pair o'them wi every purchase!" Bullock gave a throaty laugh. "Eh, ah don't think you're allowed five 'undred from the 'ole in t'wall. We'll 'ave to go inside the bank."

Cashed up and back in *Boptics,* Lostweathiel sat as they had left him, his chin on the white wiry plumage of his chest. Extravagantly, Bullock slapped down a wad of cash on the counter. An eye slowly opened and the craggy neck was raised.

"Right sir. There is one thousand pounds in cash from me and Tommy. In view of the bargain you offer us on our optics, we wish to purchase other merchandise up to that sum of money!"

Lostweathiel slowly reached out an arm, and laboriously counted out the cash. He got lost on the first and second occasion, but on the third attempt, managed to count out the notes to their correct value.

"A THOU!" he shouted, raising himself up and squinting suspiciously. "A thou? What are you wanting, my 'ole stock?? Do yers want to put me out o'business? Is it wun o' them 'ostile tekkover bids?"

"Err…no," grimaced Bullock. "We thought we might tek some coats n' 'ats n' that. And some books."

"Well, well, ta-ake what yer fancy then. An oi'll give yer change when yer be ready!"

With that, he wandered off to the back of the shop and put a rusty kettle on a leaky gas hob.

THE HIDE

Bullock and De'Ath tried on various hats, fleeces, waterproof trousers and rain-proof jackets, none of them priced. They perused the books on the shelves with Ball, insisting to buy him a history of birdwatching he seemed keen on. To finish, they bought their wives each a fluffy bird which when squeezed emitted a life-like birdsong. Bullock went for the blackbird and De'Ath for a hoopoe.

When they were satisfied that they had what they needed - and more - to sum around an estimated six hundred pounds in addition to the hugely discounted four hundred for the binoculars, they made a pile of their chosen items on the counter, and summoned the tea-slurping Cornishman from his snug.

"Roight, the last o' the big spenders...watcha got 'ere then. Lordy me."

Lostweathiel began sorting through the pile, apparently making calculations in his head. If so, they weren't adding up, as he had to keep starting again, much to the rising frustration of Bullock.

"Look, lad, count it up to a grand and if its mower, just tell us."

"A gree-and! Don't be da-aft. Oi'll tek seven ton sixty fer this lot. Ere's yer two ton forty back. Do yus want wanna these yer bags? THEM'S FIVE PENCE EACH MOIND!"

Bullock and De'Ath laughed, shamefacedly taking back the notes and appreciating the joke, as they stuffed their purchases into two large bags taken from a hook on the side of the counter. Except, as judged by the aggrieved look on Lostweathiel's face, that it wasn't a joke. He extended his gnarled arthritic palm.

"Ten new pence in total. Oi told yer! The bags ain't free no mower! ANOTHER BLIMMIN TAX FROM EUROPE!"

With a sigh, Bullock placed a silver coin in the extended palm, which closed like Gollum clutching The Ring.

"Erm, could I ask for a receipt?" asked De'Ath innocently. "In fact, if you could separate that into two, perhaps just divide between the two,

THE HIDE

of three hundred and eighty pounds each?"

This request was simply met by a puzzled frown, engendering an uncomfortable silence. De'Ath felt the need to justify himself by way of nervous blathering.

"Yes, hehe, it's just that Dot, my wife, and myself...well; we do keep joint accounts, and any expenditure needs to be well, put in the disposable income book, as it were, hehe..."

"What the wurgle you need a receipt fer, yer gurt crabstick? You gonna put them binocules straight on EBaywatch are yer? Sell 'em on, is that yer game is it?"

Bullock attempted an emollient intervention. "Well, a proof of purchase is always a good idea, Mr. Lostweasel. For you as the vendor too. For example, when we return for a service, or even a trade-in...it would be proof we bought them here and not in some other place."

"Proof? What proof you need. You bring 'em in and I fix 'em. I won't forget you two pilchards! Roight, I'll be gettin' the door fer yous. It be well aafter closing time, you know...must think oi'm a blummin suppermaarkit or summink! Open all hours be buggered boy! Off you get!"

With no further word, the baffled customers were ushered briskly from the shop as the High Street clock struck 4, and the cardboard sign was promptly turned to 'Closed'.

With very mixed feelings, the trio marched towards the High Street. Bullock spoke first.

"I feel like we just robbed a bank, but not one o' them multinationals as can afford it! And Bella won't be pleased – no cruise money for 'er! Four 'undred wont keep 'er in bingo money for long. There's nowt so queer as folk, as they seh where ah'm from. Ah think we owe you plenty for bringin' us 'ere Prof! Let's buy you a slap-up tea at Betty's anyway, c'mon!"

Over tea and jam scones, the trio picked through their purchases from

THE HIDE

Boptics. Tom put on his tracker hat and fiddled with the ear straps; Ball thumbed through his volume enthusiastically, noting various illustrations, and Bullock peered around the tea room with his Leica's, much to the nervousness of Bet, the busty waitress.

"Oooh, I spy a pair of great tits!" guffawed Ball, following the line of Bullock's gaze and exhaling scone crumbs all over the place.

"Nethen!" Bullock wagged his finger, with a mixture of disapproval and indulgent half-smile. "Though I suppose we'd better be gettin' used to birder humour - now we are ones, like. 'Ere try this one, Prof. Two vultures were in the desert eating a dead clown. The first vulture asks the second vulture, "Does this taste funny to you?"

"Heee heee, that's good, that is! Though my strong advice is - don't try jokes around Aldous on Sunday. He is very serious, Aldous. I hope it all goes well repairing The Hide - I can't join you I'm afraid, as I'll be flying the Cessna on Sunday morning. I might give you a wave though!"

Bullock and De'Ath looked at Ball incredulously. "Do you mean you can fly a plane, Professor?" asked De'Ath, in some awe and spilling tea down his beard.

"Oooh yes, I've had a private pilot's license for years! Little Oldside Airport, aaaaah! I am a fully paid up member of Tredbury Flying Club. Der-der-der-der dududer der der..." Ball raised his arms to his eyes, and inverting his wrists, made a pair of goggles with his first fingers and thumbs, humming the *Dambuster's March*.

"There really is no end to your talents, Prof," admired De'Ath, wiping his beard with a doily.

"Oooh, I'll take you up with me sometime! I can fly a glider as well, it's just like being a bird! And there's another chap in The Flying Club called Nigel, who thinks he *is* a bird! Or is it a moth...yes, he thinks he's a moth. You will meet him at Clarendon too, I expect. He goes in for this para-gliding business – now that really is like flying like a bird. Right, well...I'll be off then. Thanks for the high tea, smashing! And the book too! BYE BYE, BET!"

Bet hitched up her skirt, shot Ball a look of insouciant disdain and repaired her lipstick by bending over the counter, pouting into the mirror behind it.

"Oooh a thong!" gulped Ball. "I wish my wife would wear one of those!"

"Steady on, Prof!" hissed Bullock, trying to ignore Bet's exposed voluminous and tattooed bottom. "Get yourself away, lad, she's vicious, she is. Eat you alive and no mistake. She's got a mouth on 'er that would make Dirty Colin blush!"

Ball ignored this sound advice and reached instead to his pocket to rummage for Humphrey the Hedgehog.

"Bet, I don't think you've met Sir Humphrey Hedgehog, have you? Say hello, Humphrey!"

Alert to the danger, Bullock rose swiftly, grabbed the shopping bags and Ball's arm and man-handled him swiftly out of the tea shop. "Leave a twenty on the table, Tom. Keep the change, Bet! Tara love!"

Having hastened Ball and Humphrey on their way up the road, De'Ath and Bullock returned to the car park and put their bags in the boot of the Rover.

"Well, we are all set Tom. Perhaps we will find a way of making it up to old Mr. Lostweasel one day. Eh, just wait til they see *us* at Clarendon Marsh on Sunday…we've got the gear now, laddie!"

Tramping down the path at Clarendon Marsh, everything in the late spring Sunday morning sunshine shone with the brilliant green of new leaves. Bullock, completely bedecked in camouflage clothing and a wide brimmed Kodiak Oilskin hat, stopped to peer ostentatiously into the reeds, ensuring that the red Leica dot on his binoculars was evident to all. Seeing small brown birds flitting in and out of the *Phragmites*, he avidly consulted his various reference books stored in a green canvas satchel over his shoulder.

"Reed bunting!" he announced loudly, as two birders trudged up the path, veering around and studying the ground to avoid any possibility of human interaction.

"Cetti's!" Bullock called after them, in hope of some conversation by which to test or improve his birding progress, but their backs remained turned.

Even by birdwatcher's standards, De'Ath had made an eccentric choice of uniform. His tracker hat, despite the pleasant warmth, was buttoned under his chin and on his gillet jacket, he had pinned various badges bought from Boptics and the shop at Clarendon's visitor centre. An assortment of pens and pencils jutted from his many pockets along with at least three mini spiral note books. On his back was a large rucksack with tin mugs dangling from it, like that of an Australian outback camper. The Zeiss binoculars around his neck swung from side to side as he loped along in a pair of flappy Wellington boots and a pair of corduroys which had long lost their cord and any pretence of colour.

As they approached the broken Hide, a gaggle of Barbour-coated, mainly middle-aged gentlemen were unpacking tools from a crate. They seemed intimidated by the approach of strangers, and responded by ignoring them, though their leader greeted them sharply.

"Ten minutes late, gentlemen, a bad start," barked Aldous. "David, these are the people that broke your hide."

David Smith, under a mop of grey hair, peered sideways at them with steely eyes, but seemed vaguely amused rather than upset. He greeted them stiffly but genially.

"Oroight? Thanks for coming. I gather there was a bit of an accident, then!"

"Morning David. Yes, all very odd really. Dirty Colin…I mean,

THE HIDE

Colin, fell against the end panel and it just gave way. Then he floated off on it." Bullock pointed up the pool. "But me and Jack Ward got 'im back."

"I hear it's done 'im good. He's stopped swearing apparently! They reckon the bang on the 'ead cured his Tourette's!" Dave was chuckling, both at the thought of Colin floating up the creek and the odd appearances of the newcomers.

"Anyway, we are sorry about your hide, David," offered De'Ath. "Off on the wrong foot, as it were, and on our first trip to the Marsh as well."

"Don't worry about it, it's not *my* hide, I just put the money up, yonks ago. It's probably time for a new one really."

"Nothing wrong with this one!" barked Aldous. "Right, let's get to it, men. Most of that panel will go back on, and then we can put some new slats on it to make it good. Right, lifting party, fall in."

Puffing and blowing, the assembled company was able to lift and secure the fourth panel wall of The Hide back into place, after which followed much sawing, hammering and banging. After an hour so, The Hide was restored to an enclosed space providing relative shelter from the elements, though in Stern's words, it "looked like a patch up job."

"Right, Mr. Death and Bullock, the cost of the wood and metalwork comes to £63.45; I suggest that you split the cost between those that you hold most responsible for the damage. I will take a cheque made payable to Clarendon Marsh Volunteer Group - here is my address. Right, I must get off to church service. Alan, you will see to packing up the tools and leaving everything tidy. I will return later to see everything is made good and conduct the dusk survey." With that, he was off.

Bullock grimaced ruefully at being handed the 'cost of repairs' but unusually, he held his tongue.

"Don't worry about the bill, mate." David Smith said quietly. "It was probably in need of repair anyway by the sounds of things. It was a wonder nobody got seriously hurt. And it sounds like Colin got some benefit, bless him!"

"No, no, David, we insist. I will post a cheque to Mr. Stern this very evening. I caused the accident by gettin' me legs all tangled up in yonder benches."

"Well, if you're sure…blimey you fellers have some kit on you. Boptics bargain bins, by any chance?"

"Ah yes," admitted De'Ath bashfully, stroking his Zeisses lovingly. "I am afraid we got the Sale of the Century!"

"Haha, not just you, mate! Old Arthur is a legend round here - but you are lucky actually, 'cos he only does that for people 'e likes the look of."

"Likes the look of!" spluttered Bullock. "I don't think 'e said two words to us! And 'e called us pilchards!"

"Oh, he calls everyone pilchards. It's when he calls you other species of fish you want to watch out. Gurnard isn't good. Pollack is worse. Anyway, I daresay you'll get a chance to pay him back - look out for him. He's always getting lost - so you might need to take him home occasionally."

The party was distracted first by the sound and then by the sight of a light aircraft flying low over the Marsh. So low in fact, that the grinning face of Professor Ball waving madly from the cockpit was perfectly recognizable.

"Good Lord, it's Bally!" grinned Smith, waving his arms, as did Bullock and De'Ath.

"For God's sake don't encourage him," muttered a bald man with the hint of a Welsh accent. "If he gets any lower he'll hit the trees and then there won't be any repairing your Hide, Dave - he'll bloody well smash it to bits. It's just as well Aldous has gone - he'd have him shot out of the sky. I'm Nigel by the way, lads. Nigel Shiltberry."

THE HIDE

De'Ath recognized his name from a conversation with Prof. Ball and remembered that Nigel was probably the guy who thought he was a moth.

"Are you the para-glider, Nigel?" he ventured. "The Prof mentioned you the other day."

"Did he now!" puffed Nigel, relieved to see that the Red Baron above had circled away to the north. "Then I suppose he told you that I think I'm a moth, did he?"

"Er, no, not exactly, he just said you were a para-glider," responded De'Ath unconvincingly and inspecting the ground.

"Oh, I bet he did!" insisted Nigel. "He tells everyone I think I'm a moth. Well, I don't mind, but just for the record, I don't think I'm a moth, I just happen to be extremely interested in them. I breed them actually, and OK, my paraglider is in the shape and colour of the peppered moth…"

"Is that a moth tattooed on your forearm, by any chance? It's a biggun!" remarked Bullock.

"Erm, yeah, that is the elephant hawk moth. And I do have a few more, actually."

Rolling up his sleeves, it was clear that Nigel's arms were covered in tattoos of various moth species, together with various plants and flowers on which more moths fed or rested.

Looking at Nigel carefully, Bullock thought that in fact, there was a hint of the moth about his face, and suspected that there were probably a pair of moth wings tattooed on his back, which at least he thought, would be a change from the angel wings sported by the masses, including his daughter Wendy.

"Well, there's nowt wrong wi' tats, lad. Look, I've got one on me forearm - the Pyramids of Egypt."

THE HIDE

Nigel inspected the blue blur on Bullock's meaty forearm but was at a loss to make out anything, let alone the Pyramids.

"Yep, there is the Sphinx, look. And some birds flying too! We used to call 'em shite-hawks in the army. The black kite, I believe is its proper name. They used to feed off all the rubbish round the camp. I did me National Service y'see. Frankly, I think they should bring it back. Gave me the chance to get out and see the world."

"Erm, right. Anyway, I'd best be off, doing a bit of para-gliding today. Nice to meet you both, I expect we'll be seeing each other around if you've joined the Volunteers. I'll show you me moth trap next time if you want. Cheerio!"

"Moth trap?" said Bullock after Nigel had loped off. "Why do you want to trap moths then? Are there too many or something?"

"It's just a light in a box with some egg boxes, really. During the night, the moths are attracted to the light of course, and when they can't get out they creep under the boxes until morning. It's a really good way to survey what species are about," explained Smith helpfully, as he packed away the tools.

"Eh, haha, that reminds me of a joke, that does," grinned Bullock. De'Ath shot him a warning glance, recalling Professor Ball's advice that the Clarendon Marsh Volunteers didn't do jokes. The glance went unheeded.

"So this guy walks into a dental surgery and says, "I think I'm a moth." The dentist replies "you shouldn't be here. You should be seeing a psychiatrist!" The guy replies, "I am seeing a psychiatrist." The dentist says, "well then, what are you doing here?" And the guy goes…"your light was on." Hahahhaha-herrrrr! Your light was on!!"

Dave Smith smiled, but looked mystified. The remaining volunteers shook their heads, some muttering inaudibly.

"Soooooo….why did he go into the dentist's if he was already seeing a psychiatrist? Did he have toothache?" asked Smith, apparently innocently.

"Er, well, hehe, erm…moths…light?" responded Bullock, gingerly.

"Oh, I see!" Smith smiled as the penny dropped, and there was relief all round for both Bullock and De'Ath, who let out an audible sigh through his wavy watery smile. "So he actually *was* a moth then, was he?" laughed Smith, heartily.

Bullock and De'Ath looked at each other with alarm - the other volunteers had already packed up and scuttled off. "Aaaanyway," exhaled Bullock, "we'd best be off too, lad. Nice ter meet yer."

"Thanks for fixing up The Hide, lads. Come over to my place sometime – we do some badger watching from the hide in the garden."

"Aye, eh, we will…tara for now, lad."

"Badger baiting?" whispered Bullock to De'Ath when they were out of earshot. "That's not allowed nowadays, is it? Reet cruel that can be. They are a funny lot these nature volunteers - are they not! I thought it was the farmers that did the badger baiting?"

"Oh, I don't think he said badger baiting, Ron. Badger watching. It's like watching birds but instead, you watch, erm, badgers."

"Why? Where's the challenge in that? There ain't more than one species of badger is there? Mind you, I have never seen a badger, apart from dead on the road. Don't they come out in the dark though - how would you see 'em? Infra-red cameras or summat?"

"Me neither, I haven't seen one, although there is a sett in Bramely Woods. Now that is one thing that Dot *would* join in on. She loves badgers. Not so keen on birds but loves animals, my Dot. *And*…she is softening to thoughts of having a dog, thanks to the mighty Basker!"

They stopped at a bench overlooking a pool and decided to have a sit down for a bit. As they did so, there was the sound of a 'peep', like a pea-whistle, and a flash of iridescent blue zipped over the water.

"Blimey, that was a kingfisher that was!" exclaimed Bullock, reaching for his Leicas. "Look Tom, there it is…no there *they* are look…sitting on that branch over yonder! There's two of them, see!"

"I have them! How marvelous, this is the first time I have ever seen a kingfisher in real life. Gosh, it's better than on the telly, isn't it. Somehow more, erm… real, if you know what I mean. Wow, one of them just dived in…he's caught a stickleback, Ron!"

Both men sat glued to their binoculars, sporting great grins and watched on in wonder at the kingfisher show.

"There isn't a much finer sight in nature gents, is there?"

Dirty Colin leaned over the back of the bench, peering through his own binoculars. "A breeding pair no doubt, they sometimes build a nest in that exposed bank over there. Yep, looks like there is guano below that hole."

"Colin! I didn't think we'd see you back down here so fast – we repaired The Hide this morning. How is your 'ead? And the jaw? No hard feelings I hope, lad." Bullock stood to inspect Colin's face, which apart from a split lower lip, looked as before, only calmer.

"Hard feelings?! I owe you guys BIG time - I've only stopped doing my Tourette's sweary thing! Well, so far so good, anyhow. It might start again – if so, just give me another belt with me scope, eh! Come on, I'll buy you both lunch at Brocks - least I can do. Eh! You two have got kitted our haven't you, blimey…I can't see you Ron, you are that camouflaged! You look like a nightjar on the heath - practically invisible. As for you Tom, you look like a right tw…tw…"

De'Ath winced, suspecting that his apparel may have caused the re-boot of Dirty Colin 2.0.

"Tw…tw…twitcher! Twitcher! You look like a twitcher. Not a tw… no, I have beaten it. I am not Dirty no more!"

"Congratulations Colin, and we 'll be happy to join you for a spot of Sunday roast. We 'ave questions a-plenty for yer, lad!"

THE HIDE

With that, they sauntered up the path to enjoy a roast beef lunch at Brock's, but not before Bullock made his first entry in the Sightings Book at the Visitor Centre Reception desk. "June 2nd. Kingfisher pair. Glebe Pool. Nesting nearby and catching stickleback for lunch. RB & TAD."

"There we go Colin, first of many."

"I'm sure it will be, Ron! You are both w…w…w… WWWWWELCOME!"

THE HIDE

- CHAPTER THREE -

Puffin Billy

Wherein a trip to the Farne Islands of Northumbria is undertaken and the City of Newcastle upon Tyne is visited en route. There are close encounters with puffin and tern, in the company of Icelandic hunters. Bella reveals a family connection to pigeon fanciers.

"It's a long drive, lad. I didn't realize that Northumbria was so far from t'Midlands. It's well past Barnsley, eh?"

Bullock and De'Ath were in their usual spot in Bullock's lounge at The Nook. Bullock studied a road atlas splayed out on the coffee table, whilst De'Ath, on his laptop computer, was investigating bed and breakfast options in the vicinity of the Farne Islands.

"Do you know, I've never been to Newcastle. Not even to watch the football."

"Theeee.... *fog on the Tyne is all mine, all mine, the fog on the Tyne is all mine*..." De'Ath broke into song, and was soon joined by Bullock, who not only knew the chorus of the song, but the first verse as well.

"Sittin' in a sleazy snack-bar,
Suckin', sickly sausage rolls
Slippin' down slowly, slippin' down sideways
Think I'll sign off the dole...chorus, Tom, together now!"

"*Thhhhhe.... fog on the Tyne is all mine, all mine, the fog on the Tyne is all mine. The fog on the Tyne is all mine, all mine -THE FOG ON THE TYNE IS ALL MIIIINE!!* WOOOH!"

"Haha!" laughed De'Ath. "Lindisfarne, 1971. Yes, I have met plenty of Geordies in my time, but also never had the opportunity to visit. I believe they drink all the time and wear next to nothing in the freezing fog. I am told it's a fantastic city though, despite all that. Shall we have a night in The Toon then? And then a night on the coast - this Seahouses place looks best bet."

De'Ath resumed his accommodation search, humming as he did so another *Lindisfarne* song. He was surprised that Bullock knew that one as well, as he joined in, with his low gravelly voice.

"Hey mister dream seller, where 'ave you been? Tell me 'ave you dreams I can see? Well ah came alo-ong, just to briiiing you this song - can you spare one dream for me-eeee?"

They joined together in the chorus, De'Ath with one hand on his ear in a folk-warble.

*"Meet me on the corner, when the lights are coming on,
And I'll be there, I promise I'll be there.
Down the empty streets, we'll disappear into the dawn,
If you have dreams enough to shaa-aare!!"*

"Oh very good! Didn't know you liked a bit of folk music, Ron?"

"I don't generally, but everybody likes Lindisfarne, don't they. Eh, I wonder if Prof Ball will drive us mad if we are cooped up with 'im for three days? What do you reckon, lad?"

"Well, we will certainly have to keep an eye on him. He could get into trouble with his glove puppets. But he is interesting company. We can always put a tape on in the car if he gets too much. In fact, I'm pretty sure I have the Lindisfarne tape somewhere! I am more concerned that you have to do all the driving Ron, I am very sorry I don't drive and could take a turn. And you definitely don't want Bally at the wheel!"

"Aye that's fer sure! Not a problem for old Ronny, lad. Ah could drive through t'night and the followin' day if necessary, I thought about bein' a lorry driver for a bit. OK, let's invite 'im, shall we. His birdin' knowledge will be highly useful. But he'll 'ave to 'ave 'is own room. Don't mind sharing with you lad, but three is a crowd, as they say."

Bella entered with three mugs of coffee. "What's all this sing-songing, boys? You both seem in very good spirits. How's plans for the trip coming along? Oooh look, there's a green bird on the nuts, look!"

Since taking up their new hobby, Bullock had festooned the garden beyond the French windows with bird tables, feeders, a bird bath and a feast of various nuts, seeds and dried insects, which he carefully topped up each day. It hadn't taken long for the birdlife to find it, and a growing list of visitors were carefully noted on a list in a book kept on the sideboard. Never far from their binoculars, the birders inspected and focused on the feeder.

"I do believe that is a greenfinch, Thomas! NOT to be confused with the siskin or the serin of course…check the *Collins* lad!"

"*Carduelis chloris*. Yes, no doubt about it, Ron, look at the yellow edges to the primaries. That's a fine adult male, there."

"New one for the list, get that one on, lad. These bloody pigeons are a nuisance though aren't they? They gobble everything up, the fat buggers, and there are that many of 'em. They never came in gardens when I were a lad. They don't seem to give the littl'uns a chance."

"I get a bit mixed up with pigeons, Ron. The ones in the cities, you know, like Trafalgar Square, they are not like these ones, are they?"

"Erm, I dunno. These are wood pigeons, are they not? Is *Collins* any 'elp?"

"Page 200. Pigeons and doves. Wood pigeon. *Calumba palumbus. Best identified by large white patch on neckside…*"

"Roger that, Tom. We have the wood pigeon. I'd bloody shoot it on its neck patch me. Nice in a pie. You used to do a pigeon pie, Bella, when we lived up north."

"Oh yes, its good meat, pigeon. Can you eat these, then? Are they not dirty if they live in the town?"

"I don't know, love. I'll find out. I certainly wouldn't want to eat them ones in Trafalgar Square…or Tredley Piazza, for that matter."

"Ah!" added De'Ath, still reading. "It seems the townie ones are in fact feral pigeons, *Columba livia (domest.)* and they are all sorts of colours. They originate from the wild rock dove *Columba livia* which seems to be quite rare now, it lives in northern Scotland on sea coasts and cliffs. And the feral pigeon, or city pigeon, originate from them, having been bred in pigeon houses and escaped. And now…the feral ones are mating with the rock doves and breeding them out!"

"My Uncle Wilf used to keep pigeons in Bolton," mused Bella, crunching a HobNob, a noise that snapped Basker from his slumbers. He edged closer to his mistress, without bothering to rise to his feet, by snaking along on his belly like an overweight python. "He used to race them on Sundays. A pigeon fancier, they called them. I remember them all cooing away, loads of them. All cooped up in this old shed, pigeon loft 'e called it. He bred them too, won trophies and all sorts."

"I have heard of that Bella, but I often wondered how they know which one is the winner. I mean, I know they would take them miles away in cages and then let them go, and I suppose they would return to their loft, that's why they called them 'homing pigeons', I presume?"

"Ooh, it were quite involved, Tom. Some races were hundreds of miles. There was this thing called a pigeon racing clock. Yes, it was in a leather case - like a little suitcase - and it had, like a mechanism, you know, it looked like the inside of an old fashioned telephone, I used to think. Well, you put these rubber rings round the birds' legs, each one with a different number on it. Then Uncle Wilf would put the number in the clock, and then seal it up. Then, off go the birds, and Uncle Wilf went back home to wait. Of course, some never came home - either they just flew off or a falcon got them, or got shot, who knows. I remember once when we were all in Victoria Square – that's in the middle of Bolton, Tom - in the Wimpy Bar and there was a flock of these pigeons pecking away, and Uncle Wilf suddenly shot up and

THE HIDE

went, "That's Dolly that is!" And went chasing round the square after it - it was one of his best birds, apparently. Anyway he never caught it. I remember me Dad killing himself watching Wilf running round like a madman - he never understood the pigeons, my Dad, God bless him."

"Haha, good old Wilf, I remember him, Bella, a very kind soul. But I never knew about this pigeon hobby of his?"

"Well, in the end me Auntie Joy couldn't stand the mess in the yard and made 'im get rid of 'em. I think he went to the dogs after that - literally, well, he went to the stadium as well, to bet on the greyhounds, Tom - but he was never the same after his pigeons were gone. I've got a photo of him somewhere, I'll go and look when I finish me coffee."

"But what happened if the pigeon *did* come home Bella. What then?' asked Tom.

"Oh yes, Wilf would come home - on the bus, or I think they had a truck or something like that, and wait in the yard, smoking his Capstan Full Strength and eagerly watching the sky for a sign of his birds. When one came back, he would have to take the ring from the bird's leg and put it in a slot in the clock. The time that the ring was placed in the clock was recorded. They called it a timestamp - as I recall it was stamped onto something like a thimble that they then took it to the Club HQ. Then they could work out the speed of the bird - and the winner.

"Mind you, I was there at his house once with me Auntie Joy in the kitchen making steak and kidney puddings and outside, poor Wilf was going mad! His prize pigeon had come home – but it didn't want to go back in the loft. It just sat on the wall looking at Wilf. I think it knew that taking the ring off wasn't nice, so it just sat there, watching him. Well, he went mad because he knew that any time lost taking the ring off could lose him the race - sometimes there were only seconds in it, you see. He was up a ladder, shaking a brush at it, trying to cajole it down with *Trill* – that's budgie food, Tom - shouting at it, but it wouldn't move! I reckon that one ended up in a pie."

De'Ath was hooting away in merriment. "Oh, I love your stories, Bella, what a raconteur you are!"

"Well, it's a shame Uncle Wilf isn't around any more, Tom, because he would tell you it a lot better. Auntie Joy said he used to come home from the club fuming about the clock checkers not doing their job properly. Some fellers used to cheat by shaking their clocks about or putting them in the oven to get a better time, oh I don't know, very involved it was. Let me see if I can find that photo of 'im."

Bella shuffled off up the stairs and could be heard rummaging around in boxes upstairs.

"Well, fancier that! Get it, Tom, get it? Fancier that? Hehe, it's the way I tell 'em, as old Frank Carson used to say. Honestly, Bell, never fails to surprise me after forty years of marriage, she doesn't."

"I wonder how they navigate home - they must have pigeon sat-nav. Let's see what the internet says. Hmm…University of Oxford, they should know. Earth's magnetic field to map their position…probably false…sense of smell…probable…linked to landscape cues… probable…still much to learn…they always say that! They want more research funding to muck about with pointless experiments. A researcher friend of mine once got a grant for figuring out how many fruit pastilles it took to choke a kestrel. Well, it was similar to that anyway. Something to do with how much rubbish that birds eat and that included chewing gum and discarded sweets. "

"Yeah, they have an award each year for the most pointless piece of research, I allus follow it. They are called the 'Ig Nobel Awards'. Look 'em up on yer computer! I remember my favourite - *"Frictional Coefficient under Banana Skin"*. These Japanese boffs measured the amount of friction between a shoe and a banana skin when somebody steps on one!!"

"Haha! Ah yes, I see it! I have the webpage here. 'Dog fleas can jump higher than cat fleas', Winner Biology 2008. 'Lap dancers get higher tips when they are ovulating', Winner, Economics, 2008. That's a bit rude. What are lap dancers, Ron - have you ever been to one of those clubs?"

"Erm, ahem, well…keep yer voice down, Tom. Well, me and Barry,

THE HIDE

we were out in the field a lot y'know, selling carpets n' that, and well, Barry was a bit keen on that sort o' thing. I went sometimes, but I didn't enjoy it much. Barry did. The girls used to know 'im by name in Darlington and Dundee. All sorts 'e got up to. Eh, keep that secret mind. You know what 'is wife Belinda is like. Remember 'er at that cheffery party we did? Common as muck, that woman. "

"Are they good looking then, these lap dancers - you know alluring, as it were?"

"What in Dundee and Darlington Tom?...you must be joking. I expect they are in Las Vegas or Rio or wherever, but I especially remember one woman in Darlington, eeh dear, I would 'ave paid 'er to keep 'er clothes on, ah tell thee."

Their laddishness was cut abruptly short by Bella scurrying in with a battered old shoe box.

"What are you two chortling about? Look, I've found 'im! Wilf look!"

Bella handed Tom a creased, dog eared and tea stained black and white photo stuck on a piece of card of a flat-capped Uncle Wilf holding a large silver trophy, with several others, including some very tiny ones, on a table next to him.

THE HIDE

Uncle Wilf

"Oh very nice, Bella, those were the days. He looks like a jolly nice chap."

"Oh 'e was, Tom," replied Bullock taking the photo and smiling fondly. "But what is that concrete block doing in the picture. It looks most incongruous, I must say. Look Bella, what is it?"

"Dunno, perhaps Auntie Joy threw it at 'im! Or mebbe 'e was supposed to stand on it for the photo, he was quite short Uncle Wilf. Do you know, he wrote a book. I am pretty sure it was called *The Pigeon Fancier*. They produced a few copies of it. Perhaps cousin Les has a copy still, I will phone him up and see. It was good…you know, it described his life in Bolton, with Alf the lodger, a coal fire,

THE HIDE

Auntie Joy doing the ironing. Well, it was more of a pamphlet that a book, but he was quite proud of it, I remember that. He had some sort of nom de plume - Old Scrote, I think…"

"Old Scrote? Are you sure? Any road, we must get hold of *The Pigeon Fancier* by Uncle Wilf aka Old Scrote, Bell. Do yer best. It might come in very handy actually. Pigeons are evidently clever birds, and none knew them better than old Wilf, by the sounds of it. We 'ave to know the minds of birds ourselves, Tom. It isn't just collecting names this hobby, like collecting football stickers or stamps or whatever – we 'ave to know the behaviour, the biology, the migration patterns. There's an awful lot to this birding business you know! Look, what's that on the feeding table now - it's the thieving bloody magpie."

"One for sorrow, two for joy, three for a girl, four for a boy, five for silver, six for gold, seven for a secret never to be told, eight for a wish, nine for a kiss, ten for a bird you must not miss," recited Bella.

"Well I am counting nine then, Bell, nine for a kiss!" pouted Bullock.

"Too bad," retorted Bella, "there's only one. Sorrow for you - if you don't bugger off up north for a few days, I could do with a bit of peace from you two."

"They weren't common in the old days, the magpies" mused Bullock, ignoring his wife's evidently hollow threat. "Now they seem to be everywhere. I think they have adapted to townie life – like the wood pigeons – and foxes and squirrels. Eh up, speak of the Devil – there he is, Squirrel bloody Nutkin. Nickin' all the nuts."

A villainous-looking grey squirrel, glancing left and right like a pantomime thief, suddenly hurtled up one of the bird tables, sending the small birds scattering, and helped itself to peanuts, which it then set about burying in various parts of the garden. Bullock stood up, hands on hips and frowned in disapproval.

"I was reading that these grey ones have seen off all the red ones, you know, Tufty of the Tufty Club. You only see 'em in Scotland and Jersey now. These greedy buggers carry a virus and that kills off the little red 'uns. They are pests. I reckon we should start a cull of these vermins…if we got rid of the grey squirrels, pigeons and magpies I reckon the little 'uns would be loads better off."

"A bit of ecosystem management you mean, Ron. A bit of gamekeeping. I think that Hugh Fearnelystall eats squirrels, you know."

"I am not cooking squirrels!" protested Bella. "Pigeons yes, squirrels no. It'd be no better than eating rats."

"I used to be a top shot with an air gun. P'raps we should get one, Tom. Let's see what Prof Ball thinks of it, shall we. Bring back the Tufty Club! I've probly got me badge somewhere. Do you remember that, Tom. Road safety it were. We could do with that coming back. Well, they ride these bikes on the pavement now! Old PC Badger would 'ave clipped me round the 'ed for that! And these chavvies just walk out in the road in front of yer, as if daring to run 'em over! I would bloody love to, I tell yer!"

"Ah yes, poor old Willy Weasel in his stripy shirt was always getting knocked over wasn't he, poor chap. Getting an ice cream without his mummy, knocked over. Playing in the street, knocked over. He didn't die though. Let's see if it's on YouTube, most things are."

To their delight, The Tufty Club was soon found on De'Ath's laptop, and all three were soon respectively hooting, cackling and wheezing at the Public Information Films of the 1960's.

"Eh Petunia, ah feel like a swim…is that on?" requested Bullock. "Old Joe, with 'is knotted 'ankerchief and little moustache, and big fat Petunia with 'er big 'at and fifties sun-glasses! Bloody genius. They killed 'em off in one about worn tyres 'cos they were more popular that what was on telly."

"Aha, you are in luck! Here they are!" announced De'Ath.

"Ooooh, that's the one where they leave all the litter in the countryside. Look, Joe is chucking stones at a bottle! Find the one they are sat on the cliff and the bloke is sinking in his boat. That's the one! Dingies. That's what they call 'em, y'know, sailin' dingies!"

THE HIDE

"Cooo-eeee!"

And thus the afternoon passed in pleasant nostalgia and much merriment, though in between, arrangements for the trip to the north-east were also made; Professor Ball was invited by telephone and the invitation duly accepted; a hotel in Newcastle and a B & B in Seahouses were selected and booked on-line by De'Ath, who claimed to know what he was doing in such matters. De'Ath's wife Dot was invited to stay with Bella whilst the men were away, during which the ladies elected to book themselves into a local spa and beauty therapist for 'A Day of Pampering'. An equal sum of the money spent by the menfolk on birding equipment had been allocated to the ladies, and Bella declared that she was going to buy a dress, shoes, hat, sunglasses and handbag, so that she could be "just like Petunia".

"Right, well...I will see you on Tuesday at 9am, Ron. I can't wait to see the fog on the Tyne! Have a great time at the spa, Bella. Bye, Basker!"

The dog didn't bother to get up, and neither did his master; as ever, it was up to Bella to see De'Ath into his coat and out into the porch.

"Oooh, tell Dot to give me a ring about the spa, Tom. I'll get it booked up. We could do with some girlie fun - it's what they do these days, Tom. Girls just wanna have fun!"

"Oh I do like to be beside the seaside, I do like to be beside the sea!
Come on Humphrey, sing along - do hedgehogs like the seaside?"

After three hours of stop-start travel up the highly congested A1, and now somewhere near Harrogate, tempers in the front seat were starting to fray.

"Ah think that's enough of Humphrey for now, Prof. We are still nowhere near the seaside and you've been singing that for the last two hours. Let's 'ave a tape on Tom, and no more Lindisfarne. Let's 'ave one o' mine, shall we - 'ere look put that one on… *Comedic Monologues - The Very Best of Bob Newhart*".

De'Ath groaned inwardly but managed a watery smile, as Newhart began his infamous *Tobacco* monologue. Bullock seemed to know every word, just as he knew all the Monty Python sketches. He assumed the most awful of American accents as he joined in.

"Then what do you do, Walter? ha! ha! ha!...
You set fire to it! ha! ha! ha!...
Then what do you do, Walt?...
Ha! ha! ha! You inhale the smoke, huh! ha! ha! ha!...
You know, Walter... it seems you can stand in front of your own fireplace and have the same thing going for you! Haha, he is great old Bob int 'e!"

In the back seat, Professor Ball was listening carefully. "Is he American? What's his name, Newhart? He is talking to Sir Walter Raleigh on telephone, is he? I don't think I've come across him. Is he still going?"

THE HIDE

"Yep. Professor Proton in *The Big Bang Theory*. Well into his 80's. I don't mind him in that. It's just this earlier stuff grates on me a bit," admitted De'Ath.

"WHAT!" exclaimed Bullock. "Newhart grates on you?! Wash yer mouth out with soap, Thomas. What's this *Big Bang Theory* then? A science show?"

"Oooh, it's good that is. It's about these physicists at Caltech who share an apartment; with a glamorous waitress called Penny. Very nice she is."

"Oh, have you seen it Prof?" beamed De'Ath. "Yes, it's rather clever isn't it."

"It's not like that *Friends* is it, that one that Bella watches?" groaned Bullock. "Mind you, if Bob is in it, it must be worth a watch. Eh, listen at this one…*The Driving Instructor*, oh, this is champion, this is."

When bored, Ball had the habit of making a squeaking noise and then taking one of his sock puppets out of his pocket and having a conversation with it. He decided to have a chat with a puffin.

De'Ath toyed anxiously with the *Tufty Club* badge on his gillet that Bullock hadn't noticed yet, and looked out of the window.

"Come on, lads!" bellowed Bullock. "Get into it! This is vintage Newhart this is…Oh bugger it, turn it off then!"

There was a tetchy silence for a while.

"We could all play a game?" suggested Ball, helpfully. "We could play spot the lorry. Ron, you could be Eddie Stobart, I could be Norbert - I'm always Norbert - and Tom could be The Big Pink Lorry. Let's see who gets the most - ooh look, a Norbert!! One to me!"

"No," agreed De'Ath and Bullock in unison.

"I know," proposed De'Ath rooting in his bag, "I've got the *Birdwatch* magazine somewhere. I'll read some articles out, shall I? Here we go,

THE HIDE

'Focus on Falcons'."

This seemed to do the trick; pretty soon there was an avid conversation stimulated by the articles in *Birdwatch,* and before they knew it, the Angel of the North loomed up ahead of them.

"Ooh, let's stop!" grinned Ball. "Yes, off left here, Ron."

Admiring the great welcoming span of 'The Angel' atop its mound, the three took it turns to take the traditional photo of each other with outstretched arms.

"Hey, I've got a selfie-stick in me bag, hand on, I can get all three of us together!" announced De'Ath. I'll go and get it. I can text it to Dot then - hang on!"

"A selfie-stick, I didn't expect you to 'ave one o' them, lad!" chided Bullock on De'Ath's return. "Whatever 'appened to asking somebody to take yer picture? Much more sociable."

"Well, that's not always a good idea, Ron," countered Ball. "For example, what if there *aren't* any other folk around to take your picture. Like now!"

Bullock had to admit, that was the case; just them and The Angel.

"And…these mobile phone cameras are not that easy to operate. It's easy to put your thumb over these tiny cameras, for example. Or press the wrong button, so you take a burst of about a hundred frames. Or make a video. Or slo-mo. Or…"

Bullock got the point, and nodded.

"Or they could drop your 'phone or camera. Are they insured for breakages? Probably not! Or they might just be a useless photographer, and photograph your feet, or make it blurry and out of focus, or with your eyes shut…"

"Ok Prof, you 'ave made yer point, lad. Selfie-stick it is then….right lads, 'uddle in…CHEEEEEEESSSE! Oh Bloody 'ell, Bally, yer not in it!"

A Selfie at The Angel

"Boooo! There is no fog on the Tyne after all!" De'Ath peered down at the eponymous river as they drove over the Tyne Bridge in search of the Premier Inn on the Quayside.

"Bit windy for that, Tom. Is Bally asleep - he's a bit quiet? Eh, Prof - we're 'ere!"

After parking and settling in to their hotel rooms, they strolled up and down the Quayside, which they all admired very much, stopping to watch the Tilting Bridge wink and then walked over it to visit the Baltic and the Sage.

Crossing back from Gateshead to Newcastle on the Tyne Bridge, they were able to inspect the furthest inland colony of kittiwakes nesting in and around the bridge.

"Kitti-wake, kitti-wake, kitti-wake!" mewled Ball, peering upward in delight at the swirling white birds, though his delight soon turned to disgust. "Kitti-wake, kitti….oh dear, yuk. Yuk, yuk, yuk. Messy kitties!"

"Haha! That's what they thought of you apein' 'em, Prof! Ooof, that is a lot of bird poo, that is. Poor old Prof - covered in it!"

Completely caked in white kittiwake excrement, the Prof elected to return to the hotel to clean his cap and coat.

"We'll meet you at the Crown Possada, Prof, it's just up the hill. And I booked a table at Sabatinis, proper Italian that looks."

Just as the kittiwakes were doing their worst on Professor Ball, Bella and Dot were sitting in the bar of an establishment in Oldside known as The Pampering Palace, dressed in thick, snowy toweling robes and spa sandals. They were both puce in the face, having spent most of the afternoon in a sauna, interspersed with trips to the team of resident beauticians and masseuses.

"Cheers, Bella!" Dot raised a flute of Prosecco to her friend. "What a lovely afternoon we are having!"

"Ooh yes, cheers!" cackled Bella. "I like your nails, Dot, what did you have done?"

THE HIDE

"Well, I had a four layer Bio Sculpture Gel Overlay, and gone for Metallic Sorcery on my fingers and Gilded Reflection on my thumbs. And on my tootsies I have gone for Dark Anemone. What do you think?" Dot wiggled her toes and giggled as the bubbles from her glass went up her nose.

"Oh they are lovely, Dot. They wouldn't do my feet."

"Oh my dear, why ever not?" Mrs. De'Ath frowned with exaggerated concern and leaned forward in sympathy.

"Well, I don't blame them really," chuckled Bella, kicking off her spa sandals. "Look at the state of 'em!"

"Ah, erm…" Dot quickly averted her eyes from Mrs. Bullock's gnarled and mangled hooves, the toes of which seemed to have been bound by an especially cruel Chinese foot binder. Calluses, bunions, chilblains, varicose veins and malformed toenails abounded on Bella's neglected trotters.

"It's all these years wedging 'em into tight high heels!" laughed Bella, without apparent concern. "I always buy Size 5 even though I am a Size 6. The girl said I need to see a chiropodist."

"Well, you should, sweetie!" gulped Dot, hoping that Bella would put her sandals back on. "Anyway, wasn't that hot stone massage relaxing?"

"Oh, they were too hot for me, them stones, love. I told the woman to use some ointment instead. Sloan's Liniment, I always carry a bottle about with me. She didn't want to use it, but I insisted. It warms you through, does Sloan's love!"

"Ooh look," smiled Dot, responding to a beep on her Samsung mobile phone. "A photo of the boys! Two in fact! One at the Angel of the North and another on the Tyne Bridge. Ah, how cute they all look!"

"Let me see – haha! Look at Ron, bless 'im. What's this one – oh dear it's Professor Ball covered in bird muck! Look at Ron laughing at 'im - the sod! Here you are love, I think there's a message underneath."

Dot simpered and blushed, as a message of love from her husband appeared beneath the photographs. "They are having dinner at an Italian restaurant and apparently the hotel is fine. Do you and Ron not have mobile phones, Bella?"

"Well, we do have these little Nokia ones but we don't use 'em much. Do you think I could pop out the back and have a smoke, Dot? I feel like I am in one of those mental hospitals – just listen to that depressing music! I am going out on the fire escape - if anybody asks, cover for me, tell them I've gone for a seaweed body wrap or summat?"

Whilst Bella sneaked out and sparked up, Dot took a selfie of her nails and sent it to her husband, and then looked at the menu of beauty treatments, deciding what to do with their last hour. She decided that intimate waxing wasn't something she could endure, and thought herself too old for eyelash extensions. The Clarins luxury facial sounded nice though.

Bella returned, wreathed in the reek of cigarette smoke and looking pleased with herself.

"I thought I might have the facial to finish off with, what do you think, my dear?"

"Oh, I've already decided love! I am booked in the flotation tank with cellulite mud!"

"That's brave of you Bella, I don't think I could do that. It's like the Dead Sea isn't it, you float about in salty water in a pod thing with a lid?"

"I have no idea, Dot, it just sounded good."

The young woman who had unwillingly massaged Sloan's Liniment into Bella's back approached.

"Mithith Bullock for the flow-taythion?" she asked in a girlish simper.

THE HIDE

"Ooooh, that's me, Amber! Wish me luck, Dot!" Bella bounded up and followed the beautician down a corridor, and was escorted into a room, at the centre of which was a moulded white pod the size of a family car. The young woman lifted a lid much as the bonnet would be raised on a car, to reveal a deep blue glow, and swished her hand about in the salty water contained within.

"You ordered the thellulite mud Mithith Bullock, was it?"

"Yes, the brown mud, love. It looks a bit like a toilet, doesn't it, the flotation tank."

"Er, a toilet? Well, I never heard it described like a toilet!" giggled Amber, taking the lid off a large canister of a creamy brown substance and pouring it into the water, which then floated like a layer of sewage on a polluted blue sea.

"Yes, like a toilet, with a lot of Harpic Blue in the bowl. And I won't say what it looks like now, that would be taking the comparision too far!" cackled Bella.

"Erm, OK, would you like to choose some music – there's a litht over there?"

"Oooh, Enya! I like her!"

"Okayy…Enya…and would you like the lid down for darkneth or do you want the lid up?"

"Total immersion, love. Lid down!"

"Righto…if you'd like to step in…"

Bella removed her robe unselfconsciously, and splashed clumsily into the bath, sploshing brown muck all over the beautician's uniform.

"Oh, I am sorry, love!"

"No, no itth fine!" Amber wiped the splattered mud from her eyes as she helped Bella to recline.

THE HIDE

"OOOH! I am floating! It's lovely and warm, in't it!"

"There we are, lid down, I will come and get you in half an hour, Mithith Bullock! Enjoy!"

Bella leaned back and spread out her arms, as the strains of Enya's *Orinoco Flow* swept through the darkness of the capsule. After five minutes or so, Bella's relaxation transformed into slight claustrophobia, and she began muttering to herself.

"It's very dark! I wonder if I could sink and…drown?"

This thought continued to nag at her, as her immobile flotation turned to splashing of hands and feet.

"Oooh, I don't like this! It's like being buried in a watery grave!"

She began to panic. "Get me out! I don't like it!" But like in space, there was nobody to hear her. She banged a few times on the lid, but with no response.

"I am getting out! Sorry Enya!" Thrusting her arms upwards and thrashing about with her feet, the bath turned into a heaving quagmire of muddy, salty water, which clung to her body, and as she thrashed about, she sunk further into the morasse, her head submerged and her hair becoming caked in the mud. She began to gasp for breath like a drowning woman, and water filled her nose and mouth as she bobbed under the surface.

"AAAAHHHH! Get me out!!" she yelled, coughing and spluttering as she desperately pawed at the lid of the tank. She was grateful to feel the lid open on its hydraulic springs and she sprang to her feet. Clumsily banging her knees on the sides of the bath, she clambered out, into the blackness of the room.

Naked and panicking, and blinded by the mud, she decided to crawl towards where she remembered the door was, and flailed at the handle. To her relief, the door opened to a brightly lit corridor, and she crawled to the safety of the light.

THE HIDE

Dot was being escorted down the corridor by the mud-spattered beautician to her facial appointment, when both were stopped abruptly in their tracks, as something brown crawled out into the corridor, flailing its arms.

"Oh my God, what the Hell?!" Both women sprang back in alarm, Dot thinking for an instant that it might be a dog or a human experiment gone badly wrong.

"Bella! What…what are you doing?"

"Mithith Bullock? Erm, are you alright?"

"No, I am not bloody alright," spluttered the naked crawler, resembling the preserved remains of a woman recovered from a peat bog after thousands of years. "I didn't like it! I got out!"

The young beautician quickly swathed Bella in a towel robe and helped her to her feet, the cellulite mud gushing onto the floor and oozing menacingly. "I need a fag! Get me my smokes, Dot, they are in me bag!"

"Er, I think you should have a shower first," recommended Amber. "I really need to wash that mud out of your hair, Mithith Bullock!"

After a good hosing down, Amber washed Bella's hair and blow-dried it into her usual frizzy halo, and it wasn't long before Bella had her in stitches of laughter.

"I won't be doing again that in a hurry, Amber. And I don't think I will be able to listen to *Orinoco Flow* ever again. I don't think I am cut out for beauty parlours, me - I will stick to Curl Up and Dye in Tredley High Street from now on - they do a good rinse and perm there. Oooh Dot, look at you, your face is glowing. Is it a spray tan? Anyway, I'm not a celebrity - get me out of here!"

THE HIDE

The following morning and after a sound night's sleep assisted by Brown Ale, chicken liver pasta and a bottle of Valpolicella, the birders took a walk around the centre of Newcastle. After coffee in Grey Street, at Bullock's insistence, they had a walk round St James' Park, home of Newcastle United FC.

"It was a shame what happened to Gazza, wasn't it," sighed Bullock, inspecting the giant murals of past footballing legends of the Toon.

"Who is Gazza?" asked De'Ath and Ball in unison.

Just then, a cab pulled up, and a grizzled ruddy old man dressed only in a shabby beige dressing gown, in his mouth an unlit, broken-in-half cigarette, staggered out into the street. The taxi driver screeched off, under a volley of foul-mouthed abuse and obscene hand gestures from his passenger, whose dressing gown fell open to reveal a number of blue tattoos about his legs and chest, and what they call in the northeast, his wedding tackle. Apparently unconcerned about his state of undress, he shuffled up to Bullock, wearing a nasty cut on his forehead and a malign expression.

"'Scuse uz, lads," he started in a thick and bleary Geordie accent, his rancid breath reeking of alcohol, "Would ye myund poppin' in that offie there un' getting' us eyut Tennants Super, a small bottle o' Bells n' fo'ty B & Hayuch? A'd go in mesel', leike, but a'm banned. 'Ere's sum cash…"

The man fumbled about in his gaping robe and found a wad of twenty pound notes, peeled a couple off, and proffered them unsteadily.

Bullock inspected the man closely. "It isn't…"

"Aye, course it is, man. 'Ow d'yer do, bonny lad? Pawel Gascoigne."

Bullock shook the man's clammy hand, in shock. "Paul, oh dear, what…"

"Ah know, ah know, 'ave gone the weah 'o Georgie Best, hevvent ah. Oh, sorry, ah dint see ah was flashing ye, ah'll just belt meself up.

THE HIDE

Now - haway to the offie man. Ah'll just 'ave me fag."

Leaving a wobbly Gascoigne to attempt to light his broken cigarette, Bullock and his companions reluctantly ventured into Ace Off License.

"Is that, is that …the same guy in that big mural over there?" inquired a puzzled De'Ath. "A professional footballer that played for England?"

"It is, it is," replied Bullock, grimly. "I don't think he's fifty yet, but 'e looks eighty. One of the best footballers to pull on an England shirt, an' all."

"Is this lot for Pawel, is it?" enquired the Sikh behind the counter in a mild Geordie accent.

"Er…no?" attempted Bullock, in more than two minds about whether he should be assisting Gazza's drug-fuelled demise.

"Oh come off, I can see 'im outside. Tell him there's no charge, and he can come back anytime if he doesn't smash the place up - like he did last time."

"Er, oh, alright then. Erm…we'll tell him. Thanks."

"Paul, the feller says there's no charge for the booze and fags and you are un-barred from Ace - er, on condition that you mustn't smash his shop up again."

"Eh? Ah nivver did that! Well, ah divvant remember doin' it anyweay. Thanks lads, ya can keep the money – just get me a taxi will yer?"

Bullock hailed a taxi, giving the driver the money he had been given by Gascoigne, and helped the England legend into the passenger seat.

"Well, good to meet you lad, and, well…thanks for the memories. Ah'll never forget you at the 1990 World Cup."

"Aye, that was a long teem agoah. What yer doin' round this weah then, Yorkie?"

"We are off to the Farne Islands, actually..."

"Oh ah luv the Fawnes, them puffins eh? Ah wish ah could come wi' yer lads, but, ah've erm, got a meetin' like, this after. Tek care neow!"

"No, you take care, lad. Just try and remember how folk love you, and not just round 'ere either. If I 'ad my way it would be you presenting *Match of The Day*, not your mate Lineker!"

"Oh aye, that'd be grand, wouldn't it! Imagine the chaos, man!" The familiar crazy grin returned briefly, though it was rapidly replaced by the trademark tear in his eye, as the cab accelerated away.

"Well, that's made me right sad, that has," admitted Bullock, the glimmer of a tear in his own eye which was rapidly dried away. "Come on, let's get on the road again. As Gazza would say - Howay the Lads!"

It was a fine early evening when they reached Seahouses and located their lodgings. 'Xanadu' was a large Victorian house overlooking the coast, and as they trudged up the broad stone steps dividing an immaculately clipped lawn and tidy shrubbery, Bullock heaving his old army rucksack, Ball gripping an ancient leather suitcase and De'Ath trundling behind him a bright blue cabin case with one broken wheel, they notice a prim woman in a spotless white pinafore apron and half-moon glasses, arms folded and glaring at them from the bay window. The front door was opened to them before they arrived at the front step.

"Good evening, you'll be the De'Ath party? I was rather expecting you at four o' clock - why, it's almost five!" The woman, whose accent was derived from the posh side of Edinburgh, arched an eyebrow high into her forehead, in an expression of extreme quizzicality. Evidently an explanation was expected from the travellers.

THE HIDE

"Errr...yes, I might have put 4 on the booking form..." admitted De'Ath, sheepishly. "As a rough arrival time? We had a look around Newcastle, you see, and the traffic on the A1..."

"I don't do "approximate arrival times", Mr. De'Ath. Why, I have had a pot of tea and a plate of warm oat bannocks waiting for ye! I shall have to re-warm them now and make a fresh pot. What a bother y'are! Anyway, come in, but leave your muddy shoes on the mat there, no no, that mat, that one."

"Ah what a lovely house you have, Mrs...?" ventured Ball, wringing his hands and looking about with his few-toothed grin and doing his nervous cough.

"Pychley. Thank you, and I'll also thank you to keep it that wey! Now, take a seat in the lounge, yer trooisers are clean are they? Aye, they're no bad."

As she swept away to the kitchen, Bullock eyed the others glumly.

"I 'ate B & Bs. Dunno why you didn't book us into that nice pub in the town. Beer looked good there. Anyway, we'll go for a couple of pints later on."

"Ooooh, look at all the pictures of cats on the wall. She must like cats!" grinned Ball.

As if on cue, a predominantly white cat, with one black ear and pale green eyes in a rounded face, strolled into the room, and eyed the visitors as haughtily as had her mistress.

"Here, kitty, kitty...psss, psss!" Ball leaned gleefully forward and was roundly ignored by the Scottish Fold.

On the ledge outside the bay window sat two more cats; a Siamese at one end and a black Bombay with large golden eyes at the other. De'Ath had initially taken them for porcelain statuettes, for there were many such things adorning Mrs. Pychley's lounge, but their necks swiveled slightly and the black cat pawed the window and meowed softly.

THE HIDE

"I'm afraid Agatha isn't very sociable with men." Mrs Pychley arrived back with a tea tray, and sat down primly.

"Now then, gentlemen. It's just the one night, is it not? Breakfast is served between 8 and 8.30 - I saw no dietary preferences on the booking form so I have in smoked kippers or the full fry. After 8.30 sharp the kitchen will be closed. As I made clear on my booking form, the doors of my establishment are closed at 10pm, and I do not issue a night key. I don't entertain rowdies here."

Bullock looked over at De'Ath in fury as Mrs Pychley poured tea into china cups embellished with the Scottish thistle. De'Ath inspected the window cats with his watery smile.

"Now. I can offer you dinner this evening, it will be liver and onions with tatties, followed by Bakewell tart and custard."

"Ooooh, I love Bakewell tart!" grinned Ball., bouncing up and down on his chair. "Oh yes, please!"

Bullock, who had envisaged a fish supper in newspaper on the sea wall, eyed Ball with further fury. He briefly considered breaking ranks, and looked hopefully at De'Ath, but in vain, as he had already raised a bony index finger and sported an unctuous smile.

"That's two of you, then, and you, sir?"

"Um,…oh aye, why not then. Mek that three. All for one and one for all, as the musketeers would say!"

"And, you, ah suppose would be Porthos! Very whell, supper will be served at 7 precisely. I have noo other guests tonight, so that will be manageable."

A graceful Abyssinian cat swanked into the room swishing its tail and purring softly. After inspecting his visitors, he leapt into the lap of a surprised De'Ath, who, no great cat lover, cringed slightly as the animal padded about his thighs, cat-revolving slowly to make his bed, and swishing his tail about in De'Ath's face, who hung gamely onto his cup and saucer.

"Oh, Albert has taken a shine to you!" smiled Mrs. Pychley for the first time since their arrival. "Do you like cats, Mr. De'Ath?"

"Oh yes," lied De'Ath, Bullock shooting him an incredulous look. "I mean, who doesn't like ca-aaaaaaaaaaaaaaaaaaaaaaaahhtsssssssss?"

With a gleam in his yellow eyes, Albert extended very sharp claws from his paws and set them into De'Ath's thighs, as he curled up and began to purr contentedly. Fighting the urge to cast both cat and tea cup across the room, De'Ath smiled grimly as his cup rattled violently against its saucer.

"Whell, enjoy your tea and bannocks, gentlemen, I shall just air your rooms. Who is sharing the double?"

"Meeeee n Rrrron," confirmed De'Ath through gritted teeth, as Albert raked his corduroys.

When she had left the room, De'Ath requested assistance. "Get this cat off me, Ron, it's ripping me legs to shreds."

"Oh, I thought you liked cats, Tom?" Bullock muttered, his eyes rolling heavenwards as he took his time to offer his assistance.

However, extracting Albert from De'Ath was no easy matter. Bullock took hold of the cat's midriff and attempted to lift him off, but Albert was having none of it. Disturbed from his comfort, he assumed a wild look, and set his claws still deeper into De'Ath's legs, and began to mewl aggressively.

"Gaaah, I'll try to lift its claws out…yowch!!" Albert took a swipe at De'Ath's arm, leaving a vivid scratch, and set its other legs still deeper.

"Ooooh, shall I help?" Ball began fussing ineffectually around the now screeching cat as Bullock tried to rip it free of De'Ath's trousers. Another two cats ambled in from the kitchen to see what the fuss was about.

THE HIDE

"Right, if you'd like to come up to your rooms…what the Devil?..."

Mrs Pychley stopped in her tracks; as Albert finally relinquished his fiendish grip. There was a ripping sound, as Bullock tumbled backwards into Ball, who stumbled into the tea table, before falling on his face. Ball, Bullock, Albert and the other two cats, Princess and Ginger, sprawled about in the carnage of the overturned tea set.

"Oh dear, what a mess." As Ball stated the obvious, Mrs Pychley went a little further, turning white with fury.

"What the Hell are you playing at, you silly men? Why, poor Albert is soaking in tea! And if my tea pot is broken, you'll pay for a whole new new china service, so ye will!"

Remarkably, as the mess was cleared up, the tea set survived unbroken, though a large brown stain soaked the carpet, decorated with pulverized biscuits and half a pound of granulated sugar.

"Right, you'll all get oot of ma whay!" announced the infuriated landlady, suddenly armed with bucket, mop and a variety of cleaning fluids. "Up the ste-ars wi' ye!"

The chastised guests trooped away muttering various forms of apology, but were harried away up the stairs to the landing by Mrs P, who stomped up behind them.

"Noo then, y'say that yerseylf and Mr. Bullock are the gay couple sharing, so here is your double…"

She opened the door onto a pristine double room, completely effeminate in its pink décor; laid across the double bed was a crochet bedspread bearing a rainbow-coloured slogan - Gay Pride.

"What???" exclaimed an open-mouthed Bullock. "What the Hell…?"

De'Ath's watery smile returned, as he inspected his scratched arm. "Erm, I think there may have been some mistake, Mrs. Pychley."

"There's nae need for bashfulness, gentlemen!" admonished the landlady. "You will surely have seen in my advertisement that we are a gay-friendly establishment? Why, my own dear brother Seaton is a promiscuous homosexual and proud of it. He should be joining us for dinner later on, I am sure ye'll get on with him. Are ye also gay, Mr. Ball?"

"Look, madame," growled Bullock. "My friend appears to have made a catastrophic oversight here when he booked on-line. To be quite clear, all of us are married men - to women - and we are not, I repeat, not, homosexual. In my own case, you will not meet a less homosexual man on this planet. And I am not sharing that bed with my mate."

"I am pretty sure I asked for a twin room, Mrs. Pychley," added De'Ath, rummaging about in his rucksack for his confirmation paper, which he had printed out. "There, see…twin room…"

"Wh'ell," responded Mrs. Pychely as she peered through her half-moon glasses at the sheet, "since you ticked the box 'Gay Couple', I thought you may like our honeymoon suite, but as you must have done that in error…"

"Ah," winced De'Ath, noting the crossed box on his confirmation sheet. "Erm, sorry. I thought it was the box for 'no special dietary requirements'. Bugger. Er, I mean, bother."

"'Ave you got any single rooms, missus?" asked Bullock ruefully. "You said we were the only guests this evening? Happy to pay extra, like…"

"Wh'ell, as a matter of fact, I can oblige, as yer luck would ha' it. If you are sure? Y'know, there's nae need ter be abashed…"

"We are very sure, Mrs. P. Very sure indeed," grimaced Bullock.

"Whe'll, the other single rooms are in the attic - a bit on the small side. Here, Mr. Ball, here is your room…"

Opening the door to a pleasant room with a sea view, two more cats shot out from under the bed and sped down the stairs. "Algernon!

THE HIDE

Una! Wha-at are ye deein' in this room! Shoo wi yer both!"

"Oooh, magazines!" enthused the Professor, setting down his suitcase by the window, and picking up a pile of well-thumbed publications from the coffee table. "What's this one, oooh, *Playguy*. Ah, oh dear. Yes, and *JustUsBoys*...erm..."

"Ah ham sorry, Mr. Ball!" exclaimed Mrs Pychley, taking the magazines sharply away from him and checking under the bed. "Why, Seaton readied the room this morning and I do keep telling him that not all our guests are fond of gay pornography. And he shut Algernon and Una in! Fortunately, yer tea and coffee making facilities are all in order, at least. Right, let's get your friends ensconced upstairs, shall we?"

Bullock and De'Ath were led up another flight of creaking steps where Mrs. Pychley made a rapid inspection of the rooms for cats and gay pornography. Finding neither, she ushered Bullock into the room on the right, where he bent over to fit himself into the one part of the tiny room that he could stand up, in the dormer window. He searched for floor space sufficient to set down his rucksack, but finding none, he put it on the slim cot bed which rattled violently as the bag landed.

De'Ath was issued into an even tinier room, which improbably, had a tiny 'bathroom' fitted into one corner. "Now, the 'en suite' for you, Mr. De'Ath, just a sink for you, Mr. Bullock. Now, do make yourselves comfortable, ah must be away to clean the carpet you all but ruined!"

Thinking neither room capable of accommodating two standing people, Bullock and De'Ath hissed conversation between the two open doors on the tiny landing.

"Tom, you've gone and done it this time, lad! You've checked us into a gay hotel!"

"Not exclusively gay," corrected De'Ath. "Just gay-friendly. But yes, my mistake, Ron, I am sorry. Good Lord, if you sit on the toilet in here your legs are still in the bedroom. And the shower is minute. But you are most welcome to use it, Ron."

THE HIDE

"Well, ah wouldn't mind a shower, lad. Blimey, these towels don't cover much of yer modesty, do they? And the shower curtain 'as been ripped to shreds! By cats, no doubt. Go on then, ah'll try yer shower. Swap rooms for a bit."

With very considerable difficulty, Bullock tried to squeeze his large naked frame into what wasn't really a shower at all - it was a narrow three sided glass cubicle atop a shower pan which seemed to have been roughly sawn in half. Plumber's mastic was smeared crudely and abundantly, apparently in a botched attempt to seal the unit. The electric shower seemed to have been installed by an amateur, with wires poking out where they probably shouldn't have been. Pressing a button, the tiny shower head jolted into life, issuing needle-like jets of water from the few holes that weren't blocked with green scale, alternating rapidly between scalding hot and freezing cold. Bullock was unable to install his whole body into the narrow box, so one leg remained outside, as he tried to draw the shredded ribbons of the curtain. He lathered himself up with the minute bar of wrapped soap on the soap dish, and attempted to hose himself down, wincing as the hot/cold needles of water bounced everywhere.

In the room immediately below the shower, Professor Ball was gazing happily out to sea with his binoculars, his glove puppets lined up on his bed. He didn't notice the first few steady drips from the ceiling above, but when a steady stream of droplets started to bounce off his head, he looked quizzically around.

"It feels like its raining, Humphrey!" Looking upwards, a large droplet spattered his glasses, and turned rapidly into a steady stream. A large, damp patch was spreading across the ceiling and into the plaster ceiling rose.

"Oh dear! We've sprung a leak! I had better go and tell Mrs. Pychley!"

Moments later, Mrs P was bounding up two flights of steps, followed by the concerned Ball, who had found her chopping onions in the kitchen. Arriving at De'Ath's room and hearing the shower running, she banged loudly on the door.

"Mr. De'Ath! Stop the shower immediately! You are leaking through the ceiling!" Hearing the commotion, De'Ath emerged from Bullock's room.

"Oh, ye've swapped have ye…Mr. Bullock, please desist from your ablutions!"

Inside the 'shower' Bullock, finally cleansed of his lather, stepped out of the shower, noticing to his horror that the carpet outside the cubicle was soaking wet.

"Oh 'eck! Where's that tiny towel - that'll never go round me…"

"Mr. Bullock! I hope yer decent, cos ah'm coming in…oh my days!"

Greeted by Bullock's fulsome pink bottom, Mrs. Pychley rapidly averted her gaze to the window, her palm to her eyes. De'Ath and Ball peered round the door, both trying hard not to snigger.

"Make y'self decent, sir, if you please!"

"Bloody 'ard wi' the size o these towels, missus!" protested Bullock, holding the tiny towel over his private parts.

"You haven't used the shower curtain adequately, Mr. Bullock. The sign over the shower says it perfectly clearly…place the curtain INSIDE the shower before ablutions commence!"

"It isn't possible!" protested Bullock. "The curtain's in ribbons, and any'ow – yer can't fit a grown man in there! Look, me clothes are next door, let me get past yer and Tom will help yer clear up…"

Bullock edged his dripping and partly scalded frame past his forlorn landlady, leaving soggy footprints on the carpet.

"Mr. De'Ath, go and fetch newspaper and J-clothes from the kitchen – I will have to get this carpet raised up!"

Half an hour later, the trio were fully dressed and decided to go for a walk along the sea front before dinner, Mrs. Pychley declaring that dinner would be delayed by exactly half an hour due to "irregularities with the shower in Room 6" and they were shooed from the house, to be followed by a number of cats, some of which they had met before, others newcomers.

"This is a right rum do, this place," muttered Bullock as they trudged along, eying the gathering gloom of the bay before them.

"The Gathering Gloom"

"All my fault, Ron," admitted De'Ath. "I didn't master my brief this time."

"Oh my room is fine! Well - apart from the leaking ceiling and that unpleasant magazine - I wish I hadn't opened that. Just as well my wife wasn't with me, she would have a had a fit! Not that either of us have anything against gay people, or anything…"

"Oh me neither, Prof, me neither. Though what ah cannot understand is when they are all camp, y'know, like Larry Grayson. *Shut that door!*" laughed Bullock, doing a poor impression of the limp-wristed comedian. "There's nowt wrong wi bein' queer – they can't 'elp it - but why do some of these 'ave to parade it?"

As they ambled along, looking out to sea, a middle-aged man approached from the opposite direction, dressed in pink trousers, a yellow floral shirt, a Panama hat and a pale blue silk scarf arrayed elaborately around his neck. His gait was tremendously effeminate, his womanly hips sashaying from side to side, one hand on his hip and the other held limply aloft as he smoked a yellow Sobranie cocktail cigarette in a holder. He approached the trio with a coquettish glance and the hint of a pout about his painted lips.

"Ooooo, 'ello duckies! I 'avent seen you about? You aren't the three at Shangri La tonight are you?" His accent was softly Scottish, with a more than a hint of Kenneth Williams.

"It's not Seaton, by any chance is it?" growled Bullock, adopting an absurdly exaggerated macho stance; his legs rooted and splayed, his thumbs tucked into the hem of his trouser, his jaw jutting and his chest puffed out.

"Oh, I see my infamy goes before me, does it? What has my nasty sister Temperance been sayin' aboot me? She is sooo-ooo uptight… you know what she needs, don't you, a good, old fashioned f…"

"Mrs. Pychley has mentioned that you may be dining with us. In fact, we have made a bit of a mistake, to be honest with you, lad, because us three are about as far from homosexual as it gets, and though we 'ave got no prejudice, we 'ave not selected Shangri La because of its reputation for being gay-friendly!"

"Oh, what a shame, we could have had such fun!" declared Seaton in pantomime camp and waving his hands aloft. "But never mind! Straights are very welcome too. As long as you don't mind cats! Anyway, see you gentlemen at dinner! And if you change yer wee mind…!" he winked outrageously at Bullock, before mincing off, giggling to himself.

"I 'ope the locks work on the door, lads - old Quentin Crisp there can't be trusted!" grunted Bullock. "What a shambles this is turning into. I need a pint, and fast!"

In fact, and despite their worst imaginings, dinner with Mrs P, Seaton and a host of moggies, passed enjoyably. Seaton was well behaved, evidently having been threatened with dire consequences by his sister if he did not, and her cooking was basic but excellent. Softened slightly by a glass of fine Cote du Rhone provided by her brother, she also provided amiable company, and was able to laugh about the unfortunate events on their arrival. Seaton was an authority on the history of the Northumberland coast, and much to the appreciation of his guests, muted his camp act, and spoke authoritatively on Bamber Castle and the Farnes.

Retiring to their rooms feeling replete and slightly drunk, Bullock took the precaution of locking his door, before changing into his striped pyjamas and brushing his teeth in the sink. About to sink into bed, he suddenly realized that he needed to "pass water" as Mrs Pychley would have put it. Deciding that he did not have the energy to descend a floor to the shared bathroom, he ran the cold tap in the sink, unbuttoned his 'jama bottoms, and urinated powerfully into the sink.

Mid-stream, he was alarmed by a loud beeping noise coming from what looked like a fire-alarm fitted below the sink. Blue lights flashed from its centre, and the beeping grew in volume sufficient to wake the whole house.

"What the - is the house on fire now?" he muttered to himself. He heard padding footsteps from the squealing stair and somebody knocked on his door.

"Are ye pishing in the sink, Mr. Bullock?" hissed Seaton from behind the door, suppressing a giggle.

"Er, what if I am?" responded Bullock, as he continued to do just that.

"Wheyl, ah wouldn't, if I were you. My sourpuss sister has fitted an ammonia detector. There's a sign there somewhere. Nay urinating in the sink."

"A what? An ammonia detector? I have never heard of such a thing! Is it not the fire alarm?"

"Nooo. Push the centre button and flush the sink wi' watter, quick!"

Following Seaton's instructions, the flashing light and beeping desisted.

"If ye want a wee, dee it oot the windah! That's what I dee!"

"Er, right thanks, Seaton, good night to you. See you at breakfast."

"Aye, gi' it a good waggle oot the windah, Ron!" sniggered Seaton. "Good neet, and mind the bugs don't bite!"

Bullock listened at the door to check that Seaton had descended the stair and the door to his room closed behind him.

"Bloody madhouse," he muttered, as the bed creaked beneath his heaving weight. He was soon asleep and snoring loudly. Next door, De'Ath was kept awake for most of the night by a deafening cat's chorus conducted on the eaves of the roof next to his room. His fitful sleep was filled by terrible nightmares featuring a lion-sized Albert and a shower that would not stop running, redolent of 'The Sorcerer's Apprentice' - with Mickey Mouse replaced by a hapless Professor Ball and the Sorcerer by Mrs. Temperance Pychley.

THE HIDE

"There's only kippers, gentlemen!" announced a flustered Mrs. Pychley, as the trio gathered in the breakfast room at 8am sharp. "Seaton forgot to buy the bacon, the silly sodomite."

"Aye, sorry!" Seaton, decked in a frilly apron, waved a spatula from the kitchen. "Good mornin' gentlemen, I hope ye all slept well. I trust ye all enjoy a kipper?"

The three nodded, though Bullock was gravely disappointed - as he liked nothing better than a full English, or indeed Scottish, fry-up.

As the smell of broiling kippers began to waft from the kitchen, the cat-life of Shangri-La went wild. All twelve cats descended on the kitchen from all parts of the house and garden. Albert deposited a captured and mortally wounded sparrow from his mouth on the dining table and all the felines began a competitive, mewing, tail-swirling battle for attention.

"Get those cats oot, Temperance!" demanded Seaton, slamming the kitchen door with his foot and catching Una's tail, who shrieked like a banshee, causing De'Ath to spurt a mouthful of tea down his beard. The trio watched grimly as the sparrow made a last failed flutter for freedom from the table, only to be ripped to shreds before them by ginger Algernon.

"Doon, all o' ye!" commanded Mrs Pychley, imperiously. There was a surprising level of compliance from her feline brood, many brushing her legs and begging her attention, though the insouciant Siamese ignored her completely and sat in the middle of the dining table, staring coolly at Bullock, daring him silently to try to shove her off.

"Here ye goo, gentlemen…kippers fa' three!" Seaton kicked the kitchen door open and emerged with three bright yellow fish surrounded by bread and butter. "Now shoo, the lot o' ye, let these men hae their breakfast in peace!"

THE HIDE

Much to Mrs Pychley's evident distress, Seaton picked up each cat and rudely dispensed them from the back door. The twelve rapidly reassembled on the window ledge, vying for the best position to observe the meal, knowing that a bit of skin and bone would surely be subsequently available.

Having settled the bill and pleased to be on their way from Shangri La, the wayfarers put their luggage in the boot of their car, and swung their day packs onto their shoulders.

"Bloody madhouse," said Bullock, yet again.

"Burp. Sorry fellows. I do like kippers but they do have a habit of repeating on me. Burp. I think I'll have a smoke on that bench if nobody minds. Take the taste away."

"I will join you, Tom. Let's get the pipe's flaring, that'll cheer the day."

After a bowl of St. James flake and a philosophical discussion on the events of the previous day, the trio were ready to stroll down to the harbour to buy their tickets for the boat trip to Staple Island.

"Here he is! Puffin Billy, this is the one!" beamed Professor Ball, pointing to one of the sales booths. "Hello Billy, I don't suppose you remember me?"

An amiable seafaring chap in flat hat and checked shirt leaned out, and winked.

"Course I remember you, Professor! It's been a wee while noo, eh? How is Humphey, now?"

"Ooooh yes, here he is!" Ball rummaged in his pockets, to fetch out the notorious puppet. "And he's got a new friend…Brexit Badger! Say hello, Brexit!"

THE HIDE

"Aye, Brexit, is it, well the jury is out on all that, ah would seh. There's an old mate of yours hearabouts, Prof, are you headin' out wi' us today?"

"Yes, this is Ron, and Tom, Billy, we'd like three tickets for a landing on Staple please. I bet you mean Fred Hopple the artist, don't you, is he still about?"

"He is that, lad. He is over there, look. There you go, gentlemen, there's yer tickets, see you back here at a quarter to eleven, if you please."

Fred Hopple sat on a camping stool, daubing on a canvas propped on a wooden easel. Dressed like a cartoon artist, wearing a beret and painting smock, he smoked a thin cheroot, as he squinted over the harbor through squared thumb and forefinger, and applied thick dollops of oil paint to his current *oeuvre* with a painting knife the size of a small trowel.

Creeping up behind him, Ball donned Humprey and perched him lightly on Hopple's shoulder.

"Hooo, ah k-now 'oo, that is, reet enough - why it's a-Humprey, and that can ah-only mean one thing - Bally?"

"It is indeed, Fred, how are you!"

"Why 'am fine, man! Grey-at ter see yer. And these are yer friends, are theh? Lovely. Ah bet yer oot ter the Farnes, ter watch them birds, then?"

"Indeed we are. Ron, Tom, allow me to introduce Fred Hopple, Northumberland's finest living artist!"

"Ah, yer too kind, Bally, too kind. See, a'm just capturin' terdeyah's spawklin' leet on the hawbour. H'evereh dee, a different leet, not two the se-am!"

Peering over Fred's shoulder at the pretty scene ahead, with its

THE HIDE

colourful boats and bobbing sea birds, De'Ath was not able to recognize it reproduced on the canvas in any conceivable way, as Fred daubed another smear of red paint.

"Oh, I see - you are an abstract painter are you, Fred?" exclaimed De'Ath, in sudden realisation. "Very interesting how you artists represent the way you see things. I don't get it myself, I am keener on the impressionists, as they say."

"Abstract? What ye on aboot, Tom? Why, it's a mirrah image of the harbwah, man! In guache, o' course. Allus payunt in guache wi' a knife, ah do, costs a fowtune in payunt, meynd!"

"Really?" Now Bullock joined De'Ath to quizzically inspect the canvas, he also finding no resemblance whatsoever between the harbour before them and the great squadges that Fred was trowelling on like a good bricklayer.

"Any'ow," said the great painter swivelling round to inspect his critics with a lop-sided grin, "ah'm mower of a portraitist actually. You 'ave got a very strong fayus, son, vewy wround. Sit dowun, lad. C'mon, ah'll do yer with me charcoal!"

Whpping an A3 sketchbook from a large canvas bag, he insisted that Bullock be seated, whilst he described expansive and expressive swirls onto the paper, intently studying Bullock's face, and transferring his vision to the page.

After exactly three minutes of scrawling, he tore the page exuberantly from the pad, and signed it extravagantly in the corner - "Hopple".

"There y'are, bonnie lad - an original Hopple! Just a tenner to yous - get that framed and it'll be the talk of the toon, will that."

Bullock inspected the drawing forlornly, the grin he had been modeling for his portrait melting slowly away to a grimace.

"Sorry Fred, but it just looks like somebody 'as drawn a football on a pair of shoulders. Me eyes aren't wonky like that, surely to God? And as fo' me nose…it look's like that of a hog!"

THE HIDE

"Oooh, I don't agree!" Ball leaned over to admire the Hopple. "Fred has caught you there, Ron, yes he has. Don't you agree, Tom?"

"Well...let's see...it seems there's more than a hint of the abstract about it. Sort of a Picasso version...shall we say, a Potato Head Ron."

"Potato Head?! Yer cheeky bugger, Tom!" laughed Bullock. "Anyway, it'll give Bella a laugh, no doubt. Here's a tenner, Fred, but I don't recommend you paint The Queen anytime soon, they'll put you in the Tower of London! Now, we will leave you two fellers to catch up, I want to go and see what them fishermen are bringing in. We'll see you on the boat, Prof. Nice meeting you Fred - do Tom's portrait next time, eh!"

"Nah, why - there's nowt to capture in that fayace, a bit too wishy-washy fo' me, no disrespect, Tom. I look fo' strong 'guache faces, me. There's a thousand shade's o'pink to guache in your face, Ron. Come back any time for a sittin' in me little studio - just a thou' for you boy - think about it! Paynted by Hopple —won't that be summat to tell?! Eh, before ye go...ye me-ah be inrested in me bird awt. Come on, 'ave a look - hawf price to you blu-okes, like!"

Hopple rose slowly to his feet, guiding them to a row of canvasses propped up against the harbour wall. De'Ath and Bullock attempted to work out what bird species on Earth they were meant to represent.

"Oh, I like this one, Fred," lied De'Ath. "Is it a basking seal colony?"

"Divvant be daft! Them are wrocks, atop which perch the Aw-ctic terns!"

Bullock was trying to make out a painting which looked to him like a Pierrot doll.

"Haha! D'ye leike me puffin, do ye Ron? Ah think ah have captured the fayus just nicely, eh?"

"Oh, a puffin, is it? Erm, well, yeahhh..."

- 127 -

THE HIDE

"And this 'un! Yous know what these are, bein' bwurder men, as ye aw?" Bullock and De'Ath squinted hard at a daubing that may have been a pod of killer whales or possibly a foaming grey sea during a turbulent storm.

"Gannets!" announced Hopple, triumphally. "See how they plunge into the briny from a gre-at height. Boom, boom, boom…can ye see, lads?" The artist pointed with pride at a series of white blobs on a grey gauche so thick it was a marvel it remained stuck to the canvas.

"Ah, gannets! Yes, I see," lied De'Ath again. You have certainly caught the drama of *Morus bassanus*, plunging into the ocean there, Fred."

"Dee ye like it, Tom?" grinned Hopple, conspiratorially. "Ah can see ye do! Oh alreet then ye'll cawl me a big fool. But here. Tek it. Go on, it's yours."

The artist picked up the canvas, and inserted it smartly under De'Ath's arm. Bullock tried his best to stifle a laugh, but his best wasn't enough.

"Oooh no, I couldn't! Really, I…" stammered De'Ath.

"Nooo lad, I insist. Yours for a song. Just cos I liyke yer - yer can have it! Just gi' us fowty quid, just fo' the payunt, like. Now, if I were you, ah'd put it above a mantelpiece and get one o' them lights to illuminate h'all the various tones n' shayuds."

"Forty…oh…" De'Ath looked at the canvas forlornly; Bullock couldn't take it any more and heaving with laughter, moved away to feign a coughing fit. Reluctantly, De'Ath opened his wallet and paid up.

"Right, well, we'd best put that bargain in the car then, Fred!" Bullock decided to beat a retreat, before Hopple tried to palm off any more of his masterpieces. "See you on the boat, Prof!"

THE HIDE

"OK! Bye for now, lads, luvly ter meet yer. Enjoy ya tour with Billy. Now then Bally, how 'ave you been, me auld mayut?"

Having made their escape, Bullock and De'Ath decided on a game of crazy golf before boarding the boat. After a pot of shrimps on the quayside, they made their way early to the stone steps for the boat, and were first in the queue. Puffin Billy arrived with a brisk thumbs up, moved the rope, and guided them down the stone steps.

"Welcome aboard the *Glad Tidings*, boys, mind your step, there y'go." Billy helped them step out onto the boat, where they seated themselves to the stern, and readied their binoculars for action.

"Surely 'e can't get all those people aboard, can 'e, Tom? It's gonna be a pretty full boat if so!" Bullock observed the long queue of folk descending the steps from the quay above, as the gulls wheeled and mewed overhead.

"Where 'as the Prof gone, he'd better be quick or he'll miss the boat! Ah there he is look, right at the back, the silly sod, with Pablo Picasso up there. PROF! WE ARE ALREADY ON BOARD DOWN 'ERE!"

Ball waved, and re-joined the back of the queue, waving Hopple a jaunty cheerio. As the boat filled up, Bullock and De'Ath were soon crammed together between a young couple from Hartlepool in black heavy metal T-shirts on one side, and on the other side a family from Richmond Park with many young children, their surname being Parchment. Pretty soon, all seats on the boat were taken, Ball having to take the last seat crammed within a party of what looked like enormous Vikings - three men with red beards and two women with plaited blond hair in the style of Brünnhilde the Valkyrie. Ball was delighted to be almost engulfed by the enormous bosom of one of the ladies, and immediately fell into conversation with the party, who were from Iceland. Puffin Billy took his place at the helm and revved up the engines. He addressed his passengers in a mechanical commentary through a crackly Tannoy as he reversed the boat away from the quayside, his mate hauling the landing ropes into a neat spiral on the deck.

"We have a bit of a swell on today, folks, so please remayun seated

THE HIDE

until we reach the islands. To your left you can see a number of eider ducks, well known for their 'eiderdown feathers'. The UK's heaviest duck, and its fastest flying. It's a true sea duck, rarely found away from coasts where its dependence on coastal molluscs for food has brought it into conflict with wor mussel fawmers. Listen oot for its cawl, which resembles Frankie Hoowerd at 'is finest. Locally, we call 'em Cuddy's, after a seventh century monk called St. Cuthbert who was one of the first men to protect birds."

Bullock and De'Ath assiduously observed the black and white ducks bobbing in the harbour, and both made notes in their books, listening carefully for pantomime dame-like calls from the Cuddy's.

Even as the *Glad Tidings* left the harbour wall behind, the children of the Parchment family to the left of the intrepid birders got up and started running wildly around the sea-sprayed decks.

"Oscar, Beatrice, Alexa, Zacky, sit down, please?" Their father, a bald and chinless specimen in flip-flops, cargo shorts and a generic fashion T-shirt was ignored completely by his offspring, who jumped about, emitting various loud squeals, roars and whines. The youngest let out an alarming, piercing screech, which she repeated without fail every ninety seconds, for no apparent reason or motive. The mother, in a floral dress and expensive designer sunglasses, looked absentmindedly out to sea.

"I want a lolly!" demanded the eldest, nine-year old Oscar, as he picked up a coil of landing rope from the deck.

"I want a lolly more!" insisted his slightly younger sister Beatrice in a shriek and stamped her foot repeatedly. "I want a lolly now!"

Little Alexa was taking an interest in De'Ath, and put her small paw on his thigh and started tugging at the straps of his Zeiss binoculars. "Me want, me want, me want," she chanted.

Three-year old Zacky decided he rather liked the look of the captain's cabin, and hurried off to climb the steps thereto.

"Childree-een, come here, please? You've had two lollies each this

THE HIDE

morning, haven't you!" attempted the father, once again invisible and inaudible to his marauding offspring. For some incomprehensible reason, father Parchment stood up to adopt the posture of a gibbon, and started making chimp-like noises. Bullock and De'Ath stared at him, uncomprehendingly, wondering if his children had elicited in him a rare form of insanity. However, Mother Parchment laughed approvingly, and the four children began hopping about and making small chimp noises in return. Father Parchment sat back down in smiling contentment and kissed his wife's cheek.

Alexa entered infant chimp mode, becoming a serious nuisance as she climbed up De'Ath, using his binocular straps to hoist herself, placing one of her Clark's sandals on his right thigh and jamming the toe of the other one firmly into his crotch region.

"Ah, ooh, that's a bit uncomfortable," De'Ath smiled unconvincingly, as Alexa trampled his testicles like grapes in a barrel.

"Me want vese!" Alexa shouted in De'Ath's face, pawing the optics with her lolly-sticky hands.

Bullock eyed the parents incredulously. They both seemed to be sporting indulgent, even proud smiles, as they watched their daughter mauling about on a stranger. Evidently finding their brood the cutest and most adorable of creatures, it seemed that it was incumbent on their fellow mortals and passengers to feel the same way.

"Leave the nice man alone, Puggles?" grinned the father. "I don't think he wants to lend his binoculars to you! Oh, Zacky, darling, what are you doing up there?"

Zacky gave a grin of contentment as he waved from the top of the ladder leading to the captain's cabin.

"And what are you two doing with that rope?" called father loudly and proudly, as Oscar and Beatrice uncoiled rope and started throwing it overboard.

"We are fishing, daddy!" announced Oscar, happily.

THE HIDE

"Oh, you are *fishing*, are you?" smiled their father, looking around in search of endorsing "aren't they cute" smiles from fellow passengers, which improbably, he duly received. Though not from Bullock, who's incredulous look was turning to one of outrage.

The boat began to pitch, and as the prow hit the first of the swelling waves, little Zacky wobbled, seemingly about to tumble six feet to the decks below, but he kept his balance, turned, and went to join Puffin Billy.

"Who's child is this?" crackled Billy from the cabin Tannoy. "Please keep your children seated - we are, as I told you before, heading into a swell."

Bullock turned his gaze to the proud parents, certain that one of them would comply with the captain's instructions - but to his amazement, father put his arm around mother, and looked contentedly out to sea.

Oscar and Beatrice had now let out most of the rope, which was dragging out behind the boat, dangerously adjacent to the propellers. Alexa climbed the summit of De'Ath and sat on his head, her hands gripping his ears and her little legs swinging about and kicking him merrily in the throat.

"Eh..he he, I erm…think you should get down now, little girl?" protested De'Ath mildly through his watery smile and catching his glasses as she kicked them off his nose. "I erm, oooof…hehe, ooh, right in the mouth, that was!"

"Does she need her nappy changing?" the mother smiled at De'Ath. "I think she's a bit stinky, isn't she?" Seeming to find this amusing, she simpered at her husband, who smiled proudly back.

"I repeat!" crackled Billy. "Will the person in charge of this child - please come and retrieve, or we will have to return to shore!"

It seemed possible that the smiling parents had forgotten that they had children at all, as they still showed no sign of retrieving Zacky, or any of the others. Bullock snapped. He rose unsteadily to his feet, as the boat pitched to port and starboard. First, he ripped Alexa from

THE HIDE

De'Ath's head, and planted her extremely firmly in her father's lap.

"OOOYAH!" emitted father Parchment, as Alexa let out the most piercing of screams.

Bullock then unsteadily marched up the boat, took Oscar and Beatrice by the scruffs of their necks, frog-marched the shocked infants and flung them into their mother, who let out a cry of horror.

"Frog-marched"

THE HIDE

Turning, he hauled the trailing rope back into the boat, getting covered by salt spray as he tottered back and forth. Finally, he unsteadily mounted the ladder to capture Zacky, who was fiddling about with dials and switches, much to the rising consternation of Puffin Billy.

"Right you, yer little brat" shouted Bullock. "I'm taking you back to yer dad, and if 'e don't give you a good wallop - I damn well will!"

"You cannot let your grandkids up here, man!" chided Billy. "If you can't keep them under control, don't bring 'em oot ter sea!"

"My kids, Billy?! They are nowt to do wi' me, lad! The bloody parents are down there - they evidently cannot be arsed!"

Bullock attempted to pick up little Zacky, who squirmed away with a venomous yell. "I DON'T LIKE YOU!"

"And I 'don't like you 'an all, yer little bugger! Come 'ere with yer!"

But Zacky decided that he did not want to be captured by Bullock, and sprang to his little legs and ran away. Unfortunately for him, he ran into thin air, crashing down onto an elderly couple on the seats below who were sharing an egg sandwich from a Tupperware box.

Landing uninjured, Zacky began thrashing about with his arms and legs, sending the egg sandwiches flying and winding the elderly fellow, who bent double and gasped for breath.

"Oh dear!" exclaimed the elderly lady. "Are you alright, Norris?"

"Geh...not really dear," groaned her husband, "I....EEEEUUUUGGGHHHHHHHH!!"

Norris copiously vomited the egg sandwich he had partly ingested, together with his breakfast of smoked kedgeree, all over the horrified face of little Zacky, who disappeared under a malodourous yellow slime.

Father Parchment had finally arrived. "Erm, has anyone got a tissue?" he asked nobody in particular, as he gingerly recovered his younger

THE HIDE

son, who was now bawling piteously, from Norris' lap.

"Oh, I am most sorry," belched Norris, helping to clean the wretched child with his handkerchief. "It's just that he sort of, landed on me! From nowhere!"

"Well there was no need to be sick on him was there?" the father whined petulantly. "I mean, what's all that about?"

"Ah will tell you what that was all about, sunshine," Bullock fumed as he descended the ladder. "Take your lad and sit yourself down. Now."

Oscar was already running about again as his father sat down with the sobbing and reeking younger brother.

"Hahahahahha! Zacky is covered in sicky! Zacky is covered in sicky! I don't like that man, he hurt me, Daddy!"

"I will hurt you a damned sight more, son, if you don't sit down, right now."

Oscar's brain was demanding that he should ignore yet another hollow adult threat, but there was something in Bullock's menacing frown and pointing finger that made him wisely decide to squash between his elder sister and mother, though with folded arms and a petulant frown.

"OWAH!" yelled Beatrice at Oscar. "You hurt!"

"Right, now that we've got you all sat down," started Bullock, remaining standing and grabbing hard onto a handrail as the boat pitched to all angles, and eyeing each member of the family in turn. "I am going to say something that doesn't seem very fashionable in this day and age. Now I don't know you people from Adam, but I see your sort every bloody day, in the street and in the supermarket. I 'ave raised four kids and I 'ave six grandchildren, and I know how 'ard it can be to control children. I like kids, me, but I'll tell you this - I don't like some of their parents, and that includes you two."

He leaned over mother and father Parchment, who cowered slightly.

"YOU…and…YOU… CHIMP DAD…are an absolute disgrace. Your kids are lawless, they don't listen to you, and they don't respect you. And their behaviour, running about, shouting and screaming, especially aboard a boat crammed with other folk - should be a disgrace to you. All they want is the right kind of attention, and you are not giving it. Now, I don't care what you do when you get off this boat. But if your kids so much as move until we get to the Farne Islands, I will personally throw 'em overboard. Hear that, kids? Big bad Ronny here, he will chuck you overboard and the sharks will gobble you up in one bite! Let's see what the Chimp family make of that!
Oooh-oooh-ooh!"

Oscar was already wriggling free to test this preposterous threat, but was held back by his mother.

"Osky…noooo…"

All of the Parchment family looked sharp daggers at Bullock, who squeezed himself back on the seat next to De'Ath. Father Parchment decided, extremely unwisely, not to take his admonishment on the chin.

"So…who the Hell so you think you are then?" he ventured, staring intently at the deck, as his yellow son writhed about on him.

Exhaling loudly, Bullock stood up once again, bringing the sandpaper of his chin to rasp against Mr. Parchments' neck, and growled into his ear. "I'll tell you who I think I am, son." Then he stood up, and in a loud voice, made an announcement to the entire boat.

"This person, old Chimp Dad 'ere, just asked me who the Hell I think I am, and I am going to tell him. I am a person who believes in, and will always believe in, good manners, consideration to others, and in a spirit of community. I believe that children should behave themselves, and be made to do so by their parents. And if the parents don't even try to do that, it's the job of people at large to insist they do. That's who I think I am lad. You two, you come on this boat with four young kids, let them run about, scream and bawl, crawl about on people, chuck ropes overboard and mess about in the captains' cabin. So tell me lad -

THE HIDE

who the Hell do you think you are exactly, apart from an escaped chimpanzee?"

Bullock was much pleased to receive applause from a scattered section of his audience, though some gripped their seats in excruciated embarrassment and others pretended nothing was happening and poked their phones. Ball was in rapt conversation with the Icelanders, and was oblivious to the events astern.

"Thank you, sir," crackled Billy. "It is so important that you do remain seated during the voyage, for your own safety. Now, we are approaching Grace Darling territory - Grace was the lighthouse keeper's daughter, famed for participating in the rescue of survivors from the shipwrecked *Forfarshire* in 1838. Unfortunately, she died of tuberculosis just four years later, aged 26."

Father Parchment, aka Chimp Dad, muttered something under his breath and whispered in his wife's ear, who laughed insouciantly. It was noticeable however, that none of their offspring was willing to risk being thrown to the fishes, and they watched Bullock suspiciously and intently. Oscar decided to feign an annoying attention-seeking cough, which his parents ignored.

"Good on yer, like," offered the young man to Bullock's left, sporting a fluffy beard and a Motorhead T-shirt. "You don't often see people do summat. I saw a bloke like you go after a charve who chucked his chip paper in the road last week."

"Oh aye, and did the miscreant put it his chip paper in the bin?"

"Oh no, he stabbed the bloke in the arm and ran off," reported the lad, matter-of-factly. "Aye but they did arrest him, like. Well, he stabbed somebody else later on in the same day. But I don't know if that was about litter or not," added the lad's girlfriend, who seemed to have an exaggerated lisp and a metallic click to her diction, possibly due to her seven lip piercings.

Bullock shook his head, keeping an eye on the Parchment children, who were all wriggling about and complaining. He had already decided that if one broke ranks, he would pick up the child, and

THE HIDE

pretend to throw it out to sea. He realized that might well get him arrested, but he decided it had to be done. The Tannoy crackled again.

"Now on yer right you can see a number of seabirds - guillemot, shag, fulmar and a few puffins. We have over 40,000 puffin pairs during the summer, though we believe that number may in fact be declinin'.'"

"He, he, there they go!" chuckled De'Ath training his sticky binoculars on the flapping puffins, "yep, look at those colourful bills, Ron!"

"Puffintastic!" chortled Bullock. "Christ, is the engine on fire?!!"

Gales of smoke were wafting down the boat, Bullock immediately checking the Parchment children to see if one of them had lit a fire, but they were all still sulking. The billows of smoke were emanating from the couple on his other side.

"What the 'eck are you two smoking?! Has your beard caught fire, lad?"

"No, we are vaping, mate," explained the lad, making Darth Vader sounds as he sucked from a what looked like a large battery. He exhaled a huge plume of perfumed smoke.

"I 'ave 'eard about these! Let me 'ave a look. Me and me mate 'ere are pipe smokers, we are aficionados of the St. James Flake, aren't we, Tom."

"Have a go if you want," said the lad, offering the device to Bullock. "Just press that button and suck."

"OK then, I will if you don't mind. Thank you. Like this?....GAAAHAHAAAAAAAAA!" spluttered Bullock, coughing out smoke through his nose and mouth. "It tastes like pop!"

"Yeah, that's Cola Bunny that is. Try not to take it into your lungs. Like this look."

Taking the vape back, the lad drew a huge cloud of smoke into his mouth, and then exhaled it as a series of rings.

"Impressive smoke rings," remarked De'Ath.

"Watch this," said the lad. "I can do jellyfish." Leaning out of the wind into the bottom of the boat, he first blew a smoke ring, then puffed some more smoke through the ring. The bluish vapour did indeed resemble a jellyfish, before it dissipated in the next gust of wind.

"Haha, that's good that is, a jellyfish, very good!" commended Bullock. "Where do you get these oils then? Where do they come from?"

"What the E-liquids? Oh, there's loads of shops about now, or you can get 'em on-line. We go to Planet of The Vapes in the 'Pool, like."

"What flavor are you smoking, love?" Bullock asked the lip-ring girl.

"Just now, coffee. Do you want a blast?"

"Christ no, thanks anyway," chuckled Bullock, shaking his head. "I'll 'ave me coffee in a mug, thank you. What other flavours do you like, then?"

"Oh, pink lemonade, Jamaican rum, Red Bull, there's a new one called Monkey Fart I quite like."

"Monkey Fart?" laughed Bullock. "Well, I don't know, it's a strange world this vaping. Is it addictive then, cos that's the problem with smoking. As Tom and I say, you've got to be in control of the baccy, and not t'other way round."

"Aye well, some o' them have nicotine like, some don't. You can get tobacco or cigar flavor if you want."

"Well, I think we will stick to the pipe - I expect you have to charge them things up all the time do you yer? And they don't look cheap, neither."

"Yeah, you do 'ave to charge 'em but same as most stuff innit," replied

THE HIDE

the lad. "We make our own vapes actually, these are double turbo charged with a massive tank. This will keep me going all day, this will."

The vaping conversation was interrupted by a slowing down of the boat and another monotonous commentary from the helm.

"On your right by the rocks is a seal colony. The islands hold a notable colony of about 6,000 grey seals, with several hundred pups born every year between September and November. Grey seals eat a wide variety of fish, squid, octopus and crustaceans such as shrimp. Sometimes they eat a seabird or two. Small fish are swallowed whole, while larger ones are held in the seals mouth and torn into smaller, more easily swallowed pieces with the claws on the front flippers. Right, hold on, we are going to get close in to the cliffs so you can see the nestin' bird colonies."

"Dadddyyyyyyyyyyyyyyy? What's that horrid stink? Don't like it…." Oscar was holding his nose as they approached the guano encrusted cliffs, where masses of nesting seabirds nested and perched.

Bullock had to admit that the ammoniacal stench was overpowering, and decided to ignore the whining child, as he stood up to study the cliff ledges and inhaled the vile smell, which would have had set Mrs Pychley's ammonia sink alarm ringing for ever more.

"Blimy, Tom, just look at 'em all!" 'Ow on Earth do they find their own nests?"

"Well, I was reading that each guillemot egg has an individual pattern. That's why they were much-prized by egg hunters. Some people say the most perfect thing in the universe is a bird's egg. There is a book out about it, I noticed. Would you agree with that, Ron?"

"Nah. Fo' me, t'most perfect thing in the universe is a brand new cricket ball. Good Lord, just look at all these birds. There's blimmin' millions of 'em!"

"Reet, if you' all sit doon again," crackled Billy through the Tannoy, "we will be mooring at Staple Island soon, and those of you leaving for

THE HIDE

the island, please be ready. Those stayin' on board, please keep seated."

"Good, the horrid man is getting off," bleated Oscar. "I don't want to get off on that stinky island. I want to go home and have two lollies!"

Bullock sighed wearily at the Parchment family and shrugged - evidently his speech had made no difference, and no doubt they would continue to annoy everyone but themselves for their entire holiday, and possibly for their entire existence.

The boat moored up and was swiftly tied; Billy helped his passengers to step off the boat one by one.

"Mind hoow ye go, and back in one hower, mind! That's the we-ah, and divvant fowget ye hats - the terns are on the nest an' guardin'! Those of ye for the guided tour, meet Charlotte at the top o' the brow."

As they disembarked; Ball enthusiastically introduced his new five Icelandic friends to De'Ath and Bullock.

"Now, let's see if I can remember all your names properly. This is Oddur. This is Ragnar. And this is Baldur. Have I got that right?"

"Ferry guud indeed," congratulated Oddur, as they shook hands with Ron and Tom. "Guud to mit yoo. Ant do yoo remember also de name of my wife and de wife of Baldur?"

"Yes, now, let me think. This one is Brynhildur, no, not Bryhildur, you remind me of a character in Wagner's Ring, for some reason… Brigitta, that's it, Brigitta! And you are…Elfa!"

"Ferry guud indeed, Yon Ball!" they all congratulated.

"And…let me see if I can remember what you taught me on board… "Gaman að hitta þig"…nice to meet you!"

"Ah egsellent, Yon Ball!" congratulated Brigitta.

THE HIDE

"Come and hit a pig from me as well" grinned Bullock. "I don't think I have met Icelandish before. Swedish, but not Icelandish. What brings you good folks to our islands, then?"

"Vell, we are goink to Fraance, actually. For the Euro football. Many people in Iceland are soo proud of this team, we are going to support. We have thiss chant…"

The five Icelanders stood together, and struck up postures, as if to begin a Maori Hakka.

"HOOOO!"

After what seemed a long pause, came again in unison, "HOOOO!"

After a slightly less length pause, again, "HOOOO!"

It appeared that the chant may go on sometime, so the trio sat down on a bench and Bullock and De'Ath lit up their pipes, watching in interest.

"HOOOOO!"

The chant began to speed up. "HOOOO…HOOO…HOOO, HOOO, HOOO, HOOOOOOAAAAHHH!!!"

The five threw their arms in the air and punched the sky.

"Marvellous!" congratulated Bullock, as the three applauded. "I think you will do very well at the Euros actually, your form during qualifying was good. Never know, you might play us lot!"

"Well, that would be soo good, to get out ov the group and play a big team like England. We would try our best, so watch out!"

"You might beat us, lad. Old Woy – he 'asnt got a clue. I would soon 'ave that lot playin', if I were managin'. I support a team called Barnsley, that's where I am from, see, 'ave you 'eard of Barnsley?"

"No, but we have one of ours, Jonsson, he iss playing in the Fleetwood Town. Iss near?"

THE HIDE

"Nay lad. But my wife supports Bolton, so we know Gudni Bergsson and Eidur Gudjohnsen."

"Ah, Eidur iss in the squad, a little bit old now, but he may play."

"Me and my wife Dot would love to visit Iceland, we hear your scenery is fantastic," said De'Ath, unctuously.

"You will be ferry velkommin, Tom. You vill contact uss, and ve vill look after you. We are fery hospitable people."

"Well, let's look after you, then," returned Bullock, slapping Radnur on the back. "I think we are expected - look, that young lady is waving at us up yonder."

At the top of the jetty slope, Bullock, De'Ath, Ball and the Icelanders were greeted by a young blonde woman wearing a baseball cap with a puffin on it.

"Right, good that's the eight of you – welcome to the Farnes! I hope you had a good voyage over with Billy. My name is Charlotte, I am part of the research team here, and I am fortunate to be living on the island this summer doing a census of the puffins, and as you will soon see, they are doing very well this year, although we are seeing a general decline in their numbers, probably due to the decline of their favourite food, the sand eel. Anyway, let's start our walk round, shall we…have you all brought a hat?"

The group murmured their general assent and trooped off after their leader; Bullock yanked down the Kodiak Oilskin and tightened the chinstrap, and De'Ath buttoned the tracker hat under his throat. However, Ball rummaged his pockets in vain for his OLDNACT baseball hat, and in doing so, got left behind.

"Oh, I erm, here's Humphrey…Buzzy…erm, yes spare socks, field guide, handkerchief, er…biscuits from the hotel…house keys… damn it, where's my hat gone?"

After several more rummaging minutes and the extraction of a great number of other miscellaneous items including a spanner and a test tube rack, Ball noted he was getting left behind by the group led by Charlotte, and decided to jog after them to catch up.

THE HIDE

"Right, as you can see, the terns - and as I am sure Billy has told you, there are four species here, common, arctic, roseate and sandwich - as we are right in the middle of the nesting season, they are guarding their nests...look, those are common terns, just rising up behind us, and they can really give a nasty peck, which is why we always advise on hats...oh dear, what's happening to our friend down there?"

Below them on the footpath, the hatless and hapless Ball was being viciously attacked by a shrieking mob of common terns, who rose angrily above him and took turns to swoop to give an angry peck to the pate of his exposed head. Surprised by the ferocity of the attack, Ball dived to the shingle next to the footpath - but this made matters worse. By mischance, he landed face down in a nest of speckled eggs, which cracked and splattered all about him. At this, the birds' fury was intensified, with more outraged parents joining the attack.

"Oh shit!" exclaimed a bewildered Charlotte, who tore down the path to Ball's aid. Noting that the prostrate victim's head was trickling blood, she bravely decided to offer up her own hat, and jammed it onto Ball's head.

"Oooh, yes, nice to meet you, Charlotte!" Ball offered her an eggy hand. "They seem to have gone for me, don't they! You see, I always carry my Oldshire Nature Conservation Trust - OLDNACT, well, of course they try to call it Oldshire Wildlife Trust these days. We have common tern at Clarendon Marsh you know - they breed on the rafts we set up, well, I say we, Mr Stern and the Volunteers. Anyway, I don't know what's happened to my hat. I might have left it at Mrs. Pychley's, I suppose. Do you know her? Ooh very nice Mrs. Pychley is, what a lot of cats she has! She, well her brother Seaton actually, do you know him? He does a very good breakfast, this morning we had kippers...there was no bacon you see. Ah, I remember now! Well, when we were in Newcastle the other day, we were observing the kittiwakes under the Tyne Bridge - "kittiwkake, kittiwake, kiitiwake!" and one of them (actually it may have been more than one of them because there was an awful lot of it) made a mess all over my hat and coat, so I went to the hotel to clean everything up, ooh terrible mess it was - and I washed my cap and left it on the radiator to dry. Silly me, I must have left it there. I

THE HIDE

hope they have a lost property at the hotel - perhaps we can pop by on the way back to have a look…"

"Really, that's very interesting, but…owwww!! Oh, they are going for me now…ouchhhh!…come on, we need to move!"

Aided by Bullock, Charlotte and Ball took back to the footpath, De'Ath wafting at the angry birds with his furled umbrella. The rest of the party, the Icelanders, looked on with unease.

"It iss rarder dangerous," announced the stout Brigitta. "Iss dis men inyured?"

"Oooh no, I just got a bit of a pecking. You can't blame the birdies for protecting their nests, can you!"

Charlotte began the process of sticking the first of many plasters to Ball's head.

"Anyway," said Charlotte, trying to regain some composure, "let's get around the headland, where there aren't so many terns, and that is where you will find the nesting puffins. Please stick to the path!"

They reached a grassy knoll which resembled a rabbit warren, with many holes in the ground. Several puffins, apparently neither shy nor aggressive to humans, waddled about their business, appearing from and disappearing into various burrows, just a few feet from the footpath.

"OOOOHHH….puffin, puffin, puffin!" squealed the be-plastered Ball. "Would you like to meet Puff the Magic Puffin, Charlotte?" Ball waved his puffin puppet madly about on his hand, and began singing.

"Puff, the magic PUUUUFFIN lived by the sea,
And frolicked in the autumn mist in a land called Honah Lee!
Little Jackie Paper loved that rascal Puff,
And brought him strings and sealing wax and other fancy stuff!
Oh…"

THE HIDE

"Erm, not just at the moment, thanks, er..." Charlotte was trying to remember her script. "So, where was I, oh yeah...puffins are a red-listed bird species. This means there has been a severe decline in the population of puffins over the last 25 years. Our work on the Farne Islands is critical to the puffins' ongoing breeding success. Every five years our ranger team undertakes a full census of the puffins. By counting them we can help monitor growth or decline on the colony. This information is fed into national data that help monitor the country's wider population. Erm, what are you doing?"

Ball had crawled off, and was attempting to introduce Puff the Magic Puffin to a puffin which had just popped out of its hole. The puffin didn't seem to be impressed, and after defecating on the puppet, waddled off.

"Oooh, Puff's got pooed on. Just like me in Newcastle! Never mind, Puff, I'll soon get that off..."

"Er, it would probably be best if you don't actually put your hand, well, Puff, or whatever - in the burrow? They do have a bit of a nip, and we don't want any more accidents, do we. That's it, yes hello Puff, not too near me now, you are a bit stinky, aren't you. Erm, where was I, yes...puffins nest in burrows underground - as you can see - or under boulders, or in rocky crevices. Just one egg is laid. After hatching, the young puffin remains underground concealed in the nest, until the night comes for it to head for the open sea, not to return until it is ready to breed, usually some five years later. Early in the season, as the puffins return to the islands, they start cleaning their burrows and making a fresh abode for the months ahead. It is in these burrows here that a single 'puffling' will hatch and grow.

"Ooooh. Puffling! I like that! Did you know that you were a puffling once, Puff? Puffling. Puffling...." Ball repeated, until gently hushed by De'Ath.

"Erm, where was I...yes....so...incubation is normally around forty days, the chick developing over a period of a further forty days or so. The erm, puffling won't leave the nest until it is ready to see the world for the very first time. It eventually emerges with its parents for a trip down to the water's edge, and its first introduction to the water, its future home. Puffins live longer than you might think!

THE HIDE

Many in excess of twenty years. Some puffins around the country have been recorded at ages of over thirty years old!"

"Thirty!" wow that's a good innings, lass! You would never 'ave though that, would you. Thirty. What is the longest-living bird, Charlotte? " Bullock asked.

"Good question - I know flamingoes can live into their eighties, cranes, as well. The albatross into their sixties…"

"Why do flamingos stand on one leg, Charlotte, I always wondered that?" asked Bullock mischievously.

"Er, do you know, I don't know, erm…"

"Because if they lifted both legs, they'd fall down!"

"Ah! Yes, very good. Which bird is always out of breath, then?" reposted Charlotte.

"A puffin! Puff knew that! That's an auks-cellent joke!" Ball chuckled.

"Auk-cellent, very good, now, where was I? Oh yes, on land, puffins may appear awkward or clumsy, but on their home territory, the water, their evolutionary development shines and, like many seabirds, this is where they gain their agility. Underwater, while steering with their feet, the puffin's wings become flippers, propelling them to depths at great speed in their quest for the next meal…right, shall we move on a bit…er, are you OK, sir?"

De'Ath seemed willing yet unable to move along to the next vantage point.

"Er, I think I am stuck actually, Charlotte. I think I must have put my foot in a puffin hole. I can't budge - I think my welly is wedged."

"Jesus," muttered Charlotte under her breath. Bullock was as ever, quick to the rescue. "Right you Icelanders, form a human chain, we will yank Thomas out in a jiffy. That's it, Tom, take a grip of my arm, that's the way, and Radnor, my other arm, now PULL!"

THE HIDE

De'Ath was violently extracted from the burrow, but with the loss of his Wellington boot, which remained wedged deep in the hole.

"Well, we can't leave that in there, we'll have to get it out!" sighed Charlotte. "There is probably a puffling in there, and its parents can't get in to feed it!"

"Give me that brolly, Tom," said Bullock, thinking fast. "I will use the hooked handle to get it underneath the sole of the welly, and then yank it out."

Lying flat on his belly, Bullock inserted the umbrella into the hole. "Yep, I can feel the boot - by gumboot, it's gone a long way down! Now, just hook the handle…aye, I reckon that's got it…ready…heave!!"

Bullock's trick worked perfectly - the rubber boot was hoisted from the hole. But not just the boot. Something black and white and fluffy was perched on the instep of the boot. The young bird blinked, not used to the bright light, and looked about anxiously.

"Puffling!" shouted Ball in delight. "Take a picture Ron, it's most unusual to see a puffling!"

"Oh no, this can't happen!" exclaimed a startled Charlotte. "It's too early, it shouldn't be out yet, especially during the day. The gulls will have it! And I don't want to handle it without gloves - if it smells of human its parents might reject it or kill it. Has anyone got any gloves?"

"No, but it's Puff and Humphrey to the rescue!" grinned Ball, once more donning the sock puppets. "Come on now, little puffling, Puff and Humphrey will take you back to your burrow. Oooh don't peck Puff - he is your friend! There we are - now don't come out again!"

The puffling disappeared from sight, apparently none the worse for its unexpected extraction. No sooner than Ball had done his work, a parent puffin with a beak full of sand-eels, flew in and ignoring the on-looking humans, ducked into the burrow to feed its offspring.

"Phew, that all seems to be OK," sighed a relieved Charlotte, "right, let's all move on and leave them in peace, shall we!"

THE HIDE

"Well done, Bally!" grinned Bullock. "Got a great photo of you putting that puffling back. Eh, Tom, watch where you put yer big feet! I told you to get some walkin' boots like mine - them wellies are no good for the cliffs!"

"Now, this part of the island has our greatest concentrations of puffins, and it's a good place to get that classic photo of them perching with sand eels in their bills, there you go, look over there." Charlotte pointed at a cluster of rocks where a group of puffins sat with mime-white faces and melancholy eyes; their multi-coloured bills with limp sand eels dangling out of both sides like a silver moustache.

"Now, we are a bit worried about the lesser sand eel because the breeding success of seabirds has been proven to fluctuate in line with sand eel stocks. Clearly, sand eels are massively important to the health of the marine ecosystem, and it is good news that the commercial fishing intensity on sand eels has started to reduce in recent years, however it's… NOOOOOOOO!! Put it down! You can't do that here! What are you doing?!!"

The Icelanders were giving each other high-fives, having co-operated, much as in a rugby line out, to propel Baldur into the air, who one-handed, had snatched a flying puffin from the air as it descended to land. Baldur took the bird in his large hands, as if to break its neck - which is exactly what he was about to do.

"What the…what the Hell?" stammered Charlotte in disbelief, charging towards them in confusion and fury. "What are you doing with that puffin?"

"We will eat him offcoursse!" Elfa replied in dismay. "In Iceland, ve eat maaany puffins. We cetch wis guns or nets, but also, if you are clever, yoo can catch them straight from the air. We cen issily catch more, one for you next?"

"NO!!!!" shouted Charlotte, finally losing her cool. "We don't eat puffins here! They are protected, red-listed. Let it go!"

THE HIDE

"But… usually…" Ragnar responded sadly, "jes, ve like to rip out da heart and eat it raw. I can show you, like thiss…"

"NOOOOOOOOOOOOOOOOOOOOO!" howled Charlotte. "Give it to me! Now!!!"

Reluctantly, Ragnar handed the reprieved puffin to Charlotte, who, relieved to find it unharmed, set it on the ground. The puffin ambled off, looking slightly offended to have been snatched from the sky with a view to having its heart plucked from its body and swallowed whilst still beating.

Oddur, Ragnar. Baldur, Brigitta and Elfa looked penitent, yet baffled. "What birds doo you eat in England, then, if not puffins?" asked Oddur.

"Chickens from the supermarket mainly. But we do shoot some birds for eating," answered Bullock. "Pigeons, pheasant, partridge, grouse, that kind of thing."

"But not puffins," confirmed Charlotte.

"Poor puffins in Iceland!" ventured Ball, re-donning Puff the soiled puffin puppet. "We'd better not take you there, had we, Puff!"

"No!" laughed Oddur, "for surely ve vill soak him in salted water, smoke him vith wo-od and dried sheep dung, then boil him for two hours in a sweet malt. Then into the fridge, and finally serve him, bone-in and cold, with butter. And eat him with a glass of Brennivín and some rotted shark. Skál!"

"You see, we are a family of fishers and hunters!" laughed Brigiita. We shoot the reindeers, gooses, ptarmigan…it iss our culture. In France, do they eat the puffin?"

"Oh they eat 'owt over there, lass. Eh, let's get a picture together, shall we!"

Charlotte was pleased to see the *Glad Tidings* battling back against the swell to the jetty, and was relieved to be able to guide her charges off the island, keeping a close eye on all of them to prevent any further mishap.

THE HIDE

"Well thank you, miss," said Bullock, shaking Charlotte's hand as Billy helped the Icelanders back on board as well as Ball and De'Ath. "That really was very interesting indeed. Keep up the good work!"

"Thank you, glad you enjoyed Staple Island, that was quite, erm, eventful, wasn't it. Hope to see you again next year!" she said unconvincingly.

A senior warden joined her to wave off the boat, Ball frantically waving both Puff and Humphrey in the air as they receded towards the shore.

"Tony, are all birdwatchers nutters?"

"Well, Charlotte," he replied, putting a supportive hand on her shoulder, "to pinch a well-known phrase - you don't have to be mad to be a birdwatcher - but it surely helps."

THE HIDE

THE HIDE

- CHAPTER FOUR -

Birdfair Buffoonery

Wherein The Birdwatchers visit the annual Birdfair at Rutland Water. Celebrity birdfolk are encountered. A demonstration of mist netting and ringing is attended, with unfortunate consequences. An exhibition of para-motoring goes seriously wrong.

The weather in Rutland on the twentieth of August was far from clement as Colin's Land Rover bumped across the ruts of the 'Blue Entrance' parking field, which was turning into a quagmire. Drenched people in red vests attempted to look pleasant as they directed the traffic, but already they were having to shove motorists out of swamps, becoming be-spattered by mud as the engines revved and wheels span frantically without earthly traction. The odour of the air was an unpleasant combination of trammeled grass, petrol fumes and distantly frying onions.

"Haha, look at that berk in his Volvo! Stuck fast. Shall I give him a tow - or maybe I won't!" Colin laughed gleefully as he engaged four-wheel drive and slalomed past a long queue of cars, enraging their fist-shaking drivers and bumping the heads of his passengers Bullock and De'Ath on the uncovered metal roof.

As well as the rain, there was a turbulent and fitful westerly wind; the gusts propelling with velocity ominous black clouds and ripping the securing ropes from the flapping banner on the metal field gate that bade them - *Welcome to Birdfair.*

THE HIDE

"Well, here we are chaps. The world's biggest nature fair in Britain's smallest county. Let's go and see what we can find shall we? Bloody Hell! We have to pay fifteen quid to get in? Never! What's all this about, you never had to pay before!"

A sinister looking woman at the entrance, wearing a blue sweatshirt and a cap of grey hair that looked like a sheep's fleece after a bad shearing, bade them an unfriendly welcome.

"Have you pre-paid?"

Colin took a deep breath, quelling with difficulty an obscene reply. "OOOOF! We have not pre-paid and I think it's an outrage charging an entrance fee. We are here to spend money with the exhibitors, not to pay for you and your security henchman here!"

A security man who looked like Lennox Lewis, previously slouching in a corner and chewing a blade of grass, sensed some action to relieve his tedium, and stood up to his full six foot six, looming ominously over Colin.

"Got a problem, bruv?" he sneered, flipping the grass out of his mouth with his tongue.

Bullock eyed Lennox up - as ever, fancying his chances in a bruise up.

"It's you who'll have the problem son, if you pick on us. The harder they come, the harder they fall, as they say where I'm from. Which is Barnsley by the way. Bruv."

"Actually it was Jimmy Cliff dat said dat," corrected Lennox. "Anyway, are you gonna pay your money or just piss off?"

A weird glimmer of what might have been a warped smile passed briefly over the fleece hat/hair woman. She evidently preferred that they would choose the latter option. She was disappointed. Bullock slapped some notes on the table.

"There's fifty quid. Three adults. And put the fiver towards a lesson in customer service. Bruv. Come on lads, let's see if the rest of the

THE HIDE

Birdfair staff can possibly match the levels of rudeness on the gate!"

Bullock wasn't to be disappointed. As they ambled around Marquee #1 among stalls displaying artwork of dubious quality, a lecture was taking place in a droning voice about the birding paradise to be found in Borneo.

"SHHHHHHHHHHH!" A woman who may have been the twin sister of the fleece hat/hair woman only much wider, put her finger to her lips in the direction of Bullock, in the manner of a Victorian schoolmistress.

"Ah didn't seh nowt!" protested the Yorkshireman.

"You were about to! I saw you put your hand over your mouth and lean towards your associate."

"Well, you are talking now!"

"I'm allowed to. I am a Birdfair steward. See…badge."

"It is a badge, er…Madge," squinted Bullock. "But you are not very fair, madam. Anyway, I might as well be hung for a sheep as for a lamb, as they say where I'm from. EXCUSE ME, MATE!!" he hollered at the nasal-droning speaker, who looked shocked to have his monologue interrupted.

"Er, yes…"

"ARE THERE ANY TOUCANS IN BORNEO? I LIKE TOUCANS, ME!"

"Err…no, there are not toucans in Borneo. But there are hornbills, some of which look similar to toucans. Toucans inhabit Southern Mexico, Central and South America and the Caribbean region. Do you mind if I take questions at the end, if that's OK?"

"Well, I do have a follow up question!" bellowed Bullock, Colin and De'Ath beginning to find proceedings extremely amusing. "Do toucans actually drink Guinness?"

The flustered speaker appeared to confer with a seated panel, the chair of which looked vaguely recognisable to Bullock, and who rose to address the issue.

"Sir, I don't know who you are, but obviously toucans do not drink Guinness. I think you are weferring to a TV advertisement of yesteryear. I daresay that chimps don't like tea either. Now, would you mind if Bwyan continues his lecture and we will take some sensible questions afterwards?"

"It's Packman!" exclaimed Bullock to his chums. "'im off Springwatch! I don't like 'im one bit…I will sort his hash out, watch this!"

"Is that a question, Mr. Packman? Cos if it is, yes, I do mind. What if you have a question and then forget it by the time he has finished ramblin' on? What then? It's not like the telly you know, where you get to address a captive audience and shut Michaela up whenever you want! Toucan play at that game, Sonny Jim! "

Aside from a few embarrassed titters, the audience gripped their chairs in anxiety and stared hard at the floor.

"Look," sighed the disgruntled celebrity, "if you came in here to cause diswuption, I'm afwaid I am going to have to ask you to leave."

With delight, the wide hat/hair woman scuttled off to fetch Lennox, but unfortunately for her, he had disappeared on one of his many tea breaks.

"Disruption? What are you on about, disruption? I am just asking a civil question. And a good clear answer, thank you. I certainly won't be going to Borneo for me hols then. I will go and see toucans in Meeexico! Ay caramba! Anyway, come on lads, let's get to another tent. I won't stay where ah'm not wanted!"

Like three naughty schoolboys, the trio left under the quizzical gaze of chair and panel.

THE HIDE

"Right, sorry about that Bwyan, I think that man may have had a few too many Guinnesses for his own bweakfast! Do continue, please…"

Bryan, the panel and the audience issued relieved and servile laughter, and the monotone duly continued.

"Hoho, you are good fun, you are Ronny!" chuckled Colin. "They used to chuck me out of here regular 'cos of me Tourette's. Honestly, they can be such a bunch of humourless b-b-b….ay-ay-ay… not doin' it, not doin' it….grrrrrr!!"

"Blokes?" interjected De'Ath.

"Thanks Tom, yeah, humourless blokes. Let's skip these next marquees and get some brekkie shall we? Just more holiday tours in there anyway."

Striding off to 'Cook Street', they found various food vans serving burgers, pizza, fish and chips, and vegetarian food.

"I don't suppose that 'bird' is on the menu here, is it," laughed Bullock. "I can't even see chicken, let alone pheasant or grouse. Or Peking duck…or fois gras! "

"I didn't think about that!" chuckled Colin. "Mind you, you can sign a petition over there to ban the eating of ambelopulia - the forbidden delicatessen. It's the Cypriots - they catch the little birds like robins and black caps and roast 'em on skewers or even pickle 'em. Absolutely disgusting in this day and age. And the French are as bad – they catch Ortolan buntings, fatten 'em up on millet, drown 'em in Armagnac, roast 'em, stick cloths on their heads and eat 'em up whole. Mitterrand had 'em at his death bed feast, apparently. "

"Oh, there's no need for that," agreed De'Ath, grimacing. "I mean, four-and-twenty blackbirds baked in a pie must have gone out in Tudor times, Colin."

"Well, I suppose you have to accept that different cultures eat different things, even nowadays. They eat puffins in Iceland, apparently. Rip the heart out and eat it whilst it's still warm."

THE HIDE

"Jesus, don't remind me about that – didn't we tell you about what happened in the Farnes? Old Ragnar caught a puffer and was about to break its neck - good job that young Charlotte was on hand to stop 'im. As for French food, Col," Bullock shook his head and paled a little. "Me and Tom went snowboardin' in the Alps a couple of years back. I shall never get over that tarteflette. Ooof, and that weren't the worse nither. Lambs' brains. I will never forget that, so long as I live."

"Snowboarding? Blimey that was intrepid of you fellers! Not skiing?"

"Nope. We must 'ave been the oldest boarders ever to learn. It was Bella's fault. She bought a holiday by mistake. But we did it, din't we, Tom?"

"Well, we did Ron. What a trip that was, we survived an avalanche, death by freezing, Ingvor's cooking…and what about that little monkey man!"

"Oh aye, what was 'is name? Blangard! What a mystery 'e was! Anyway, that's another story for another day, as they seh. Nethen, if we can't get a nice buzzard buttie, I suggest we go The Whole Hog. Pork sandwich fo' me, fellers," decided Bullock. "Ah love a pig roast, ah do."

"Make that two, Ronno. I'll pay, since you shelled out for the tickets. Tom?"

"Yep, pork bap Colin, thank you. No apple sauce for me."

As the three stood at a table chomping and crunching their enormous crackling-filled floury rolls, a colourfully-dressed band, redolent of Morris Dancers though dirtier and scruffier versions, started tuning up their folky instruments on a small stage opposite.

"Oh for f-f-f-f-f…." grimaced Colin.

"Flip's sake?" improvised Tom.

"Thanks, Tom. For flip's sake. It's the Hurdy Grinders. I though they

THE HIDE

must have retired or died ages ago."

"Ah one, ah two, ah one, two, three, four...*oh, let six pretty maaaaidens with a bunch of re-ed roheses, six pretty maaaaidens for to sing me a song...*"

An aged whiskery fellow put one hand over his ear and started stomping one buckled shoe in time with the thudding of the bass drum harnessed to the shoulders of a sturdy fellow behind him, and the arrhythmic tootling of a tin whistler took flight. The vocalist warbled unmelodiously forth.

"Then upon the pe-aaace of my ducks and my geese, he bo-holdly did intrude..."

Bullock and Colin peered scornfully away into the mid-distance, but De'Ath, an unrepentant fan of English folk music, put down his bap, put one hand in his trouser pocket and started hopping about, roughly in time to the music.

"Let me so-hoar with the ea-gal and make merry, me men! That's the spirit, sir, make ye merry indeed!" encouraged the singer.

"For God's sake lad..." hissed Bullock, but in vain, as De'Ath was caught up in the accordion solo and pirouetted wildly about.

"Yeah, erm, sorry about this, Colin. Tom is usually a very sensible chap, but we all 'ave our Achilles heels don't we. Mine is me knees, actually. Tom's is folk music."

The players were amused and encouraged by De'Ath's whirling antics, giving him the thumbs up and grins lacking many teeth.

"For we'll make merry, merry, make merry, merry, yes we'll A-MAKE MERRY, MEHERRRRRRRY....IN AULD ENGARLAND'S WIYNNDY LAH-HHHHHHHAAAAAAAAAANNNNNNES...AH!!"

The song ended with a triumphal punch of the air by the wizened singer. There was perfunctory scattered applause, mainly from De'Ath.

THE HIDE

"Thank you indeed, thank you, we are the Hurdy Grinders, making mischief and merry, wherever we go…mainly mischief, as it happens, with old Burbot on the fiddle here…"

The rest of the band sniggered their approval, though 'Old Burbot' merely stared into the heavens. Bullock recognized the vacuous stare beneath the red knitted hat.

"Hang, on that's old Lostweasel on the violin!"

"So it is! Hallo Mr. Lostweathiel!" grinned De'Ath with a wave, pointing at the Zeiss binoculars around his neck.

The Cornish shop-keeper and fiddle-player gave De'Ath an unrecognizing frown, before being distracted by the throb of the drum announcing another song, which he struck lively into.

"The daaay the hey nonny lolly ca-aame te town…"

"Right, ah think that's quite enough o' that," announced Bullock, swilling down the dregs of his coffee and wiping his face with an enormous pocket handkerchief. "You can stay and make a spectacle of yerself if you want, Tommylad, but I am off to explore."

"I'm with you, Rhino Ron. That pork bap should set us up for the day - let's do a bit of bird ringing shall we?" Colin simultaneously belched and farted loudly, earning Bullock's visible disgust. "Ooof. Better out than in, Ronno!"

"Not in my book, Colin. You'll be standin' alone if you do that again. Any 'ow what's this bird ringin'? Chatting up ladies on the 'phone is it?" guffawed Bullock. "Or is it like bell ringin' but using jackdaws instead o' the bells!"

"Hahaha, you are the one, Ronny! I like that…jackdaws, you could have a line o' them couldn't you, you know, like those handbells…tiny little wrens at one end and owls on the other!"

"I tell you what, I wouldn't want to ring 'is bell - but I wouldn't mind wringin' 'is neck!" hollered Bullock, pointing at the lead singer of the Hurdy Grinders, who was warbling about the many virtues of mead.

"Bird ringing, did you say, Colin?" De'Ath reluctantly tore himself away from the music, following his mates towards what looked like a cricket net, only with a much finer mesh.

"Yeah, look, it's my old mate Olly. He's got all the licenses to do all this ringing - English Nature, Scottish Wildlife, the lot. Alright Olly, boy!"

"Mr. Col! How are you - you f*#@ing old c#@*?"

"Ah, now then, old son! Thing is, I don't swear no more, me! I'm cured, well, been two weeks only, but so far so good, like. Meet my new mates here, Ron and Tom. It's a long story, Olly - but made short, they clobbered me with a 'scope, I demolished a hide at Clarendon and ended up floating up the lake unconscious!"

"Crikey mate, is that what they call shock therapy? Sounds a bit brutal!"

"No you b-b-b...."

"Blackguard?" suggested Tom.

"Berk?" offered Ron.

"Berk! That'll do. Thanks gents. No, it was all an accident, not a very happy one at the time, but - well, for now anyway - I am tic and sweary free. So don't set me off again, Olly. Now, what are you up to you old, c-c-c-cuckoo, that's it, cuckoo."

"Well, Col," replied Olly, looking mildly confused, "I've got the old mist net out, as you see, and I am giving a bit of a ringing demonstration...sorry lads - Olly Nice, good to meet you. Do you want to have a go? See, we've caught something over there, looks like a long-tailed tit to me. Let's put a little ring on him, shall we?"

Something small, dark and fluffy was bulging part of the filmy net that

THE HIDE

ran some thirty yards towards the nature reserve of Rutland Water. Olly carefully extracted the bird and held it gently but firmly, so that its head and legs were visible in his nut brown and somewhat scratched and scabby hand.

"Right, this is a tiny little feller, so we'll have a B-ring for him - just pop one in the ringer there Col, will you?"

Bullock and De'Ath peered at the little tit, admiring the long dark tail feathers which gave its name, and felt sorry for it. Bullock said so.

"I feel sorry for that little feller, Olly. Why are you putting a ring round its leg? It's like clapping a man in irons or putting one of those Asbo tags round his ankle. What's the point of it?"

"Ah," smiled Olly, in a way that suggested he had been asked the question a thousand times before. "First off, it won't feel like it's got anything on its leg - it's like you wearing that wedding ring on your finger. And it gives us loads of information, like how old they get and where they get to. All the info gets sent to the BTO to put on their database, helps with the conservation, like."

"Jesus, what are you doing with those pliers? You'll have its little leg off!"

"Don't worry!" smiled Olly. "I've done this many, many times...there you go, little feller. Just put him in the book - male LTT, one year old...off you go, chap!"

The bird took back to the skies with a relieved "peep".

"Oops, there's another visitor to the net! Well I never - a juvenile nuthatch...don't see many of them here...do you want to do this one, Col?"

"I can't mate - I had to give up 'cos of me Tourette's. I squashed a swallow in me hand during one of me spasms - I tell you, I am not over it to this day. Whenever I see a swallow I feel a pang of guilt, oh dear, that was a terrible day, that was." Colin literally hung his head in shame, and a tear glistened in his eye.

Bullock put a hand to Colin's shoulder in sympathetic support. "It weren't your fault, Colin, lad. But best you don't do no more ringin' til we know yer fully Tourette's-free. In the meantime, I will 'elp Olly wi this 'un!"

"Go on then, Ron," smiled Colin sadly. "I loved to handle the birds, I really did. That little fluffy ounce of beating life…there is something precious having a bird in your hand. One day, perhaps, I will be able to do it again."

"Well, a bird in the hand is worth two in the bush, anyway," wisecracked Bullock, feeling the need to lighten the mood. "Right, give us that nutcracker, or whatever it's called, Olly. I have a very steady hand, I have."

"Right you are, Ron. OK, I want you to curl your fingers into my palm to take the bird…no, the other way, that's the way…good, and firmly but gently take him, good, that's perfect. We'll be needing a tiny A-ring for this little feller. Just look at that beautiful blue-grey plumage and the russet at the neck. And the black eye-stripe of course."

"The Mask of Zorro!" declared De'Ath peering at the birds head, held captive in Bullock's meaty paw. "Ooh, and a sharp little beak, too…"

"Bill, Tom, remember, not beak," corrected Colin. "And it *is* as sharp as a needle, ain't it! Needs to be - for picking bugs out of the bark and breaking up acorns."

"OK, hold it still, Ron, just…"

At that moment, a posse of indignant-looking people came striding towards them, including a raddled old gentleman in country attire and an officious-looking young woman in a pencil skirt carrying a clipboard and three mobile phones. At the forefront was the lecture chairman and TV celebrity Chris Packman. The hat/hair woman scurried along beside him, trying to protect him from the rain with a *Birdfair* umbrella.

Approaching Bullock, who was hunched over the ringing in a tight circle with Olly, Colin and De'Ath, Packman tapped him sharply on the shoulder.

"You there, I want a word with you!"

Bullock, feeling an unwelcome jab at his scapula, spun round in reaction, raising his right fist.

"You have a nuthatch in your hand! I jolly well hope you are a wegistered permit holder!"

"Packman!" exclaimed Bullock. "Erm…permit holder? No, I don't think so, I am just helping Olly out here..."

The young nuthatch felt the grip of Bullock's hand loosen a little from its body, and it was suddenly able to swivel its head around. It saw its chance to escape from its prison - it drilled the needle of its black beak hard into the soft muscle below Bullock's thumb.

"YEEEEOOWWWWWWW!" roared Bullock, instinctively flinging his hand open, and propelling his tiny assailant to the ground. The nuthatch was briefly stunned as it hit the grass, lying face up with its wings outstretched.

"You clod!" yelled Packham. "You can't chuck nuthatches about! You've gone and bloody well killed it!"

"It pecked me!" protested Bullock, stemming the blood flowing freely from his hand, "and you poked me in the back whilst we were ringing it, you nincompoop!"

Happily, the spread-eagled nuthatch was not dead, and began to recover its senses. Out of its beady eye, it spied a dark crevasse of safety from the many looming and babbling humans above and flipping over onto its legs, it made a scuttle for it. But the dark crevasse it thought might have been the hollowed-out root of a tree was in fact the flapping hem of Packman's baggy country corduroy trousers.

"The nuthatch lives!" cried De'Ath in delight. "It's disappeared up Mr.

THE HIDE

Packman's trouser!"

Indeed the nuthatch had. Finding itself in the dark, much like it would if on the trunk of a beech tree, it quickly scampered up Packman's leg.

"Ah! Oooh! Cripes!" The celebrity naturalist hopped around, just as De'Ath had been doing during the performance by the Hurdy Grinders, though with significantly greater agitation.

"Help me get these twousers off!' he yelled at his entourage. "I'm wearing bloody bwaces - I'll have to get me waistcoat off first!"

Bullock and De'Ath didn't imagine, on the occasion of their first visit to the world's biggest nature fair in Britain's smallest county that they would be called upon to de-bag one of the nations' leading ornithological experts, but they set about their task with determination.

"Easy, Tom, don't yank 'em off like that, we might injure the nutpecker. You'd best lie on the grass, Chris. You don't mind me callin' you Chris, do yer?"

"Call me what you bloody like, just weleased the bird!" yelled Packman, assuming a recumbent position on the soaking grass.

"Well, I 'ope you are wearing yer undies, Chris, cos…here goes! That's the way, over 'is bum, lads…roll 'em down…there it is!"

The nuthatch, relieved to see the light once more, perched briefly upright on Packman's knee, inspected the growing throng of curious faces, and restored to health, it flew off.

"Blimey, is that a pouch you are wearing, Chris? What does it say on it? *Ornithology Isn't Just a Science It's a Lifestyle*. Is that a birding joke, Colin?"

"Er, I don't think so, Ron. Oooh, he's drawn a bit of blood up and down yer leg there, Chris. I hope your tetanus is up to date. Best get these wounds dressed in the Medical Tent."

"Give me my twousers, you bunch of imbeciles," demanded Packman, rising to his feet. Assuming that he was acting out a sketch for a comedic episode of *Springwatch* perhaps related to *Children in Need*, the growing throng began to applaud and cheer.

"Nice thong, Chris! Nice arse as well!" cheered a brazen woman in a green *Birdfair* T-shirt, videoing on her I-Phone.

"Post that on social media, and I will have you sued!" Packman shouted at her, attempting to get back into his trousers and adjusting his amusing pouch.

"Right, get me out of here Amanda; I want the helicopter here in ten minutes. And I want to be in the Azores by midday tomorrow. And get some TCP and sticking plasters for me legs, for God's sake."

Amanda the PA began barking orders into two of her three mobile 'phones, and the disheveled celebrity was led away by his entourage.

"No time for a quick pint, Chris?" Colin shouted at the departing posse, receiving a single, middle-fingered gesture from Packman without so much as a look back.

"Jesus, I wish I still had me Tourette's!" growled Colin, through his teeth.

"No you don't lad," responded Bullock, sucking the wound on his hand and spitting out a red gob. "But I definitely do want a pint. Olly, thanks for the demo mate, sorry you didn't get a ring on the nutwarbler, but through no fault of mine! I wish it would've been a bloody big Woody woodpecker – that would have served old Packman right. What was that on his undies anyway - it wasn't even funny! *Ornithology Isn't Just a Science It's a Lifestyle?* What's all that about?"

"Not sure," admitted Colin, as they entered the beer tent. "Oh 'eck, talkin' of celebs - here's another one – the lesser-spotted Oddie. You'd think he was a Tourette's man as well. Let me introduce you."

"Alright Bill? How are you do…"

THE HIDE

"Colin, don't f******** interrupt me like that, I was just telling these people about my adventures in Armenia. Now go and buy me a drink for your many sins - Old Stinkful, pint of. Now, where was I…" With much animated effin' and blindin', 'effin' and jeffin', Oddie, clad in a striped rugby shirt, resumed his tale with considerable animation.

Heading to the bar, Colin issued some advice to Tom and Ron. "Don't ask him about *The Goodies*, he doesn't like to talk about those days. And try not to challenge his authority on anything."

"What the Devil is wrong with these TV people?" muttered Bullock. "I'll bring the bugger down to Earth, you watch me. Yes mate, over 'ere…four pints of Old Stinkful, please."

Returning with a tray of beer in plastic glasses, the trio watched Oddie giving an impromptu reading to a small and grinning group of Malaysians, all wearing the same yellow T-shirts emblazoned in red with *Kuala Birdwatching Tours*. He read from his autobiography *One Flew Into The Cuckoo's Egg*.

"And so there I was as a young boy, creeping about in the hedge after my tennis ball in Rochdale, and I found my first nest! Four blue eggs and one round whitish one. It was none other than a cuckoo's egg…"

"I didn't know you were a Lancashire lad, I thought you was a Brummie?" interrupted Bullock and handing Oddie his pint. "My wife is from Bolton. I s'pose that's where you got that Eckythump from? Eh - "there's nowt wrong wi' owt what mitherin' clutterbucks don't barley grummit"! Haha, that was great when you kept clobberin' Brooke-Taylor and Old Garden wi' that black puddin'!"

Colin gave Bullock a puzzled look which suggested 'what part of *"don't ask him about The Goodies, he doesn't like to talk about those days"* had Bullock not understood, exactly?' whilst De'Ath made a watery smile in the direction of Oddie, wondering if a raging fury, possibly involving a black pudding, might next ensue.

In fact, Oddie's response was to take a sip from his pint, raise an eyebrow slightly, and then to ignore Bullock completely.

THE HIDE

"A cuckoo's egg! Well, of course, I didn't know that at the time, but that was my moment of awakening, my epiphany. So, you'll all want to buy a copy of *One Flew Into The Cuckoo's Egg*, I expect. I have also written many other books, here they are on the table over here, come with me…here we go, take your pick… *Bill Oddie's Little Black Bird Book, Bill Oddie's Gone Birding, Follow That Bird, Bill Oddie Unplucked* and of course, *Gripping Yarns*. You will probably not know, being from foreign climes, that 'Gripping' is to see a rare bird when your friends haven't, and that actually this is a bit of pun on '*Ripping Yarns'* which was a BBC series once. But never mind about that, I am sure you will enjoy all of them, and as a one-off I can offer a pound off the rrp - and sign them for you as well in the bargain! Sooo…"

The Malaysians looked politely at the books, and then started to wander off, smiling profusely. Oddie became furious.

"What! Where the f*** are you going?! I haven't wasted my time giving you a reading for you to all just to sidle off! Come back here! Oh, you bunch of total wankers, I don't think you understood a single word, did you, you…"

Indeed, the group of Malays fortunately possessed no English whatsoever, as they were making their first ever foreign trip, and their translator had been left manning their stand. In response to the volley of abuse they were receiving from Oddie, they merely grinned broadly and applauded meekly. Bullock and De'Ath looked on in shock, though Colin did not seem a bit surprised.

"F****** unbelievable!" ranted Oddie, returning to his pint, which he supped venomously. "Absolute timewasters!"

"Er, I will buy one of your books, Bill, if it's any consolation to you," ventured Bullock. "I quite fancy that *Gripping Yarns* if it's about twitching. Pound off and signed though, mind. You weren't in *Ripping Yarns* were you, it was the Monty Python lot wasn't it? *Like that Rutland Weekend Television*. I expect you knew the Python boys didn't you Bill? Ho ho, I bet you could tell a few tales about comedy in the 70's, eh!"

THE HIDE

Oddie's small blue eyes twinkled mischievously, as he took a copy of his *Gripping Yarns* from the table.

"Not really. Eight quid then. What name shall I put?"

"Erm, *"To Ron"*, please Bill. No 'ang on *"To Ron, good luck with the birding, all the best, Bill"*. That'll do. Here you go, eight quid."

"Uh huh," responded Oddie, scribbling in the book with a Biro, his tongue between his lips in concentration.

"There you go, Ron. Thanks for the beer Colin, I'll be off. I expect they'll want me for the quiz."

With that, the diminutive, barrel chested writer, composer, musician, artist, ornithologist, conservationist, television presenter and actor, stomped off into the beer tent crowd.

"Right!" grimaced De'Ath into his beer. "Not quiiite what I thought Mr. Oddie might be like!"

"Well, he's had his battles, you know, Tom. Depression, bi-polar, that sort of thing. He can be absolutely charming, but also, as you have seen, he can be…what do they call it - irascible?"

"Irascible! That's an understatement!" laughed Bullock. "Them poor Chinese fellers got both barrels, dint theh! Anyway, Bella will be very happy I 'ave a signed book. She is a big *Goodies* fan she is. Let's see what he wrote…'ANGONAMINUTE!!"

Bullock's face turned slowly purple as he pointed in exasperation to the frontispiece of his book. Colin and De'Ath exploded in laughter, the latter spilling most of his pint down his beard. Bullock read Oddie's message aloud in disbelief.

"Ron, sod off and mind your own business. Bill."

THE HIDE

Having had a couple of pints, a pork pie each and a good laugh, the trio explored the rest of the fair, taking in stalls of binoculars, telescopes, cameras, tourism, campaigning, arts and books, as well as a live exhibition of birds of prey. Bullock was especially keen to get a photo with an enormous black eagle on his arm.

Also in the outdoor exhibitions area, something was getting a lot of attention and they moved over to join a growing throng to see what was going on. Reluctantly, Bullock passed the black eagle back to its owner, having briefly considered making an offer to buy it, but then reconsidered when he thought of what Bella might say on his return to The Nook with a huge bird of prey.

A hook-nosed chap was strapping onto his back what looked like a giant electric fan, and stepping into a harness behind which trailed long cords leading to an arc-shaped parachute, held into shape against the buffeting wind by a couple of helpers. The man looked familiar to Bullock.

"I've seen that guy somewhere before, haven't I? What the heck is he up to?"

"That's Nigel Shiltberry from the Clarendon Volunteers, isn't it? - the one that thinks he's a moth!" remarked De'Ath, remembering the hawk shaped profile of the fellow now donning a safety helmet.

"The very same!" confirmed Colin. "Apparently he is putting his paragliding skills at the disposal of the Wildfowl and Wetland Trust. They are tracking the migration of the Bewick's swan from the River Thames to Russia, apparently. Three thousand miles and ten weeks. He must be bonkers."

De'Ath retrieved a field guide from his satchel, and read aloud.

"Bewick's swan. *Cygnus columbianus*. Bewick's swan was named in 1830 by William Yarrell after the engraver Thomas Bewick, who specialised in illustrations of birds."

"Yeah, but the taxonomy gets a bit tricky, Tom, there is a sub-species issue here. They also call them tundra swans, the Bewick is a sub-

THE HIDE

species, *bewickii* -'cos you also get the sub-species *columbianus*, which is an American vagrant with a black bill. Yeah, I saw one in a group of whoopers over at Cley in Norfolk year before last. Blimey, up he goes look!!"

'Midst great applause from the admiring crowd, Nigel started galloping into the gale, and the parachute quickly hoisted him into the grey sky, where he settled expertly into his trapeze-like harness into a sitting position, and activated the giant fan. Despite the buffeting he was taking from the wind, Nigel was able to control the para-motor craft to encircle the fair, giving a thumbs-up to the support crew below.

"Wow, that takes some nerve," remarked Bullock. "Just look at 'im go. Eh look, he is beaming video from a camera on 'is 'at on that screen, look. There's us - wave!!"

"Excuse me, sir!" A ruddy and earnest young woman, with a terribly posh voice and wearing a shapeless sweatshirt adorned with a swan in flight, approached them with a clipboard. "Would you care to sponsor our *Flight of The Swans* project? They are declining, you see, and we want to find out exactly, ahm, why."

"'Ow are yer gonna do that, lass, by chasing 'em about wi' a man tied to a giant fan? You'll scare 'em off! I'm not sponsoring Nigel buggering about - if 'e were running a marathon or summat, that might be different. Any 'ow - 'e is never gonna make it as far as Russia, look at him up there! 'E'll be lucky if he gets back down at all!"

"Oh no, he'll be absolutely fine I am sure, he is one of the best para-gliders in the team. We are backed by Sah David and Ranulph Fiennes, you know."

"Sir David, yer say? And Ranulph! Oh well, that's different that is. Well worth a fiver, then. When are you off? Like marathons, I only pay if you make it, mind!"

"Well, we start in the Russian tandra in Septembah – and it's bewah of the polar bars of course, what fun!" The young woman shook her frizzy ginger mane and grinned her gappy teeth. "Then through Finland, Estoniah, Latviah, Lithuaniah, Powland, Garmany,

THE HIDE

Dyenmark, Netherlands, Belgium and Fwance. Then cwowss the Chennel to Landon."

"Are you related to royalty, love?" asked Colin. "You look a bit like that Prince Harry?"

"Thaard cousin!" she beamed. "He is such a larff, vewy nice parson."

Bullock narrowed his eyes. "Listen my dear, I don't want to be funny or 'owt, but my money aint going to the royalty. You lot 'ave got enough. This fiver is going to Sir David or Ranulph, and only if - and ah do mean *if* - yer get back alive, and find out whayt's 'appenin' to the Airwick swans. Here, I will write my address down, and pledge you five quid. There you go. But if you get savaged by a polar bear, don't come blaming me for sponsoring your expedition! I expect you'll be gettin' the bus back from Helsinki, chuck. That fan ain't gonna mek it to Latvia, that's for sure!"

"Ah, oh, thanks vary much, have a laverly day at the show!"

The trio hustled away, watching Nigel circling above them, no bigger now than a moth in the angry grey sky.

"Right, let's go and see those ospreys shall we," suggested Colin. "I reckon the last chick will be off any day now, so we'd better get cracking. Let's get back in the car before all the traffic starts moving and drive round to the Lyndon Visitor Centre and get in the Waderscrape Hide."

Back in the Land Rover, they bumped and slewed across the parking field where it had finally stopped raining, and resumed the main road.

"So these ospreys, Colin," said De'Ath studying the *Collins* guide. "It says here that they are very rare breeders here in England. Mainly in Scotland?"

"Ah it's a great story, Tom. It was once a common bird in England in places like the Fens just out east from here, but they reckon by the 1840s it was extinct because of drainage, egg-collecting, taxidermy, hunting and so on. Even in Scotland they went extinct a century later

THE HIDE

but then slowly recovered from Scandinavian bird populations. You could see 'em stopping off here in the 1980's on their way to Africa for the winter. Well, we put an artificial nest back then in the top of a tree to attract them to stop and breed but it was no good. Little did we know - it needed a lot more than that! So what they decided to do, was move some Scottish chicks down here, so that when they came back the next summer, they might think, well, this is home and this is where we need to breed. They are like that, ospreys. Home-loving."

"Didn't the Scots mind?" growled Bullock. "Not like them to be generous wi' owt. Like us Yorkshire. And I presume there must be ospreys in Wales too, 'cos that's what they call the rugby union team in Swansea, The Ospreys. Good team they are."

"I dunno about that - I think they lost their ospreys too in Wales. Anyway, there were quite a lot of breeding pairs in Scotland, and as I recall they agreed a license to move about a dozen chicks about twenty years ago. They did loads of work, radio tagging, behaviour specialists, vets, the lot. They carried on translocating and then in 2001 they started breeding here again! The first one was *Mr Rutland* – well, they give them numbers mainly rather than names, he is number 03 -97. He's had 32 chicks, 46 grandchicks and 15 great-grandchicks! What a stud, eh!"

"That's incredible, Colin. Just to think of all that work that goes into bringing back lost species."

"And still does, Tom. But talk about eco-tourism - over a million people visit Rutland each year, and many of them come just for the ospreys. Not bad for a bloody reservoir built in 1975 for drinking water, is it! Right, here we are. It's a bit of a hike down to Waderscrape, but it'll be worth it. I am bringing me 'scope as long as you both promise not to attack me with it. Unless I start me swearing again! Eh, so far so good on that front!"

After a pleasant walk, they arrived at the Waderscrape Hide, which proved to be little like their 'home' Hide at Clarendon Marsh. The long and spacious pine building more resembled a plush Swedish cabin than a shed. Some of the viewing windows were glazed; there were huge professionally-printed panels with information on the

THE HIDE

Osprey Project and other birds to be seen on the water, and at one end, a TV monitor fed by a live webcam. Over twenty birders were already present, including an evidently well-trained and enthusiastic 'Osprey Volunteer', identified as 'Malcolm' by a lapel badge on his blue polo shirt, emblazoned with an osprey. He greeted the newcomers graciously.

"Good afternoon, gentlemen, if you haven't visited us before, there are a couple of 'scopes set up on the ospreys, for your use."

"Not necessary, Malcolm." Colin breezed past him, and began scanning the horizon of open water and trees beyond. Bullock and De'Ath continued to notice that birdwatchers weren't in general very civil to each other - yet not much offence seemed to be taken. It seemed to them that being vaguely rude or at least, indifferent, was the norm. Nobody else in the hide so much as looked at the new visitors, let alone considered a greeting.

"There they are, boys. Your first ospreys!" beamed Colin. "See those two big posts, look like telegraph poles in the water, in the bay there…?"

Bullock and De'Ath sat down at an opened window and peered out intently, training their binoculars.

"Ah, there he is…Mr. Rutland! I see him!" exclaimed De'Ath.

"Actually that isn't Mr. Rutland, that is a female." Malcolm came over to offer his guidance. "On the other pole you can see the nest, with one chick, that is T8, that is. The other two have fledged and gone, just earlier this week."

"Oh, bugger off Malc, we don't need your help! Go and help them out over there, they don't known an osprey from an ostrich, that lot!"

Malcolm seemed used to routine abuse and went without complaint to help a lady who had made it to the hide with the assistance of an electric power mobility scooter.

"Why do they like these poles then, Colin, what do they do if there

THE HIDE

isn't one of those handy? Oh I see, there's the camera sending video to the telly on the wall up at the other end."

"Well Tom, they usually would nest at the very top of a tree, usually a pine or old Mr. Rutland, he likes an oak - that one over yonder, see? It's like at Clarendon Marsh, where we put rafts on the gravel pits for terns, or that thing we built for sand martins. Same principle; giving nature a helping hand. Let's get the 'scope on the chick shall we. I'll get some photos with me telescopic as well. Eh look! Here comes the male with a fish!"

"Ah brilliant!" grinned Bullock. "It's a nice trout that is! Look at him rip it up for the littl'un!"

"Oh look, a pleasure boat! What's it called, the *Rutland Belle*?" De'Ath squinted down his bins at a steamer-style craft, evidently packed with birders, all with their optics trained on the pole-nest, which they were fast approaching. "It looks a bit like the *Glad Tidings* at Seahouses."

"Yeah, a bit overpriced if you ask me. Twenty-two quid for an hour and a half. And some of the guides don't know what they are on about. Like old Malc over there, for instance." Colin thumbed at Malcolm, dismissively, who was being verbally abused by the invalid lady.

"Call these disabled facilities!" she was shouting. "Where is the disabled toilet, man? Where are the wheelchairs? Not even guide-rails! Disgusting. Absolutely dis-gusting. What is it that you have against disabled people here? Just wait 'til the council hears about you and your discrimination. Now help me onto that seat or I will disable you - with me stick!"

"Look, what's that coming in over yonder?" Bullock detected a speck in the sky, getting bigger as it approached, buffeted around by the wind.

"Use the jizz, Colin!" demanded De'Ath. "Is it another osprey? Is it Mr. Rutland?!"

THE HIDE

"Oh, shut up about Mr. Rutland, Tommy, you are a man obsessed! Even I can tell yer, that ain't no osprey!"

"It certainly isn't, Ron," agreed Colin. "That's a bloody huge bird - it can't be an eagle, can it? Maybe it's escaped from the birds of prey exhibition at the fair?! Perhaps it's the black eagle coming for its master!"

Bullock beamed. "It could be, Col! I think we formed a bond!"

The growing UFO was now absorbing the attention of all the observers in the hide. The disabled lady was of the opinion that it could be a Californian condor, as that was the only bird she knew with a three metre wingspan and she had seen one once in Arizona.

"Daft old coot. Condor! Some muvvers do 'ave 'em." muttered Colin scornfully. "Anyway that ain't a bird, lady, it's a bloke. It's old Nigel the Moth and his paramotor! And he doesn't look very stable to me."

Up at 400 feet, Nigel had been having a torrid time in the buffeting winds. After take-off at the fair, he initially had been blown some distance off course, and on attempting to make his way back against the headwind, the fan motor had packed in some time ago - and so had his radio transmitter and helmet-cam. He was trying to control the parachute so he could make a landing somewhere near the Birdfair. In the panaroma below, he could see the whole of Rutland Water and the tiny marquees and car parks of the fair.

"Come on, Nigel!" he muttered to himself. "You are in a tight spot here, mate. This bloody wind - should never have come up! I told them - but oh no, don't listen to me, do they. Too busy showing off and shaking tins. Crikey, I am losing height fast here. Don't want to land on the water. I can just about clear it, I reckon. Gaah, no, that wind is taking me down! Oh no, one of me rigs is snagged up now. Fecking Hell, I'm losing control!"

Down below, in the Waderscrape Hide, all optics were trained on the stricken para-glider.

THE HIDE

"Blimey, he is in trouble, you know," frowned Colin. "He is going to come down in the reservoir. I think his motor fan thing isn't working and his parachute is all crooked."

Nigel strained frantically on the 'chute cords to maintain height, but the wind was driving him down. The water, looking grey and choppy, was hurtling towards him, and without being able to eject the fan motor contraption strapped to his back, he thought he might sink straight down to the thirty-four metre bottom of Europe's largest man-made lake. Perhaps, like Donald Campbell at Coniston Water, his body might take years to discover. In his peripheral vision, he spied a boat, the *Rutland Belle,* circling around two tall poles in Manton Bay. He figured if he could just land somewhere near it, they may have enough time to get a rope to him before he sank. He gritted his teeth and held his course towards the boat, attempting to slow his speed as best he could with the crippled parachute.

"Here he comes!" Everyone was on their feet in the hide, some screeching like barn owls, others turning their faces away or biting their nails, fearing a horrible and possibly fatal crash landing.

"Jesus, Nigel, slow down, lad! This is gonna be nasty!" winced Bullock.

"He has slowed it down a bit…atta boy, Nigel. Keep it smooth, boy. We can swim out from here and get you if you can stay afloat!" Colin peeled off his Barbour, in readiness for a rescue.

Nigel's heels skimmed the water, sending a flume of water in his trail like a bouncing water-skier as he managed to slow down against the wind, but he no longer had any control over his direction. He realized that he was heading straight for one of the telegraph poles – he thought perhaps he could grab one and wrap himself round it for a bit.

"Here goes nuthin'!!" he shouted out to himself, which even in that instant he thought might be odd last words.

THE HIDE

"Here Goes Nuthin!"

"He is heading straight for the pole with the nest on it!" exclaimed De'Ath. "He is....he is...on it!!! Oooof, that must have hurt...but he is hanging on the pole!"

Some people in the hide decided to applaud, in the manner of a safe landing at an airport during a high wind. Perhaps inappropriately, Colin began to laugh heartily.

"Haha, look at him. He's like a monkey on a greasy pole, look! He is trying to clamber up! Hang on, T8's mum doesn't like the look of this – she is giving him the eye!"

"Ah yes, the greasy pole contest at the Egremont Crab Fair," grinned Bullock, pleased that Nigel appeared to have escaped serious harm, "good fun that is. Along with the Gurning World Championships, of course. Looks like old Nigel is doing a bit of gurning too, by the looks of him!"

THE HIDE

Grateful to be alive and not at the bottom of Rutland Water, Nigel, still strapped to the fan contraption and parachute, which had flopped into the water below him, wrapped both his arms and legs around the pole for all he was worth. He could feel himself slipping gradually down the smooth wood, but was able to shin upwards through sheer determination and will to survive. His efforts were not helped, however, by the close attention of the female osprey, who swooped her talons to rasp his helmet. He recalled the fate of renowned bird photographer, Eric Hosking, who lost an eye to a tawny owl.

"Blimey, out of the frying pan and into the fire - I'm being savaged by an osprey!" he exclaimed to himself. "Well, I'd rather take my chances with the birds than drown I reckon, so better up than down! Onwards and upwards, mun!"

He continued to shin up the pole, until his head reached the plate at the top of the pole, where chick T8 eyed him suspiciously.

"Erm, any room for a littl'un?" Nigel asked the chick, politely. T8 didn't seem to object, but his mother did, and continued to dive bomb the stricken pilot.

"Look, he's on the webcam!" announced the disabled lady, pointing excitedly to the television screen.

"Haha, so he is!!" laughed Colin, as Nigel's puce and perspiring face filled the TV screen. "Oh I must get a picture of this, just look at him!"

And so the observers of the drama at the Waderscrape Hide were able to view in close up television Nigel's heroic attempt to haul himself onto the nest.

"Oh dear, he is destroying T8's nest," sighed Malcolm. Chick T8 decided it had better be off, and took to its wings, its mother following it to the shoreline trees.

"Don't be so bloody silly, Malc, there is a man's life at stake here! The chick has finished with the nest anyway and we can always re-build that. I say bravo, Nigel. The Human Osprey is on his nest!"

THE HIDE

Colin began whistling *The Great Escape* through his pursed lips, quickly joined by Bullock and De'Ath.

Hauling himself into a seated position on what remained of the bashed-up nest, Nigel was able to unstrap and ditch his motor and parachute, which he watched disappearing beneath the grey water, reflecting that he would have certainly joined them.

Breathing a huge sigh of relief, and noting the camera above him, he gave the thumbs up to the people waving from the shoreline hide, receiving a thunderous round of applause not just from the hides, but also from the passengers of *The Rutland Belle*, which was rapidly coming to his rescue.

"I think that he should be prosecuted under the Wildlife and Countryside Act - intentionally destroying the nest of any wild bird whilst it is in use!" roared Colin, slapping Bullock on the back.

"He should be, he should be!" piped Malcolm, who seemed close to tears. "What the Hell is the man doing flying about near protected and endangered breeding birds. The fellow is a wildlife criminal!"

"He is saving the Bewick's swans, you p-p-p, oh no, I must not start swearing again!"

"Prat," added Tom helpfully. "There we go, he's aboard the boat now. What a drama!"

"I reckon I will be able to sell some of this video I took to the telly people!" grinned Colin. "Come on, let's get back to the fair before ITV turn up!"

That evening, back home at The Nook, Bullock and Bella tuned eagerly to the regional TV news, *Midlands Today*. Nick Owen was gravely introducing the story from Rutland Water.

THE HIDE

"And finally...a birdman had a close shave today as he made an emergency landing at Rutland Water, disturbing the local ospreys. Bob Hockenhull reports..."

"He-heeey!" shouted Bullock, gleefully, through a mouthful of mashed potatoes. "I 'ope this is recording, Bell! Yep, that's Colin's footage, that is! They wouldn't pay 'im owt for it though."

"This is the moment that paraglider Nigel Shiltberry managed to crash-land onto one of the poles at the top of which was an osprey's nest. He was able to scramble up the pole, despite being mobbed by an angry osprey parent, and perch alongside a nesting chick. He was rescued by the Rutland Belle, a pleasure craft on hand to take the Birdman of Rutland to the safety of the shores. The captain of the Rutland Belle is "Froggie" Morton."

The report cut to a close-up of a grizzled face consisting almost entirely of beard.

"I was just turnin' like, and one of the passengers shouts – "he's up on the nest!" So I heaved 'er starboard and I am glad to say we managed to get him aboard. I have never seen nothing like it in forty years at Rutland Water."

Then the reporter was on the shores of the reservoir, interviewing another man.

"Colin Dredge was observing the ospreys from one of the many hides at Rutland Water, and watched the drama unfold. Colin, what did you see?"

"It's Colin!" Bullock exclaimed, "that's Dirty Colin - look love! Me and Tom are in the background...look, there's me givin' it the thumbs up and dancin' around! I AM ON THE TELLY! YEEEAAY!!"

But Bullock's antics were not on screen for long. The camera zoomed into Colin's ruddy face and wry smile.

"Well, Bob, I was just in the Waterscrape Hide with my mates Ron and Tom, we'd been at the Birdfair you know, and out of the blue, well, out of the grey as it happens, comes this object, we thought it

THE HIDE

was a UFO or escaped eagle at first, and then we realized it was old Nigel, who we had seen take off at the fair, you know, supporting the Bewick's, to be fair. It was obvious he was in trouble like, he was coming down at a fair lick, and somehow he's grabbed onto one of the poles and shinned up. He is a lucky man I tell you. WIZZLER!"

"Wizzler indeed, Colin! I don't suppose he will be wanting a repeat performance anytime soon!"

"F-f-f-f-f-f-f-f-f-ff-ff-fffff...."

"Oh no!" groaned Bullock. "Colin's Tourette's must have come back during his interview. Live on *Midlands Today*. We couldn't hear what he was sayin' 'cos of the wind. What the heck's he gonna say?"

In fact, Colin said nothing more, as the report swiftly cut to a chaotic scene of a man being assisted into the back of an ambulance.

"Nigel! They are calling you the Birdman of Rutland!!" Bob the reporter was proffering a furry microphone in the direction of a highly ruffled and annoyed Nigel Shiltberry, who seemed to be having an argument with the posh carrot-haired girl in the swan sweatshirt.

"No comment! I told you, no bloody comment!" complained Nigel to the reporter, pushing his hand into the camera. "Interview her - she was the one who bloody sent me up there!" With that the door was closed and the ambulance sped off.

"Clarissa Foxman-Hunt of the Bewick Swan Adventure Project did agree to speak to us shortly afterwards."

This time the camera was in the scarlet face of the intrepid Clarissa.

"Wall, obviously it was a bit of a disahstah today, but we at the Bewick Swan Adventure Project will be doing our best to continue with the *Bewick Swan Adventure Project* as soon as possible. We are twying to wecovah the equwipment fwom Wutland as we speak, and then continue with the *Bewick Swan Adventure Project.* If anyone would like to donate to this important pwoject, *please give at...www* dot *Bewick Swan Adventure Project* dot *org."*

THE HIDE

"Well, as we can see, a few feathers have been ruffled here at Rutland today – and not just those of the ospreys! Back to the studio - Nick."

Back in the studio, Nick was wearing his serious face, and added *"and we understand that we can reassure our viewers that Birdman Nigel is making a very fast recovery and has been discharged from hospital, and also that none of the ospreys have been affected by the incident. They will be off on their winter migration to Africa soon, so let's join Shefali for the weather news to see if the wind is blowing the right way for them. Shefali…"*

"Hoooooo! Hoooooo!" Bullock was leaping around the living room like a Red Indian.

"Sit down you idiot! I want to listen to Shefali and see if it's a good washing day tomorrow. Trust you to get into a drama, Ron Bullock. Ooh, you've bought a book! Bill Oddie, I liked him when he was in *The Goodies*. He is on the *Springwatch* sometimes."

"Er, yeah, he…"

"How nice, he's signed it for you! What does it say? *Ron, sod off and mind your own business. Bill.* Well. That's a bit rude, in't it!"

"Aye, yes love, it was a bit rude," agreed Bullock, rubbing his chin, ruefully. "Chris Packman is the same. I tell yer, they are a rum lot, these TV birdwatchers."

"Well, I don't know, Ron. Trust you to get involved with mischief and mishap. I thought when you and Tom took this up, it would all be nice and civilised. Whatever next?"

"Well, its' reet good fun! My Year and Life List is growing look, love – over 100 bird species already! Colin says September and October is a really good time for seein' more, an' all - some leave and some arrive y'see, it's called the autumn migration. All sorts of birds can arrive, some blown off course from America or Siberia. Looks like me and Tom are gonna be pretty busy. Now then, where's me *Collin's* – I have some studyin' to do….oh, look outside - those bloody pigeons…scoffin' all the bird grub again. I tell you,

- 183 -

THE HIDE

Bell, I am gonna get an air rifle and plug that lot. Greedy buggers… and they crap all over the place."

"Fine by me, Ron. You shoot 'em and pluck 'em, love, an' I'll cook 'em."

- CHAPTER FIVE -

Take Aim!

Wherein Colonel Sykes is consulted on the use of firearms in respect of birdlife. Wood pigeons are targeted, with mixed results. There is a speed-birding tour of Lancashire and Cumbria where there is twitching and grouse shooting. A Knight of the Realm is harried by a television presenter bearing banners.

"Ron, what an absolute pleasure to see you again, do come in. And Basker too! The General will be so pleased to see you, boy! Come through into the drawing room, won't you?"

Colonel Sykes lived alone with his black Labrador, The General, in one of the more gentrified areas on the outskirts of Oldside. He had become friends with Bullock and De'Ath after they had met at a county cricket match several years earlier, a friendship cemented following a disastrous dinner party the year before, when The Laboratory was in full flow. Sykes had also looked after Basker during Bonfire Night celebrations; the bloodhound and Labrador were on good terms, having endured a torrid evening of mayhem the previous November.

"Drink?"

"Bit early for me, Colonel, but go on then, a whisky no ice - if you are having one."

"Now Ron, cheers. Do have a pew. Now what's all this about

shooting, then? The Glorious Twelfth got your juices flowing has it? What!"

"Well, I 'avent shot a gun since I were in the army like - well apart from at the fairground. Never a problem fo' me winnin' a goldfish. Thing is, me and Tom have taken up birdwatchin'..."

"I say - I thought you were supposed to watch them rather than shoot them, old son?"

"Well yes, but it's more in the way of a bit of conservation, as I see it. The garden is full of wood pigeons and I thought I might do a bit of culling, you know...Bella makes a good pigeon pie and it creates a bit more, what do they say - biodiversity or summat?"

"I am certain your good lady does make a good game pie, and certainly nothing wrong with a bit of gamekeeping. Good for the game AND good for the biodiversity as you put it. I am a long-standing member and former trustee of the British Association for Shooting and Conservation - BASC - do you know it, Ron?"

"Can't say as I do, Colonel."

"Well, founded as the Wildfowlers' Association of Great Britain and Ireland in 1908 by Stanley Duncan and Sir Ralph Payne-Gallwey. They found it necessary to defend the sport of wildfowling against the growing enthusiasm of extremists bent on total protection of wild birds; you see the RSPB, in those days the Plumage League - it started as a movement to ban the wearing of plumage feathers in hats, you know - well, it was gaining ground, shall we say. Not that I am anti-RSPB you understand, very important organisation, over a million members and all that, but I suppose the subject of shooting game and wildfowl is no less controversial in 2016 than it was a hundred years ago. Some of the conservation element talk a lot of guff about what goes on up on the moors, gamekeepers killing raptors and the like, but the fact is, Ron, without managed shooting there would be a lot LESS bird biodiversity. Just like your back garden - our countryside is managed and the fact is, and some of the badger-huggers don't want to face this - that involves culling and shooting. Anyway, most of what is shot is eaten. And it provides a lot of rural employment, I can tell

THE HIDE

you. I rather suspect that a lot of the antipathy we face is from these lefty vegetarian city types who have no clue whatsoever about the countryside. Drop more, old chap?"

"Aye, just a tad. I know what you mean, Colonel, I 'ave been reading about how these gamekeepers shoot or poison eagles and harriers and the like, 'cos they eat the gamebirds…"

"Utter tosh, Ron!" fumed the Colonel, becoming ruddy and animated. "We at BASC have had to counter-react to this stuff, and in fact we have just commissioned a film called 'No Moor Myths'- I am sure you can find it on your computer. The game shooting SUPPORTS the conservation – and the local economy. I mean, that Packman feller - he has no right to use his position of privilege on the BBC to attack us BASC people."

"Oh 'im!" spluttered Bullock. We met 'im at the Birdfair, we did! Oh deary me, what a day that was!"

Bullock recounted the story of the nuthatch running up Packman's trousers, which delighted The Colonel, and evidently The General as well. They both roared with laughter.

"Oh, I say, a nuthatch! How perfectly marvellous! Well, hopefully that has shut him up for a bit. Anyway Ron, you say you want to do a bit of gamekeeping of your own with these pigeons." Sykes sprang to his feet and unlocked a metal cabinet in the hall, next to a chiming grandfather clock. "Here's what you need for the woodies, Ron. Webley Stingray Quantum .22."

Sykes unzipped a gun bag and handed Bullock a sleek-looking air rifle and a box of pellets.

"Come along, have a go in the garden. It's a bit early in the evening but there may be a rabbit or two in the field over the back of the fence. Come on, General and Basker, you might do a bit of picking up."

"Well, don't mind if I do, Colonel. Nice rifle, sir."

Having strolled through Sykes' immaculate lawns and shrubbery, the

THE HIDE

shooting party took up positions at a five-bar gate at the end of the garden, which backed onto a grassy field. Skyes pinned a paper target on the gate and retreated thirty paces to a stone urn mounted on a plinth, on which he leaned his elbows and squinted through the telescopic sights of the rifle. Having made some adjustments, he broke, loaded, took aim and fired at the target.

"Bit off to the left." Sykes adjusted the sights again, and this time, having reloaded, hit the bullseye.

"Should be OK now. You may have to adjust it for your eyes a bit, Ron."

Bullock took the re-loaded rifle and after adjusting the focus slightly, leaned over, squinted hard and pulled the trigger.

"I say, dead centre! Go again…"

"Crackshot shooting Ron! You ought to have been a sniper. Now then, let's see if the General can still pick up, shall we. Just a moment, I have a decoy pigeon in me shed, I'll go and place it in the field, see if we can attract a few woodies, there are usually plenty about."

Basker eyed up The General, a dog he much admired. In anticipation of some shooting, the Labrador became keen eyed and assumed a sitting pose ready for a run. Basker copied his pose exactly.

Sykes returned with a highly life-like plastic model of a wood pigeon, and paced down the field, placing it on an area of short grass, where he cast some seeds from a box. Returning, he closed the gate, and suggested they return inside for another drink, whilst they waited for pigeons to inspect their fake mate.

"Is that it?" gestured Basker forlornly to the Labrador, as they trundled back up the garden after their masters.

"Oh, no. The fun will start later. Patience, old son!" winked the Labrador.

After further refreshments, Sykes suggested they return, but this time

THE HIDE

in camouflage gear, which he went to fetch from his washroom.

"Good Lord, Colonel - what the heck is that you've brought?"

"Oh swear by these, I do. Four part Ghillie Suit. Never see us in these, the blighters. Come along, buck up and suit up, man."

Basker was much amused by the two men, who now looked like walking clumps of lichen.

"Always suit up in me Gillie on Hallowe'en. Sees the trick-or-treaters orf like lightning."

"I look like the abominable yeti, me!" laughed Ron.

"Now, I suggest we crawl and then slither to the gate, Ron. Complete silence everyone. Forward!"

Bullock, fully entering into the commando spirit, silently crawled after Sykes and his creeping Labrador. Basker did his slither slalom along the grass, and the four reached the gate, where to Bullock's astonishment, a flock of woodpigeon had gathered, strutting about and packing the seed. Slowly raising themselves to standing positions, Sykes passed the rifle to Bullock, whispering his instructions.

"Don't shoot unless you're sure, Ron. No wounding - bad form. Head or neck please - the frontal shot is a no-no as their crops can be absolutely stuffed like a flak jacket. Texas arse shot is also inclined to persuade them to head south and not book a landing, but I don't recommend on this occasion."

Wondering what on Earth the Texas arse shot was, Bullock took the rifle, braced the butt into his camouflaged shoulder, adjusted the site focus, and picked out an especially portly pigeon, watching its head bob and rotate. Focussing intently on the white patch on its neck, he squeezed the trigger…PHUT!"

"Hard cheese, but better a miss than a wing. Haven't disturbed 'em. Let me have a shot."

THE HIDE

Bullock, feeling a sudden sense of extreme disappointment and failure, handed the rifle over. Silently breaking the rifle to re-load, Skyes leaned forward on the gate and picked out his target. The flock exploded with a wing-clapping chorus into the air, leaving the decoy with an equally lifeless friend.

"Stay still, Ron. They will soon be back. Over to you."

This time, Bullock was determined to make a kill. He was soon back in action, as the flock returned. Picking out his bird, he looked at its curious eye down the telescopic sight, - it seemed to peer back at him in recrimination as he pulled the trigger.

"Oh bugger, he's winged!" announced Skyes, observing Bullock's quarry flapping and blundering as it attempted to join its airborne crew. "General! FETCH!"

Like a black arrow, The General romped through the gate that Skyes had opened and galloped towards the injured bird. Basker followed in lolloping and gamely pursuit. The Labrador hit the injured bird hard on the run and put it instantly out of its misery.

"Pick the other one up, there's a good chap, Basker?" winked The General nonchalantly.

Basker was delighted to pick up the bird shot by Sykes, and they returned in pride and glory to their masters, their soft mouths around the limp birds.

"Good boys!" congratulated Sykes. "General - drop!"

The Labrador skirted his master's heels, expertly deposited the bird at his feet and sat down panting.

"Now, Basker - drop!" Basker had a strange taste in his mouth - the taste of warm blood. A trace of evil disobedience flashed in his eye.

"Basker - drop it!" encouraged Bullock. Basker eyed his master with a hint of disdain.

- 190 -

THE HIDE

"Why should I? he thought. "Why should I? I went and got it. It's mine, isn't it?"

"DROP IT, BASKER!" ordered Bullock. Basker's instincts were mixed. On one hand, he would gain a lot of kudos by copying the trained gun dog, who was now watching him with concern.

"Come on, old thing, play the game?" The General suggested with a movement of his eyebrows.

"But on the other hand…" thought Basker's bad side - which suddenly won the day. The bloodhound simply ran off into the shrubbery with his catch, and when well into the undergrowth, savagely tore the pigeon apart.

"Bad form," sighed The General. Bullock ran after his miscreant dog, swearing profusely.

"Come out, you silly bugger!" shouted Bullock, on all fours on the grass, peering into the branches, where Basker's face, covered in blood and white feathers peered out with an expression of guilt tinged with primal fulfilment.

"Oh never mind," smiled Sykes. "Basker can't be expected to pick up like a gun dog. The General has had years of training. Anyway Ron, let's take a few of those pigeons out with the old shotgun, shall we? You wait here with the rifle, and if you see a rabbit or the pigeons come back, feel free to have a pot. The General will pick up for you, if you give him the command.

Sykes soon returned with a H. Beesley side-by-side shotgun and a bag of cartridges. "Any luck?"

"No nowt, Colonel. Perhaps they got scared off by my crap shot on that last bird."

"Nonsense, Ron, don't be hard on yourself. You are a good shot, man. Has Basker come out of the bushes, yet? Ah, here he comes - you bad lad, just look at you!"

THE HIDE

Basker came out wagging his tail and looking rather pleased with himself.

"Oh Jesus, look at the state of you!" sighed Bullock. "We'll 'ave to clean you up before you go 'ome! Sit down 'ere, you clown!"

"Ah look, here come the woodies again, right on cue. We can take them in flight with the shotgun. Ever used one, Bullock?"

"Can't say as I 'ave, Colonel. But I wouldn't mind a go!"

"Right, well watch me, the trick is to aim just in front of them, here comes one now…"

Sykes put on a pair of ear protectors and raised the gun to his shoulder, following the flight of a landing pigeon with the barrel as it came overhead.

"BLAM!...BLAM!" The pigeon dropped like a stone in a plume of white feathers. Basker's fear of fireworks and associated loud noises returned, and he stared at the smoking gun and then quaking, made a dash for the bushes again.

"Great shot, sir!'" applauded Bullock. "Eh, let's 'ave a go!"

"Nice and smooth, Ron, don't snatch the shot," coached Sykes, reloading and handing the weapon to his novice. "Here's a couple arriving from the west…train the barrel, that's it…"

Bullock grinned broadly as he followed on of the birds…"BLAM!...BLAM!" He felt the recoil judder back his shoulder, but watched in delight as the bird fell stone dead.

"Excellent shooting, Ron! General - fetch twice!" The Labrador bounded off and retrieved first one and then the other bird.

"Right, let's skin these three and you can take the breasts to your good lady wife for her pie. I think we'll leave the one Basker savaged for the foxes, shall we."

THE HIDE

Taking a skinning knife from the gun case, Sykes expertly butchered the birds and threw the carcasses into the field. The two men strode through the gate to retrieve the decoy.

"Now of course, I don't suggest that you use the shotgun in your garden, Ron, but the air rifle will do nicely, just make sure that the pellets stay on your property."

"What, I can borrow it? Don't you mind, sir? Don't I need a license or summat?"

"No. They are always on about licensing air rifles but I don't suppose it will ever come to much. You are most welcome to borrow it, and if you get the bug, I will take you over to Gunny's to buy one of your own. And if you fancy a bit of upland shooting, I belong to a shoot up north. Pheasant, partridge, grouse, woodcock, that sort of thing. I'm sure I could invite you as a guest, if you would like? Best leave old Basker out of it though, I reckon!"

Basker sidled nervously out of the shrubbery, hoping that the loud bangs had desisted.

"That would be grand, Colonel! In fact, we are supposed to be going up to the north-west with Colin for a spot of bird watching in a couple of weeks, so perhaps it could fit in?"

"I don't see why not - end of September is a pleasant time. I will give my chaps a ring, and see what's what. Meantime, happy culling and do give my best regards to Mrs Bullock. Come along, General, it's time for *The Archers!*"

A couple of days later at the Nook, Bullock decided to wait until Bella had gone shopping to slip the air rifle out of its case and to set a trap for the wood pigeons in his back garden. Loading his largest bird table with bread, seeds and nuts, and placing the decoy lent to him by Sykes in the middle of it, he retreated to the shed, where he had built a

THE HIDE

makeshift hide. Basker watched plaintively from behind the French windows, as he had been incarcerated in the lounge. It did not take long for the fat and cooing victims to arrive.

His sights centred on the first one's neck and squeezed the trigger. "PHUT!" From ten yards, the hit was easy and the bird dropped dead to the lawn. Its partner fluttered off in alarm.

"YES!!" Bullock's heart beat with the adrenaline of the hunter, as he emerged to inspect his kill, and to pop it in a plastic bag. "Crackshot, I am!" He pumped his fist, gave the thumbs up to the watching bloodhound, and retreated back to the shed where he sat and lit up his pipe.

Undeterred by the sudden demise of its mate, the second pigeon soon came back and began gorging on the seeds. Bullock rose slowly again to his firing position, and took aim, this time attempting a 'headshot'. "PHUT!...PING!" The discharge of the airgun was followed a metallic ring…a last second duck of the head had saved the pigeon, and the pellet had struck something hard in the base of the bird table. Bullock had calculated that a miss would result in the high velocity pellet being embedded in the wooden table, or in the fence ten yards behind it.

"AYYYYYAH!" came a cry of pain from the ginnel adjacent to The Nook, beyond the privet hedge. Bullock rushed out to the bird table, noting that the pellet had struck the head of a clout nail at the base, and evidently ricocheted somewhere. His first instinct was to hide the gun in the shed and lock it. Within seconds he was smoking his pipe and feigning ease at the patio table.

At the instant of Bullock's second shot, Bella was trudging back from the local shops with two bulging carrier bags in each hand. It was not rare for her to bump into Maurice with his gasping border terrier, Sherry, as he often walked his dog through the ginnel leading to the road on which he lived. She always tried to avoid him - Maurice was known locally as 'The Black Cloud' as he usually carried with him tales of doom and/or disaster, usually involving some form of ghastly illness or injury to himself, his dog, or a member of his family.

On this occasion though, she couldn't help but stop, as he was sitting

THE HIDE

forlornly on the kerb, inspecting his lower leg with his trousers rolled up to the knee.

"Oroight, Bell! Oi reckon oi just been shot! Just look at me blimmin' leg!"

"Are you sure, Maurice?" Bella put down her bags of shopping and leaned over in concern.

"Yeah! I 'eard it an all' - bloody air rifle! It'll be one o' the local kids, that's what they do. Do you remember when they got me, the Wellard Possee, with that spud gun in that droive-by shootin' what they do? Look around yer, Bell…they moight be training the gun on you next!"

Bella inspected an angry red dot on Maurice's shin, her thoughts now racing to the borrowed air gun that her husband had brought back from Sykes, announcing his intention to add to the pigeon meat he had put in the freezer, whilst simultaneously "improving the garden ecology".

"Erm, kids, you say, Maurice?"

"Probly up in that block o' flats opposite. Well, it weren't a direct 'it, thank God. It's a ricochet job - it ain't pierced me skin, or gorn through me trouser, but it don't half sting."

"What's goin' off 'ere, Maurice?" An ancient gaunt gentleman clad in a long shapeless cardigan, tiny white shorts and gumboots clumped up The Nook to see what the commotion was about.

"Oroight, Mr. Sellars. Oi bin shot wi' an air rifle."

Sellars stooped grimly to inspect the wound. "Shure you ain't bin stung boi a bee, boy? Looks more loike a bee sting ter me. Oroight Bella. Tell Ron me layke will be finished soon an' e' can come an 'ave a fish. 'Alf price to Ron."

Mr. Sellars indicated with his thumb a muddy pond where his front garden used to be. "Stockin' it this winter. Ca-arp, ba-arbel, tench, the lot."

THE HIDE

"Ah OK love, yes I will do. Maurice, let me get some TCP and a bandage for you. I don't think you need go to the hospital."

"No, oi think we'll be oroight, Bell. They see me dayn there often enough as it is! Oi'm just worried abayt 'em 'avin another shot at me. Let's goo dayn yer layke, Mr. Sellars, they don't 'ave vantage over your place. Ah, blinkin' 'eck, Sherry!"

Maurice's inverted U-shaped mouth transformed to an O-shape, as he rose stiffly to his feet. "Oi can't even get shot in peace and turn me back on you can oi? Sorry 'bout this, Bella..."

Diverted by Maurice's injury, the crafty border terrier had noticed Bella's untended shopping bags, and had rootled around in the contents to find chicken thighs in a polystyrene tray wrapped in Clingfilm. By the time his mischief was discovered, he was more or less done with eating the raw chicken, packaging and all.

"Oh, it doesn't matter, Maurice," reassured Bella, with other things on her mind. "I'll be straight back with that bandage."

Hastening into the house, she found her husband smoking insouciantly on the patio, though wearing a furtive frown.

"Ron, Maurice has been shot with an airgun pellet," she hissed urgently, peering into the cul-de-sac beyond the hedge, where Sellars was helping Maurice to limp away, and leading Sherry with the polystyrene tray hanging out of his mouth.

"Oh Christ!"

"Was it you?"

"Er, yeah, it must've been. Trust The Black Cloud to be walking by - it could only 'appen to 'im! The pellet must've bounced off the bird table and gone through the 'edge. Freak accident."

"Freak accident it may be, but you've shot 'im Ron! Fortunately, he thinks it was some kids firing at 'im from the block of flats."

THE HIDE

"Really! Good old Wellard Possee givin' me the alibi!" grinned a relieved Bullock. "Phew! 'Es not very bad is 'e, love? It can't 'ave gone very fast after it come off that table, surely?"

"No, it's just a graze really. I am taking him some TCP and a bandage. You better go and see him and apologise, Ron."

"Apologise? For what?" he winked at his wife. "I am in the clear, and you must be my accomplice!"

"Bah, shame on you, Ron Bullock. Well, you can get that gun back to Colonel Sykes or I'll grass you up. Now get goin', you menace to the public!"

"Mornin, Maurice, what's all this, then?" Bullock found Maurice sitting with his usual inverted U-shaped mouth expression sitting on a bench outside of Sellars' house, in front of the muddy pond. A hand-painted sign jutting out of the water read *'Sellars' Fisheries'*.

"Mornin' Ron. They gone too far this time, the Tredley Massive. Shot me in the leg with a blimmin' air gun. Mr. Sellars is mekin me a noice cuppa to soothe me nerves."

"The little buggers. Don't you worry, Maurice, I'll pop round this afternoon and 'ave a word - I know where they live. That'll be more effective than gettin' the law on the case."

"You sure, Ron? Oi mean, they moight think they can get away with it, next thing you know they've got Uzis and grenade launchers. It's them video games, that's what it is. And crack cocaine in them vape pipes. Oi reckon oi should let the police know what they are blimmin' up to. They wus probly aimin' at poor Sherry 'ere and got me on the ricochet. Sherry? Oh bloody 'ell, Ron, 'e's gone and slipped the leash again! 'E's 'avin a swim in Mr. Sellars' pond! SHERRY! GIT AYT!"

Sellars shuffled out of his house still in his gum boots and handed

- 197 -

THE HIDE

Maurice a chipped mug celebrating Queen Elizabeth's Silver Jubilee of 1977.

"Jesus, there's a water rat in me layke! 'As the world gorn mad?!"

"That aint no water rat, it's Sherry! 'E loikes a swim do old Sherry. PAAAH! This tea is stone cold, Mr. Sellars!

Sellars inspected the tea he had made with a frown and stuck his grimy index finger in it.

"Oh. Mustn't 'ave boiled the kettle. Still, drink it dayn, it'll do you good, Maurice. Mornin' Ron. Oi was sayin' ter Bella, me layke will be finished soon an' yer can come an 'ave a fish - 'alf price to you, son. Stockin' it this winter. Ca-arp, ba-arbel, tench, the lot. Oi, Maurice, don't pour yer tea in me layke! That's water pollution, that is. And get that ruddy dog ayt!"

"Well oi aint drikin' no cold tea, am oi? Sherry! Git ayt 'ere!"

With difficulty, Sherry clambered up the greasy mud which formed the banks of Sellars' Fishery, and shook himself, vigorously spraying his master with silty water.

"Oh luvly, Sherry. Nay oi'm wet through as well as crippled in me leg. Ah…'ere comes me Florence Noitingale, God bless, you Bella."

Sellars slumped onto the bench next to Bullock and Maurice, wrapping his cardigan about him and watched Bella swabbing Maurice's wound with TCP.

"Owww, that stings, duck!"

"Don't fuss, Maurice, it'll clean it up. Stop wriggling about!"

"I was just saying to Maurice, Bell, I'll pop round this afternoon and 'ave a word with them little villains with the air gun - I know who it'll be. That'll be more effective than gettin' the law on the case, wouldn't you reckon?"

THE HIDE

"Er, yes, I would, Ron," responded Bella reluctantly - she hated lying or lies of any kind.

"Good then, that's settled then, Maurice, leave it with old Rhino Ron. I'll put the fear of God in 'em!"

"Well…oroight…if you both reckon it's the best course. But me n' Sherry will 'ave to give the ginnel a miss for a bit oi'm afraid. Loightin' do strike twice in the sayme place - oi should know, it 'appened ter me!"

"Oh, that'll be a shame not to see you both in The Nook, Maurice," responded Bella as she fastened a bandage to Maurice's leg, getting into the swing of bare-faced lying.

"What do you mean, you got struck by lightning twice, Maurice?" Bullock was genuinely interested and wanted to move the conversation away from Maurice's unfortunate shooting.

"Oh, few years back nay, oi was ayt wi' old Sherry 'ere, up on the Common, y'know, and the auld skoi sta-arts da-arkenin' - before yer know it, we are caught in this torrential rain and thunder storm. Well, we set off fer 'ome sha-arpish, and this bloody bolt o' loightenin' comes flashin dayn ayt o' the skoi knocks me flat on me back! Oi wakes up, old Sherry lickin' me fayce, weren't yer boy. Oi gets up - got no further than ten ya-ards, and it blimmin' 'appened again! Splayed ayt on me front this toime, eyebrows singed off. Oi gets, up, and we run 'ome loike Usain bloody Bolt – no pun intended, loike."

Had anyone else but Maurice told this tale, it would have been dismissed out of hand, but Bullock and his wife knew enough about the misadventures and mishaps of Maurice and his family to credit its truthfulness.

"Oi got struck boi loightenin' wunce," announced Sellars. "Playin' golf. Everyone else on the course 'ad gone wisely 'ome, but oi stayed ayt. Got me puuter ayt, sixteenth green…BOOOM. Put me on me arse and me 'air stood on end. One o' me noine lives that was. What's yer dog doin' now, Maurice?"

THE HIDE

"Eh, you know what you should've done, Mr. Sellars," Bullock was now feeling relieved enough to be off the hook to crack a joke. "You should have stood there, got a one-iron out of your bag, and held it aloft to the storm. 'Cos even God can't hit a one-iron! Haha!"

"Aaaaaaaaaaaaah, that's a good 'un, Ron, wun iron, loike it, boy! Aaahaaaahaaa!" Sellars choked on his rasping laugh and started coughing. "Maurice! Aaah, khoff khakhak! What is that dog... haakkaa...doin', boy?"

To everyone's dismay, Sherry was retching wads of polystyrene and chicken bones into Sellars' pond. There seemed to be much more being emitted than Sherry could have possibly consumed from Bella's shopping bag.

"More bloody watter pollution! It's just as well me stock ain't in, Maurice, cos oi'd 'ave to inform the National Rivers people abayt this. You'll 'ave ter keep yer 'ound away when oi'm up and runnin'!"

"Fair comment, Mr. Sellars. Oi'll do me best. "E is a bit of puker, old Sherry, to be fair."

Maurice's mouth resumed its inverted 'U'- shape as he grimly observed his retching mutt heave the final contents of its stomach in a yellow spume into Sellars' pond.

Bella and Bullock decided to leave the grisly scene, Bullock with a stern and theatrical promise to "sort those bloody kids out!" Bella took his arm and led him briskly away up The Nook; preparing to give her miscreant husband a severe admonishment for his gun crime.

"Good morning, Bella, is it? Not wearing your Queen's Commendation for Brave Conduct Medal this morning?"

Bella opened the porch door to a ruddy portly man bearing a smirk and

THE HIDE

all the *accoutrements* of a seasoned birdwatcher.

"Eh?"

"You know, for being married to Ronny?"

"Oh, you are Dirty Colin are you…or Cheeky Colin, perhaps? Come in, love…yes, I've seen you on telly, haven't I! Oh, is that Tom in yer jeep…COME IN TOM! RON AIN'T READY YET!"

De'Ath scuttled out of Colin's Land Rover and joined them in the hall.

"Morning Bella, morning Basky!" Basker came to see the visitors, ignoring De'Ath's greeting and sizing up the newcomer.

"Hmm, bit cocksure of himself. Think I can smell a rodent on him."

"Do you mind dogs, Colin? If you do, yer in the wrong place!" cackled Bella. "Say hello, Basker!"

"I'm more of a reptile kinda guy," advised Colin, giving Basker a perfunctory pat on the head as he was ushered into the kitchen, where Bella put the kettle on. "I keep pet snakes - I got a Ball Python and a California King at the moment. And - I recently obtained a special license to keep highly venomous snakes. I am looking after a green mamba at the moment that was found on a ship full of bananas in Aberdeen. Still waiting for the anit-venom to arrive from London Zoo – it's quite hard to get hold of apparently."

"Oh aye, married are yer?" asked Bella bluntly, lighting up an Embassy. "Smoke?"

"No and no, thanks anyway. Was married, did a bit too much twitchin' for her tastes, anyway, her loss, as they say. Just me and the snakes now! Yeah, one sugar, ta."

"What do you feed them on then? Do they live in a tank or summat?"

"Ta muchly, oh, no biscuits for me thanks - fat enough already. Crickets, mice, occasional rat…yeah they live in a vivarium in me lounge, I get 'em out sometimes, have a cuddle, like!"

"What do you do with them when you go away - like today, Colin? Does somebody have to feed them?" enquired Tom, sitting in his usual place at the kitchen table. "Thanks Bella, lovely cuppa, that."

"That's one o' the advantages o' snakes, Tom. I can leave 'em for weeks. Just drop a mouse or two in…they don't need food for ages."

Basker thought about snakes. He had encountered a grass snake or two on his meanderings on the common – one had exuded a foul smelling liquid onto his paw, and he avoided them after that. He decided that Colin wasn't of much interest to him and he lolloped away into the hall. He was sad to see his master's rucksack packed up for a journey, and gave Bullock his sad look as his master bounded down the stairs.

"Sorry Basky, cant tek you on this mission, you won't like it where I'm off to!" he footled the bloodhounds ears affectionately. "But let's see if I can bring you summat tasty back, shall we? Sorry lads, couldn't find me thick socks anywhere. Mornin' Col, you've met me beloved, I see. Aye, thanks love, a quick coffee would be just the job. Are you and Dot all sorted for Friday?"

"Yes, I got the tickets in the post just now - look!"

"*The "Make Mine a Murder Theatre Company" present – Murder on the Orient Express*," read Bullock from a sheet of paper clipped with two gilt-edged tickets. "An exciting evening of murder mystery at The Boughton Hand Hotel." Eh, that sounds great - I would've fancied that! And look, they are doing another one in three months – the 007 Club Mystery! Eh Tom, du-du- duder- dududu…diddlydah, der-der-der - the name's Bullock, James Bullock. Yeah, look good in a tux, I do."

"James Pillock, more like!" reposted Colin. There was a frosty moment of silence - Bella shot Colin a look of stern admonishment. De'Ath looked out of the window in embarrassment with a watery smile.

THE HIDE

"I know you suffer from Tourette's love, Ron told me, but we don't have bad words in this house. And I might say that the last man that called my husband a "pillock" end up getting chucked through a pub window." She took an insouciant drag on her Embassy and blew the smoke out of the opened window.

"Sorry, Bella," replied a reddening Colin, "just a bit o' banter – no offence meant. Besides, is pillock a bad word? I 'ope not 'cos these lads cured me of me Tourette's, well so far any'ow…"

"On this occasion, Col, I won't throw you through the winder," Bullock winked at Bella, remembering just how much he appreciated his wife's tenacious protection.

"Any'ow, we best get movin'. It's all worked out well, so I will see you soon, Bella - two days wi' these lads and then meeting Colonel Sykes on Sat'dy for the shoot. He will bring me back - Tom, are you SURE you don't wanna join me on the grouse shooting?"

"No Ron, I don't think I would feel good about shooting birds, to be honest with you. But…I won't mind eating them when you bring back your brace of pheasant!"

"Brace? There'll be game to last the winter after old Crackshot Ronny gets goin'!"

"Don't you mean, Crapshot Ronny?" guffawed Colin, his lesson unlearned.

"Right, that's enough of you, Colin - off back to yer jeep before Ron *does* have to chuck yer through winder. Bye Tom, have a lovely trip, and 'ope yer see lots o' new birds. Here's yer bag, Ron, here I made you some butties for the journey – spam and piccalilli!"

"Oh thanks love, what would I do without yer. Call yer when I get up ter the Lakes. Eh, and no flirting wi' them actors on Friday! Come 'ere - big hug!"

"Get off yer silly bugger," laughed Bella, pushing her husband away and into the bench seat of the Land Rover alongside De'Ath.

THE HIDE

"Love of a good woman you got there, Ron, sorry for any offence. My ex-wife always told me I didn't know when to keep me trap shut. Well, you can't when you've got Tourette's."

"None taken, Col, Bella is a very fierce woman. You don't wanna cross her mind, cos she'll bite yer like yer green mamba, and there is no known antidote! Right foot down, Col - let's hit the north, boys!"

The first stop on their tour of the north-west was Brockholes - a Lancashire Wildlife Trust nature reserve near Preston, just off the M6.

"It's a bit new, lads, old quarry system a bit like Clarendon, but wait til you see the Visitor Centre. It definitely beats a bucket of Starbucks coffee and a Burger King Big Woppa at Charnock Richards Service Station!" Colin swung the Land Rover off at Junction 31 and they were soon parked up. "Gotta pay for parking, but hey-ho, it's worth three quid for an hour."

"Wow! It's a floating village!" De'Ath was more than impressed with the futuristic buildings nestled into a natural reserve.

"Eh, nice restaurant, it looks, an' all! Beef n' mushroom pie lads, that'll do me!" Having consulted the lunch menu, Bullock got up and looked about for the toilets. "Ah'm just off for a Jimmy Riddle. Ah wonder where the wee goes - I expect they compost it or summat, eh?"

Standing at the urinal, Bullock was surprised to hear a knocking sound behind him, coming from one of the locked toilet cubicles. A plaintiff voice with a strong Lancashire accent called out.

"Ellooo? Can sumbudy'elp me please? Ah can't get owt!"

Zipping up and washing his hands, Bullock peered under the locked door to see a pair of hob-nailed boots with polyester trousers furled around them, attached to a pair of elasticated braces.

"Ah think me bwaces are stuck!" called the voice again, evidently

THE HIDE

belonging to an older-generation Lancastrian. "They've got wurapped awround the torlet seat or summat -ah can't bloody budge! Every time ah try and get up they spring me back down again!"

"Can yer open the door, lad?"

"Aye, 'ang on a minute…there. Coom in. Ah've managed ter get me underpansies up."

Bullock peered around the door, to see a worn flat cap and a ruddy grizzled face bearing a bulbous purple nose beneath profuse white eyebrows and beady blue eyes.

"What's the trouble, olt feller? Oh, ah see, yer've got 'em caught on the flush 'andle. 'Ang on…there yer go, chap…"

"Oh thanks ever ser much. They get caught up some times, don't they, bwaces." The old fellow wriggled back into his trousers and snapped his braces over his bony shoulders. "Let me wash me 'ands. It's gereat 'ere, in't it?"

"Yeah, first time fo' me, lad, we are just on our way up ter the Lakes for some birdwatchin' and we thought we'd pop in for a bit o' dinner."

"Oh, bird watcher are yer? Me too - ah coom 'n volunteer Wednesdays. Coom on, ah'll show yer round. Cyril, bah t' way. Pleased ter meet yer."

"Come an' 'ave a bit o' pie wi' us, lad. Me wife's from Bolton – ah'm a Yorkie, me! Ron Bullock."

"Yorkie married to a Lanky lass - that'll niver last!" chortled Cyril.

"Aye, that's what 'er mother said, - fo'ty years ago!"

Cyril and Bullock met Colin and De'Ath in the restaurant and all four chomped on pies and mash, Cyril giving a potted history of the reserve.

"We're in t'floodplain o' the W-ribble, y'see lads. Ah used ter work on

THE HIDE

t'quarry before it were shut, so you could say - ah made this reserve! Pass the brown sauce, Ron - why do they put it in likkle packets like that - what's wrong wi' a bottle? An' as fo' them likkle jiggers o' milk - they mek me reet queasy they do."

"What have you seen here then, Cyril? I guess it's not long established, is it?" Colin trained his binoculars to the lake beyond the window where they sat.

"Well, y'd be surprised. We've got the otters, bittern, ospreys…"

"Ha, don't tell us about ospreys!" laughed Bullock, who recounted the tale of the Rutland para-motoring fiasco.

"Oh, ah saw that in t'paper!" laughed Cyril. "Ah couldn't believe it were true, that! Eh, anybody want an Eccles cake, ah'll buy yer one for extractin' me from t'lav!"

Despite protests, Cyril insisted on buying four Eccles cakes, which they took out and sat, legs dangling, from the jetty overlooking the pool. A gang of young schoolboys were romping around.

"Eh mister, can we fish 'ere? We've got nets!" A freckly-faced ginger lad, looking like the cover boy of *Mad Magazine*, hurtled towards them, panting with boyish enthusiasm.

"Aye, go on then, but don't wet me," advised Cyril.

"Do you know who that lad looks like," said Bullock chomping into his Eccles cake and watching the group of boys enthusiastically wafting their nets about in the water.

"Alfred E. Neuman. It was a face that didn't have a care in the world, except mischief!"" answered De'Ath immediately.

"Exactly, Tom! Eh, the Mad Comics, eh! Oh, great they were! It's never still going, is it?"

"I believe it is, Ron! One of the best things to come out of old USA, I reckon."

THE HIDE

"Eh, watch what yer doin', yer daft beggars!" protested Cyril, "yer wettin' me!"

"Sorry mister," responded 'Alfred'. "Eh, ah've caught some tiddlers! Come and see!"

"Oh, well done boy, they are sticklebacks, them. Three-spiners. And see, a minnow an' all. See what else yer can catch, lads. Perhaps ye'll catch a wopper!" Cyril winked at his new friends.

As they reminisced fondly about their own childhoods with 'tiddler nets', suddenly one of the lads in the group, the smallest one by a foot, starting shouting urgently - the cane handle of his net was arching over into a hoop.

"It's a biggun! Ah've caught a biggun!" he exclaimed, straining to heave up the little mesh net.

"Don't be daft, lad, you'll 'ave got it caught on the bottom, come 'ere...I'll 'elp yer," chuckled Cyril, carefully creeping to the edge of the jetty.

"NO! It is a biggun! 'Elp me!"

"Eh up – it IS a biggun!" exclaimed Cyril. "Have you ever seen such a thing – it's a perch! More than 'alf a pound, an' all!"

The kids and adults gathered around the landed fish, which laid out on the decking was much longer than the mesh net which caught it.

"Well done, James!" grinned 'Alfred' patting his diminutive school mate on the back.

"Eh, Tom - that reminds me of old Reakes trying to bring them fish back to life last year - what did he call 'em...ferch! Well done young man, that is by far the biggest fish I have ever seen landed in a fishing net. By gum, you'd need a big jam jar to put that 'un in!"

"Can you take our photo with me I-Phone, mister? James, you must

THE HIDE

hold the biggun!"

"Nine year olds wi' I-Phones, well, I don't know," muttered Bullock. "That must take a lot o' pocket money!"

"Now mind its sharp spines," Cyril cautioned. "Hold it up like this look, that's it, lovely."

James held the fish up proudly, the other boys standing around him with fishing nets and 'thumbs up' gestures.

"Eeeh, that's a crackin' photo boys! Nethen, put 'im back in t' watter, nice and slowly, that's it…e's off. To fight another day!"

"Thanks, mister!" The lads tore off to show their teacher their photo, and Little James duly became the talk of the school.

"Eeeh, that were nice weren't it, lads. Nice to see that likkle lads are still likkle lads, even in this day n' age. They will talk about that fish for years. Mind you, so will I - I 'ave never seen such a fish caught in a tiddlers net!"

"Well, we better be off, boys," said Colin stretching. "They are a bit keen on their car park fines 'ere so we'd best not exceed our hour. Nice to meet you Cyril, and good luck to you with this place, it's the best motorway stop-off in the country!"

"Eh, if you lads come back - 'ere's me phone number look. Let's 'ave a better look round together next time. Where are yer off ter next?

"We are on a speed-birding mission, Cyril. Getting these fellers' Year List up a bit - Leighton Moss, Morecambe Bay, Meathop Fell and up Great Gable. All in two days."

"Well best o' luck wi' that, lads. I 'ope you brought yer rain gear, 'cos the forecast is terrible. But you know what we say up 'ere – no such thing as bad weather, just t' wrong clothing!"

As the trio clambered into the Land Rover and roared away back to the M6, Bullock reflected on how nice it was to see a gang of young lads

THE HIDE

in short trousers still able to engage in enthusiastic pursuit of tiddlers in the great outdoors.

"You 'ear a lot about 'ow rude and badly behaved kids are nowadays, so it were good to see young Alfred and 'is little mates behavin' 'emselves and bein' polite to old Cyril, there, weren't it boys?"

"It was indeed, Ron," agreed De'Ath. "Perhaps we should commend the school in question, on Trip Advisor, or something?"

"Yes, why not!" added Colin. "I like to see praise where it's due as well as criticism. Let's do it when we get back. We can easily ask the Visitor Centre what school it was and write a letter. Why not."

Sadly, back at Brockholes, a contrasting postscript to the eulogising tale of innocent youth was unfolding.

Just as two long-suffering teachers were attempting to round up their flock by the school coach, Alfred had noted that old Cyril had been left alone by his mates, and was bending over the wooden jetty and peering into the water, no doubt looking for more perch and sticklebacks.

"Eh," winked Alfred to his mates. "That old codger wouldn't take much pushing in! Let's rush 'im!"

Needing no further encouragement, the gang of young hooligans hurtled en masse towards the pensioner who, hands on knees, was oblivious to all, in his pantheistic reverie. This reverie was violently broken as the lads roared towards him, yelling "GET 'IM!! PUSH 'IM IN!!"

The little one who had caught the perch, James, was caught up in the mob, and as the others veered away, it was little James who, more or less involuntarily, barged into Cyril's backside. The impact was enough to send Cyril squawking into a pretty good swallow dive. He hit the water with an almighty splosh.

James looked on, shocked at what he done, but Alfred and the others were doubled up in hysterical laughter.

THE HIDE

"Haha, look at him!" gasped Alfred, "he's like a big frog!"

Cyril gasped and flapped as he got to his feet, up to his waist in the now muddy water. He took off his cap and poured a pint of water out of it, causing the lads even greater merriment.

"Yer writtle buggers!" he gargled, "yer've wet me! Ah'm reet weet through!"

As he staggered back to shore, covered in weed and mud, one of the boy's teachers came striding angrily toward the jetty.

"You boys! Get 'ere, NOW!"

"Oh no, it's Mr. Fartbreath, guys," hissed Alfred, "we better make a run for it. Come on, I know the way back to Preston, we don't need that stupid coach! Head for them woods yonder!" As they belted off, the ginger kid turned chuckling with a parting shot to old Cyril.

"Eh mister! Go and jump in the lake, you old frog!"

"JOCKY FLINTOFF! COME BACK HERE AT ONCE!!" bawled the teacher, as he helped Cyril to the shore, where he stood gasping on the wooden jetty, water pouring off him. "I am very sorry, sir, let me help you…"

"Flintoff, y'say?" grunted Cyril removing his sodden boots. "Is 'e…?"

"Yeah, fraid so. It's not the first time I'll be 'avin a word with 'is dad, either."

As the teacher, Mr. Fortbrough, grimly led the dripping pensioner for a change of clothing in the hiking shop at his own expense, he would little expect to find in the mail to Ribbleton Primary School during the following week, a letter from Messrs. Bullock, De'Ath and Dredge commending the refreshing and delightful behaviour of a group of youngsters and their tiddling nets, led by a freckly-faced ginger lad, who looked like the cover boy of *Mad Magazine*. The effusive and complimentary letter, evidently meant to be read out in morning assembly or pinned on the school noticeboard ended: *"Who says the*

THE HIDE

youth of Britain today isn't every bit as respectful and pleasant as yesteryear?"

"I do," would grumble Mr. Fortbrough, as he tossed the crumpled letter in the bin and fumbled about in his desk drawer for his blood pressure tablets.

As Cyril was getting his soaking, his gloomy weather forecast to the voyagers began to manifest itself as they reached the RSPB Reserve at Leighton Moss, where heavy rain began to fall.

"Right on with the wet gear lads, I hear there's a yellow-browed warbler about. Good tick that is. They reckon these days it ain't so much a vagrant - blown off course like, but a genuine migrant - pioneering populations looking for new places to over-winter. I mean, you'd get bored of South-East Asia after a while wouldn't you! Why not Blackpool! Anyway, we'll make for the Eric Morecambe Hide." Colin yanked the handbrake of the Land Rover and began to clamber into a black waterproof that made him look like the Michelin Man, only much darker.

"Eric Morecambe Hide? What, the one and only, Col?"

"Oh yes! Eric was very keen on birding, you know. His daughter opened up a hide in his memory just a few years ago. Come on Tom, look lively, mate!"

Bullock was very pleased with this news. He had been starting to think that he didn't really fit in with the birdwatchers he had thus far met, many of whom he would generally describe as 'odd-bods'. But if this hobby was good enough for Eric, it was definitely good enough for him!

Kitted out and wet through after ten paces, the trio marched steadfastly onto the reserve, and after a few minutes, passed a troupe of caped and saturated folk coming the other way.

THE HIDE

"Any sign of the 'yellow-browed', guys?" asked Colin.

"Aye, up yonder showing nicely - just up the path and in scrub on the right. You'll see the crowd."

"Ta muchly. Good weather for ducks, eh?"

Further up the path, Bullock and De'Ath were surprised to see a substantial huddle of people, all with telescopes and binoculars, riveted on a clump of hawthorn. Colin bustled in, setting his tripod up with great speed.

"Eh, watch out, Dredge!" complained a surly and shifty-looking fellow with an ear ring, leaning back on a shooting stick.

"Oh Christ, if it isn't the Son of Darkness himself. What the f…flip are you doing here, Robards?"

"Same as you by the looks of it. No big deal, the *Phylloscopus inornatus* but I hadn't seen one this year. What's yer year list then? Over the 300 yet?"

"No business of yours. Now f-f…flip out of me way before I kick yer stick out from under yer. Come in here, lads, don't mind this berk here. Eh listen, "soo-ee, soo-ee!" – old yellow-brow is a-warblin' to us!"

Bullock inspected the latest 'character' to be encountered on the birding circuit, who curled up his lip in a deeply unpleasant manner and despite the hurtling rain and lack of cover, managed to roll up a cigarette in one hand whilst observing the bushes through his binoculars with the other. 'Sonny' Robards was notorious on the twitcher circuit, the self-proclaimed 'King of the Twitchers'. Deeply unsociable, tremendously unhelpful and unfriendly, his only goal in life was ultra-competitive twitching, and to top the UK sightings list each year, a feat he had achieved twice and was intent on doing again.

"He-hay…there he is, yeller-brow!" smiled Colin. "Follow my finger - bit like a goldcrest, well, not that you've seen a goldcrest yet…"

THE HIDE

"I see him!" shrieked De'Ath excitedly. "A tiny little migrant from Siberia! He is green! And he HAS got a yellow brow!"

"Not seen a goldcrest! Blimey, leading novice tours now are you, Dredge? Bit of a come down for you, isn't it? Lost the urge, have we? Eh?"

Colin Dredge simply ignored Robards' unpleasant sneering, as he focussed his telescope on the delicate and graceful little migrant, but Bullock didn't. He simply kicked the shooting stick from under Robards, who fell backwards into the mud with a winded grunt.

"Oh, sorry mate!" he grinned. "Silly me, let me help you back up!"

Robards naively fell for Bullock's gambit - taking Bullock's paw as he heaved himself up, the Yorkshireman simply let go and the 'King of the Twitchers' landed back where he started, with another soggy jolt.

"Might be a novice with the birdies, son, but I ain't wi' me fists, if you fancy a bit more?"

"Yeah, piss off, Sonny!" laughed Colin. "You don't want to mix it with old Rhino Ron 'ere, I can tell you!"

Evidently too much of a sneak for confrontation, Robards glowered darkly as he retreated down the muddy path, pointing the sharp end of his shooting stick at Bullock.

"See you around, buddy boy. Anyway, I'm off to see a proper bird - over Yorkshire way. Siberian accentor. Mega rare migrant. 2nd for Britain. Great to grip you off, Colin!"

Colin winced visibly and gulped. "Siberian accentor? It can't be. In Yorkshire?" He fiddled anxiously with the Bird Alert app on his 'phone. "Christ, it is! Er, lads, erm, you don't fancy a quick diversion to east Yorkshire, do you?"

Bullock, already underwhelmed by his sighting of the little flitting greenish bird in the copse, certainly did not. "Why, what does it look

THE HIDE

like? Isn't that what the dunnock ought to be called, an accentor?"

"Yeah, bit like a dunnock, but nice yellow line above the eye - here's a photo look…"

"Looks just like the ones in our garden to me! Sorry lad, not up for a wild dunnock chase. You go at the weekend if you want, but we've a made a plan, let's stick to it. Nethen, let's get on - we've got bearded tits and great white egrets to tick off, 'ave we not?"

"Yeah, yeah, you are right, Ron," responded Colin as he packed up his kit, sounding a like a drug addict attempting to avoid free heroin. "Much nicer birds to see here. Nicer ones. Nicey-nicey. "

"Oh, and I believe the red deer are rutting here! I saw that on *Autumnwatch* last year! That would be worth seeing, wouldn't it, boys!"

"Don't be daft, Tom!" scorned Bullock. "You don't get a 'tick' for red deer rutting, do yer Col!"

"Haha, you certainly don't, Ron! Right, this way for the egrets, could be three ticks going there if we see the 'little' and the 'cattle' as well as the 'great white'."

The speed-birding continued at a frantic pace. In the Eric Morecambe Hide, as well as two of the egret species, the trio ticked their marsh harriers, water rails and wigeon; on the way back they saw their first goldcrests and tree creepers; and from the windows of the café over a warming pot of tea, they were all delighted to watch bearded tits feeding from grit trays.

"Really, they should be called 'the moustachioed tit' observed De'Ath. "They don't have beards at all!"

"Just cos you want to be the bearded tit!" Bullock chided the obvious.

"Well, once again, it's a misnomer," added Colin, "not only is it not bearded, it isn't, like Tom, a tit! In fact, it's more of a lark that adapted to reedbeds, so it should be called the 'moustachioed reedling'! Let's

THE HIDE

put that in the sightings book at Clarendon, shall we - see what old Aldous makes o' that! Right, if we've all dried out a bit, should be time to take in Morcambe Bay from the cliffs and do a bit o' sea watchin' before it goes dark. Fish n' chips at Kenny's and early night at Mrs Winterbottom's. She's a bit of an old battle-axe, but I've been staying in her guest house for years. She's the second most bad-tempered woman I have ever met, just behind Mrs. Llanfairpwllgwyngyll of Rhyl. Great fry-up at Mrs. Winterbottom's though, and she don't mind getting up at five to do it. Well, I say she doesn't mind, she moans like buggery about it, but she does it, at least. I wanna be back on the road by six tomorrow."

"Six!" groaned Bullock. That's a bit fanatical ain't it?"

"Oh, the early bird catches the worm at this game, y'know, Rhino Ron."

"I reckon I am more of your night owl kind of birder, Col. Ain't there any birds we can watch at night?"

"Well, yeah - we could go and have a watch of the nightjars next year, owls, o'course - the old bittern is a bit crepuscular, creeps about at night."

"Tommy is a bit – what did you say – crepuscular? Aren't you lad – 'specially on a full moon!"

"That's right, Ron, I am literally a lunatic, Colin. Full moon, I go a bit odd. I like a bit of a walk on the night of the full moon – mind you, that nearly did for me in The Alps. There's a nice book I was reading called *Nightwalk* by a fellow called Chris Yates. It's about a country walk he takes - but by night. I would like to do that, but I wouldn't do it on my own! Are you guys up for it?"

"We'd probly get arrested creeping about at night!" protested Bullock, getting ready to face the rain outside again. "But you know me, Tom – ah'm up for owt I am! Right, forwards, men! To the seaside! It's a reet shame we ain't got time to see the illuminations at Blackpool, we used to love it there, me and Bella did, on the top o' the tram. Though I imagine it ain't the same as the old days…"

THE HIDE

The rain had just about cleared as they reached the coast, and set up at a vantage point known locally as 'Jenny Brown's Point', where the Kent estuary met the open Irish Sea. Huge flocks of geese, ducks, gulls and waders picked at the estuary mud or wheeled around in the gusty south-westerly wind, filling the air with melancholy and plaintiff choruses.

"Time to get that list cracking, lads!" shouted Colin over the swirl of the wind and the din of the birds. Just look at that curlew flock! And the knot - there must be 10,000 of them! Look out…peregrine falcon - pair of!"

De'Ath managed to pick out the peregrines as they menaced a flock of gulls at high speed, and watched in awe as they plunged and veered. Among his burgeoning birding library, he had begun to read J.A. Baker's *The Peregrine*, and he could now easily imagine how the 1930's Essex bird watching prose poet had become fixated and obsessed with these birds.

"I do believe we 'ave a bar-tailed godwit down yonder, Colin…in that group of redshank down yonder!"

"Well done, Ronnus!" shouted Colin, "you are making a birder now, me old mate! And there's a black-tailed over there with the green sands. Now then, there's a spot, see that flock of gulls just in front of us – mainly BH and LBBs, yeah – see there's a gull there called the Mediterranean gull, yep, and there is a little gull…wow, look here come the pink-footed geese…just listen!"

Great skeins of geese in arrow formation passed low overhead. "I expect your mate will want to pop a few of these, Ron! Shooting geese is very popular round these parts - but not with the RSPB of course! Lads, whilst you round up the duck list, I'm gonna have a seawatch up on the top there. Come and join me when you are ready. It's not as good as the cliffs o'course but you never know what might

THE HIDE

turn up."

"Tom, are you ID-ing the ducks, or what? We've ticked the peregrinos off already!"

De'Ath could easily have spent the rest of the afternoon and evening watching the falcons – he was hoping to see one swoop onto a gull – but he dutifully joined Bullock in listing off the dozen species of duck bobbing in the estuary before them. Then they headed up the path to join Colin, who was sitting on his camping stool gazing out to sea through his telescope, in the company of another fellow doing the same.

"Guys, let me introduce you to David Lindo - another of our birdwatching celebrities. You may have seen him on the *Springwatch*?"

"Hiya fellers, nice to meet you!" Bullock and De'Ath were relieved to meet a bird watching celebrity who seemed genuinely affable. He welcomed them with a London accent full of enthusiasm. "Come and join me and Col - we reckon there's Leach's petrel zooming around out there."

Bullock hadn't seen Lindo on the TV and was pleasantly surprised to meet a birder who wasn't white and middle-aged, and said so.

"It's nice to see a black feller birding, I know yer can't say much for fear of being called a racist, but you don't see any Asian or black people at our local patch - though there's plenty such folk live nearby. My dentist is a Sikh, y'know."

De'Ath inwardly cringed and studied the dots on the horizon that might or might not be birds. Though he was thinking the same as Bullock, he thought it rude to articulate it. Therefore he was relieved with Lindo's reply, which contained no trace of offence.

"It's absolutely true, Ron - we people of colour are completely under-represented - not just bird watching but getting out and about generally in the countryside. Did you know, black people in the UK are more likely than white people to be diagnosed with mental health problems?

THE HIDE

I am a massive believer in the power of nature to relieve stress - man, if I didn't get out regularly - even if it's just half an hour on my patch - I'd go bonkers meself!"

"Well, why do you think that is then, David? There's obviously no problem getting coloured lads out on the footie pitch – 'alf the England team are black or mixed race!"

Lindo laughed. "True dat! I dunno, there's more black people in cities like London and Birmingham than in the leafy suburbs - that's why my passion is to get more city folk of whatever race to get out and relax in the green spots."

"They call David the *Urban Birder*," added Colin still staring out to sea with his binoculars. He's written a book about it, haven't you, mate."

"Yeah, it's sort of my autobiography and about my local patch in London, Wormwood Scrubs."

"Wormwood Scrubs! That's the prison ain't it?"

"Yeah, that's right, Charlie Bronson, Pete Doherty, Keith Richards, they all did some *bird* there,' laughed Lindo. "Get it? *Bird?!*"

Bullock did get the joke and was hugely appreciative of at last finding a birder who not only *got* jokes - but cracked them as well!

"Ah, that's a good 'un that, lad. Bird. OK then, where do birds invest their money?"

"Ahhh, I know that one, don't tell me, don't tell me…" Lindo tapped his forehead as he wracked the part of his brain that stored bird jokes. "Naaaah…go on then, put me out of my misery…"

"In the stork market!" guffawed Bullock.

"Owwww!! Alright then, now, OK, I gotta do this one in me West Indian accent, here we go – bless up, why couldn't anyone see da bird? Pretty topical actually, cos I cannot see that Leach's petrel anywhere!"

"OK mon," started Bullock, in an impossibly bad, Yorkshire-flavoured Jamaican accent, that he thought might sound like Courtney Walsh, "why couldn't anyone see da bird, De-avid?"

"Because, mon," grinned Lindo, "it was in da skies! Get it?… disguise… da skies?"

"Haha - corker!!" exploded Bullock. "Crawb up, paadie!"

"Ah y'know a bit o' patois, Ronny, you da man, a mi fi tell yu!"

"Yeah, ah went to watch the cricket in Jamaica a few years back. Me n' Courtney Walsh 'ad a reet laugh together we did!"

'Midst the general conviviality, and taking a break from peregrine watching, De'Ath unwisely added a birding joke that he had that moment made up.

"What kind of mathematics do birds like?"

"Oooh, I know, it, I know it! " Lindo tapped his head again. "Naaaah…go on then, put me out of my misery…"

"Algebra."

There was a stony silence, as the three other men tried to figure out the pun.

"Algebra, Tom? Don't get it," frowned Bullock. "Why would birds like algebra? Is it summat to do wi' an abacus?"

"No, Ron, not really."

"Is it something to do with 'an equation', Tom?" asked Lindo.

"Not strictly speaking, David."

"Well, none of us get it, Tom. Say it again," frowned Bullock.

"OK. What kind of mathematics do birds like? It's not very good really, to be honest, let's forget it. Owlgebra."

"Oh, "owlgebra"! Yeah, it is crap, but you said "algebra" first time. That's why none of us got it, yer daft 'aporth!"

"I didn't say "algebra"; I said "owlgebra!" whined De'Ath plaintively. "Why would I say "algebra"? It wouldn't be funny, would it?"

"Well, it weren't funny anyway, was it, let's face it," moaned Bullock.

Moods darkened further as Colin suddenly took his bins from the horizon and entered the fray.

"What do you do if a bird shits on your car?"

"Dunno, Col," chuckled Lindo. "What do you do?"

"Don't ask her out again." Colin and Lindo exploded into laughter, but the still embarrassed De'Ath resumed peregrine watch, and Bullock shook his head, though with a concealed grin.

"Oh, trust you to lower the tone, Colin. That's the vestiges of yer Tourette's that is. Reet that's enough of the crap jokes, lets spot that leech bird or whatever it is, shall we? And what was it you were sayin' about Wormwood Scrubs, David - before you led us down the Ken Dodd path?"

"Yeah, my fault! But seriously, it is great birding at the Scrubs, Ron. Around 140 species - not bad for a place with no standing water, eh! And rarities too, I've had Ortolan bunting there…"

"Ooh, is that the one they eat in France, Mitterrand's last supper and all that?" De'Ath asked, attempting to move on from his joke fiasco.

"Yep," replied Lindo grimly. "it is improving, the protection of birds in France, but it certainly still goes on. I've had my favourite bird down there at the Scrubs - the ring ouzel!"

"Ring ouzel! Crikey I am hoping to show these boys a ringy whilst we

THE HIDE

are up here - fancy that, seeing one on the Scrubs, David!"

"Yeah, I reckon it's on their migration path, Col, I see them pretty much every year. Yep, that's definitely Leach's petrel out there, lads."

Bullock and De'Ath scanned the horizon, De'Ath looking up the petrel in his book.

"Now...how...exactly..." Bullock peered out to the horizon with his Leicas, seeing only moving dots which he conceded could conceivably be birds, "...can you fellers identify anything from this range?"

"All in the jizz, Ronny," smiled Colin. "Think I've got a black-throated diver, David. Dagger bill, feet well back on the body, no collar on its goose neck, head tucked down..."

"Got it, Col, got it...confirm that - got the fulmar coming across beyond it? Stiff wings, grey rump?"

"Roger that, David...got a sooty shearwater mid-distance..."

It was all beyond the wit and ken of Bullock, but since he had seen the dots, and the dots had been identified by two experts, he saw no reason not to add to his burgeoning list, and scribbled like a dictation secretary in his notebook. De'Ath's binocular gaze though had turned back to his peregrines, which he followed in continued awe, remembering that he had read somewhere that they were the fastest beasts in the animal kingdom.

"We are heading for the Lakes tomorrow, David, what about you? Back to the Scrubs?" asked Colin, taking a nip from his hip flask.

"Nah, off to Tallin in Estonia to do a bit of urban. Got this great gig with *Birdwatch Magazine* where they pay me to go off to various cities. Flying from Manchester later on. In fact, I'd best get going. Lovely to meet you fellers, good luck with everything and welcome to the club! If you are ever down my way, just give us a shout, Col's got my number. It's in 'owlgebra' though, Tom! "

The Urban Birder packed up his things and left with a grin and a

THE HIDE

cheerful wave.

"What a nice bloke!" remarked Bullock. "Quite the nicest chap we've met on our travels. You'll 'ave to lend me his book, Colin, ah'll 'ave a read o' that."

"No worries, Ron. Now then, who's for fish and chips? Then, a pint of Lancaster Red in The Palatine, would be rude not to."

"It would indeed, Colin, it would indeed. Sounds like we need a bit o' fortification before we meet this Mrs. Winterbottom. If we can tear yon man away from 'is peregrinos, that is…"

At five-forty the following morning, a bleary and barely conscious Bullock stumbled down the rickety stairs of Mrs. Winterbottom's Guest House to join his pals, not sure if he was ready to face the full English. The landlady's filthy temper was in full effect.

"Yer late down! Mr. Dredge told me 'alf past five – 'e's got 'is already. And yer mate 'as an' all."

"Mornin' Ron," garbled Colin, through a mouth full of macerated sausage.

"Morning, Ron," parroted De'Ath distractedly, picking at his breakfast with a fork, whilst thoroughly engaged in his book, *The Peregrine.*

"Mornin' all," croaked Bullock in reply. "Er, just a bit o' toast fo' me, missus, thanks."

"What?! You ordered a full English. Well, yer payin' for it, anywhichdayothemonth!"

"I'll 'ave Ron's if he don't want it, Mrs W. So good, I'll eat it twice!"

"You are welcome, lad," groaned Bullock, sitting down and reaching

THE HIDE

for the teapot. "Sleep well?"

"Like a log, Ronno. And after a few pints of that Lancaster Red, who wouldn't?"

"I have to say that I couldn't put this book down last night - oh do excuse me, reading at the table, rude of me."

"You carry on, lad. I ain't speakin' for at least another hour."

By just after six, the bill paid, breakfast consumed and seen off by a landlady's scowl that would turn butter rancid, Bullock slumped down in the front of the Land Rover, hand on forehead, as Colin roared off to the first destination of the day, Meathop Fell. The van was quiet, as Bullock half-slumbered and rocked about, De'Ath avidly read, and Colin silently questioned the wisdom of consuming two of Mrs. Winterbottom's full English fry-ups, which she still did in lard.

Suddenly, the silence was violently broken.

"THHAAAAAAAAAAAAAAAAAAAAAAAAAAAAARRRRRRRR RRRRRRRRP!!"

"What the Hell…" Bullock stirred from his semi-slumber in outrage, "what in God's name was that?"

"Ah, really sorry, Ron," muttered a reddening Colin, hastily winding down the windows as an evil sulphurous stench rose like marsh gas from the driver's seat.

"Jesus H Christ, Colin! Was that the longest fart in history? It went on for a full thirty seconds! If the McWhirther twins were still alive, they'd put you in the Guinness Book o' Records, though I don't suppose they would wish to be incarcerated in 'ere for very long to do the verification! Pull over, man, I think I am gonna throw up!"

A chastened Colin did as he was told and pulled into the next lay-by.

"That's it, open the doors up. Jesus, Colin, if it weren't bad enough gettin' up at this hour, then I 'ave to smell your 'orrible trump gas. I

THE HIDE

'ave told you before, fart in your own face, not mine!"

"Yeah look, really sorry, Ron. Just couldn't keep it in. Old Johnny Fartpants took over there. Doesn't look as though old Tommo minds, though?"

De'Ath didn't seem to have noticed Colin's intestinal explosion or even the car pulling over; he sat wreathed in gut gas, a beatific smile on his face as he scanned the pages of JA Baker.

"My Lord, that must be a good book, Tommy. It's rendered you nasally insensitive. Right, I think the air has cleared sufficiently, but if you do that again wi' me in the car, Col, I'll shove you out of the driving seat and leave you for dead on t'road."

"Yep, fair enough, Ron, fair enough. Anyway, it's woken you up!"

"Yeah," replied Bullock with the hint of a smile. "I remember my army mate, Tony McGarry, 'is name were. He had summat called the McGarry Alarm Clock. He used to creep over to one o' the bunks butt naked and fart in a bloke's face to wake him up. It were quite funny - til he did to me one day!"

"Oh dear, what happened to old McGarry when he gave you the alarm, Ron?" smiled Colin, "I am guessing something bad?"

"Haha, you got it, Col. Nobody likes a fork up the porkus, do they! I kept one from the mess one under me pillow - just in case!"

"Ooooooh," squirmed Colin. "I wish you 'adn't told me that, Ron. I've gone over all funny. Christ, I bet that was the end of the McGarry Alarm Clock then?"

"Yep, for some strange reason, it stopped tickin' after that,' grinned Bullock. "And by the way, Col, I've got a little fork on me Swiss Army knife - just in case you start thunderin' again!"

"They don't like it up 'em, Captain Mainwearing!" cackled Colin. "Right, we are going to start the day at the riverside, chaps. Let's see if we can get you a marsh tit on the way through the woods."

THE HIDE

Even Bullock had to admit to the autumnal splendour of dawn at Meathop Fell on a chilly but dry late September morn. The mist rose above the River Winster and the chatter of birdlife abounded. Crouching silently on the river bank, Colin indicated in silence a chestnut brown, thrush-like bird with a striking white breast patch flitting about the foundation stones of a road bridge.

"Dipper!" he whispered.

"Just look at that grey heron in the mist!" marvelled De'Ath.

"Grey heron! That's not a tick, Tom, we see loads o' them at Clarendon," muttered Bullock grumpily. "What's that 'un, Col? Flippin' its tail about?"

"Well done, Ron, grey wagtail! And see that duck up yonder – red-breasted merganser. AND…goosander!"

"They both look the same to my eyes, Colin. How can you tell the difference?" whispered De'Ath.

"Good question, Tom. Both part of the sawbill family - their beaks are long and serrated for catching fish. Both those birds are male - see the goosander has a dark green/black head, but smooth - now look at Mr. Merganser - can you see the difference?"

"He's got a 'Mohican'!"

"That he has, Tom! The tufts of feathers are the way to tell. No females about that I can see. Eh up – kingfisher alert! Up in the willows, look!"

"We've got 'im an 'all,' moaned Bullock. De'Ath had had enough of Bullock's tick-box birdwatching.

"For God's sake, Ron! You cannot see enough kingfishers - or herons,

THE HIDE

for that matter! I am more interested in the joy of seeing these creatures than ticking new ones off!"

"Each to their own, Tommyboy. It ain't gonna lengthen yer list though. Just sayin'."

"Blimey Ron, its going to be you vs Sonny Robards at this rate! Anyway, let's walk up through the woods lads, and get Ronny his marsh tit tick before he gets any grumpier!" Colin led De'Ath reluctantly away from the magic of the river, and they made their way silently up the woodland path, autumn leaves beginning to flutter down.

"There he be look - *Poecile palustris*. Rather similar to the willow tit you've seen at Clarendon, but you can take it from me."

"Tick! Eh, there's old woody woodpecker in the trees look – any chance of a lesser spotted, Col?"

"Not up here I'm afraid, Ron. That's a greater spotted, for sure."

THE HIDE

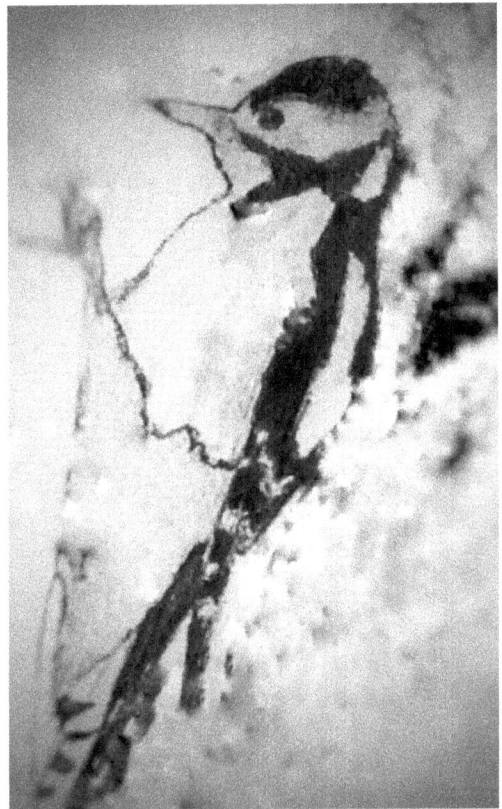

"A Greater Spotted, For Sure"
(Silas Ross-White)

"Bah, seen them at the feeders at Clarendon. Common as muck. But 'ang one - what's this up the path - it's a jay! There's another tick for auld Ronnus!"

"Wow, what a bird - I have never seen a jay before!" enthused De'Ath. "Well, apart from that juvenile one in Jack Ward's caravan at Clarendon Marsh, that is."

"Yeah, Tom, it's a shy bird, the jay. Just look at that blue flash and white rump. Listen for the call, lads, like ripping cloth. They call'em

THE HIDE

'the screamers of the woods' in Wales. Look, he is burying acorns! You get quite a lot over from the continent some years, to add to the natives. I have seen quite big flocks of them, to be fair."

Moving further up the slope, they came to a stand of tall conifers, which Colin studied intently. "Now then, some more ticks for you here, boys. I've got redpoll, siskin...and I think that's a crossbill up there. Yep, see him? He is quite pinkish?"

"Got him!" smiled De'Ath. "What a strange beak. It's all twisted..."

"Bill, Tom...I keep telling you...bill! Yeah, it's so they can get the seeds out of the pine cones y'see. There's the female, look, all olive green."

"I can see the siskin but where is this redpoll, Col?" Bullock anxiously scanned the trees for his tick.

"There look, red blob on its head. Birch catkins is what they usually like. Used to be very common, they did, you'd see them on the Marsh sometimes. Oh, bloody 'ell it's rainin' again. Got to crack on up to the moor though...there's more ticks up yonder!"

The visibility closed in as they climbed Meathop Fell, but Colin stopped suddenly near a rocky outcrop, where he saw something move out of the corner of his eye.

"Now then! It's Lindo's favourite, so it is! Meet...Mr. ring ouzel!

"Looks like a blackbird ter me," scowled Bullock, the rain bouncing off his nose.

"Well, they do call him the mountain blackbird, Ron. He'll be off to Africa soon - perhaps he'll pop into Wormwood Scrubs for a chat with Lindo on the way down. Look, he's off!"

"Don't blame 'im, Col. What's that little feller boucin' about on yonder wall?"

"That's your winchat, Ron...and I do believe I can hear his cousin, the

THE HIDE

stonechat. Hear that tapping sound? "Flint-on-flint ticking," as the poet said. Can't see him though, probably hunkering down in this rain."

"Bollocks to him!" fumed Bullock. "Show yerself, chatstone!"

"Never mind, mind Ron - you can still tick him off, you know!" chuckled Colin. "I can confidently confirm that is the call of the stonechat!"

"Really? Don't need to even see 'im? Brilliant. In the book with 'im!"

Colin spent the next hour desperately trying to find a wheatear, but as the rain got harder, none could he find. In fact, not a single bird or other creature was seen, and spirits began to sodden.

"Come on, let's head back and grab a coffee somewhere. This is no good, I can't see me hand in front of me face. We've dipped on the wheatear, I'm afraid."

"I'm with you, Col! Lead on Gunga Din!"

"Gunga Din? Who is that then, Ronnus?"

"Do you not know yer Kipling, Col?! Oh aye, we learned it in school, Gunga Din."

To the amusement of De'Ath and Colin, Bullock enlived their squelching descent with a spirited rendition of the 1892 poem.

" Now in Injia's sunny clime,
Where I used to spend my time
A-servin' of 'Er Majesty the Queen,
Of all them black-faced crew
The finest man I knew
Was our regimental bhisti, Gunga Din.
He was "Din! Din! Din!
You limpin' lump o' brick-dust, Gunga Din!
The uniform 'e wore

THE HIDE

Was nothin' much before,
An' rather less than 'arf o' that be'ind,
For a piece o' twisty rag
An' a goatskin water-bag
Was all the field-equipment 'e could find.

It was "Din! Din! Din!
"You 'eathen, where the mischief 'ave you been?
"You put some juldee in it
"Or I'll marrow you this minute
"If you don't fill up my helmet, Gunga Din!"

"Bravo, Ron! spluttered De'Ath though the rain driving into his face.
"I don't think I ever knew that one!"

"Eh, I 'avent finished yet, Tom... *I shan't forgit the night*
When I dropped be'ind the fight
With a bullet where my belt-plate should 'a' been.
I was chokin' mad with thirst,
An' the man that spied me first
Was our good old grinnin', gruntin' Gunga Din.
'E lifted up my 'ead,
An' he plugged me where I bled, An' 'e guv me 'arf-a-pint o' water green.
It was crawlin' and it stunk,
But of all the drinks I've drunk,
I'm gratefullest to one from Gunga Din.

'E carried me away
To where a dooli lay,
An' a bullet come an' drilled the beggar clean.
'E put me safe inside,
An' just before 'e died,
"I 'ope you liked your drink" sez Gunga Din.
So I'll meet 'im later on
At the place where 'e is gone
Where it's always double drill and no canteen.
'E'll be squattin' on the coals
Givin' drink to poor damned souls,
An' I'll get a swig in hell from Gunga Din!

THE HIDE

Yes, Din! Din! Din!
Though I've belted you and flayed you,
By the livin' Gawd that made you,
You're a better man than I am, Gunga Din!"

"Haha!" applauded Colin, "You're a better man than I am, Gunga Din! Hold on, lads, got something for yer. Atop them trees over there. It's the mischievous raven!

"Is that not just old Joe Crow, Col?

"Come on Ronnus – it's massive! I love ravens, I do. They mess about for fun. I saw one once sledging down a snowdrift like a child at play, he was."

De'Ath, peering also at the fearsome black bird, cleared his throat and began his own recitation.

"Back into the chamber turning, all my soul within me burning,
Soon again I heard a tapping somewhat louder than before.
"Surely," said I, "surely that is something at my window lattice;
Let me see, then, what thereat is, and this mystery explore
Let my heart be still a moment and this mystery explore
'Tis the wind and nothing more!"

Open here I flung the shutter, when, with many a flirt and flutter,
In there stepped a stately Raven of the saintly days of yore;
Not the least obeisance made he; not a minute stopped or stayed he;
But, with mien of lord or lady, perched above my chamber door
Perched upon a bust of Pallas just above my chamber door
Perched, and sat, and nothing more.

Then the bird said "Nevermore!""

"Bloody 'ell, Tom, that's a bit dark! That's never Kipling!"

"No it isn't, Ron. It's '*The Raven*' by Edgar Allen Poe. I can't remember more of it - but I recommend you hear Christopher Lee's reading - it's on the internet somewhere."

THE HIDE

"Oh now, then, Christopher Lee, now yer talkin'! Fireside tales, eh, Hammer Horrors, oh yeah. Died last year, didn't 'e. 93 he was. Nevermore!"

"Nevermore!" croaked Colin.

"Ah, I've got a song about a raven, too. Listen, You can both join in!" De'Ath started skipping, and began a folky warble.

"Well, a farmer went trotting upon his grey mare,
Bumpety, bumpety, bump,
With his daughter behind him, so rosy and fair,
Lumpety, lumpety, lump.

A raven cried "Croak," and they all tumbled down,
Bumpety, bumpety, bump;
The mare broke her knees and the farmer his crown,
Lumpety, lumpety, lump.

The mischievous raven flew laughing away,
Bumpety, bumpety, bump,
And vowed he would serve them the same next day,
Lumpety, lumpety, lump."

"YEAH! I remember that one, it's a nursery rhyme, in't it!" laughed Bullock. "They didn't mess about did they, them auld nursery rhymes like the Grimm's Tales! There was one called the Hobyahs that right put the wind up me when I were a nipper! Eh, that mischievious raven, eh! The horse went lame and the farmer smashed 'is 'ead in! And "he vowed he would serve them the same the next day!" What a devil! Come on, let's sing it together!"

Their spirits restored by walking song, the rain suddenly desisted and the sun came out to illuminate a ploughed field ahead of them, where they were rewarded by a huge flock of golden plover, gleaming greenish gold in the low sun.

Back at the car, they peeled off their sopping gear and sat steaming in the Land Rover. Colin was about to reverse from the verge and to find

THE HIDE

a place for elevenses, when he turned off the ignition and leapt out of the car.

"Lads! One more for for yer from Meathop! Get out and bring your bins. Hen harrier. Female. Get it ticked before the grouse shooters blast it out of the sky!"

Wheeling above them in the sky was a harrier, with long, broad wings, but with a barred tail much longer than that of the marsh harrier that they had ticked the day before. Through their optics, they got excellent views of the mottled brown bird against the white clouds, and thoroughly contented with their morning's work, headed for Cartmel in search of toasted crumpets.

Back in Oldside, Bella and Dot were at a charity shop in the High Street, searching for items for their Murder Mystery Evening at the Boughton Hand Hotel. The theme was 'Murder on The Train', so they had decided to dress up as characters from the 1974 version of *Murder on the Orient Express*. Bella was to be Lauren Bacall's Mrs. Hubbard, and Dot Wendy Hiller's imperious Princess Dragomiroff. Bella found the perfect 1960's black cardigan to match the brown turtleneck dress she already had, and was able to drape herself in several brown-beaded necklaces. Dot bought lengths of black lace and a dark blue feather boa to drape about her, along with some white face paint and a white wig. Well satisfied with their purchases, they set off for a well-earned coffee at Lucia's.

Up north, the rain began to lash down again, and the planned trip to the mountain of Great Gable was beginning to seem less and less attractive, despite Colin tempting them with possible sightings of the elusive wheatear, and the small upland falcon, the merlin.

"No chance of an eagle, then, Colin," asked De'Ath hopefully.

"No chance, Tom. There is a male golden knocking about somewhere in the Lakes, but tough to find, especially in this weather. Somebody told me he had died actually. We'll have to go to Scotland if you want to see the big eagles."

"Well, it don't sound worth the climb in this rain to me, Col. We could go to the Tower Bank Arms in Sawrey, sup a few pints, sort our lists out, go and see Beatrix Potter and get the Windermere Ferry back to our digs. I need an early night, early starts do me in. And another early start tomorrow, Sykes wants me in Slaidburn by 9."

"Suits me, boys. Eh, Tom, after we've dropped Ron off, do you fancy a detour over Yorkshire way to see this Siberian accentor? We could grip old Ron off here and you'd be one up on your list!"

"Ah, can't really, Colin. I told Dot I would be back around lunchtime and she might be a bit worse for wear – her and Bella are off to one of those Murder Mystery things tonight, and I gather they can be rather boozy affairs."

"As you wish, Tom, good to get your priorities right – I didn't and that's why the missus hopped it. Don't want your old lady running off with Hercule Poirot, do we?"

"Sorry Colin, but I do object to you calling my wife the 'old lady'. And as for her running off with Albert Finney, well…"

"Apologies, Tom, probly another reason Betty cleared off with the postman. My big mouth."

But Tom was already anxiously fiddling with his mobile, and sending Dot a text saying that he hoped that she wouldn't find Hercule Poirot too attractive. Bullock was more assertive.

"Well, if my Bella runs off with anybody, there'll be another murder on the Orient Express. They'll call me the Barnsley Strangler!" he grinned. "Right boys, let's get to the Tower Bank – I can taste that Hawkshead Bitter already!"

THE HIDE

After a pleasant and restful afternoon and early evening, the lads (who didn't bother with Beatrix Potter World, as there appeared to be a queue of several hundred Japanese people at the entrance) were having a nightcap at their lodgings at the Eagle and Child in Staveley just as Mrs. Hubbard and Princess Dragomiroff entered the bar of the Boughton Hand Hotel. They were immediately approached by an actor who was conspicuously playing Hercule Poirot. He kissed both their hands, before wiggling his false moustache and greeted them profusely.

"Mes dames, 'ow merveilleux you 'ave come as ze characteurs! Most of ze uzzer guests – zey 'ave not bozzerred!"

Dot sneered in character at her fellow guests who were quaffing merrily at bar tables. Some had a managed to put on a suit or dress on but one man had come in a T-shirt and his wife in an ill-fitting vest top and torn jeans. Hercule fed Dot a line.

"You never smile, madame la princesse?"

"My doctor has advised against it," responded Dot deadpan, bang on cue and much to Hercule's delight.

"Bravo, bravo, madame! Bravo! I can see we weel 'ave some fun togezzeur, ce soir! Bon…GOOD EVENING, MESDAMES ET MESSIEURS!"

Hercule banged a table with a tablespoon to get the attention of the guests. "Zere are twelve tab-els for dinneur in ze dining room, or should ah say, ze dining carriage - where you weel meet ze characteurs. We must first say – zis is NAT ze same storee as Agatha Christie. And…onlee ONE of ze people haz done ze crime…what crime, you ask…?"

"AAAIIEEEEEEEEEEEEEEEEEEEEEEEEEEEEE!" came a woman's scream from the staircase outside the bar.

"Zut alors! We must investigate! Come, mes amis!"

Everyone rushed excitedly out of the room, to find an actress in a

THE HIDE

thirties maid's outfit, the very woman who had screamed and dropped her tray of drinks. She was quivering over what looked like a horribly mutilated body.

"Mon dieu! Nobody touch ze bodee! When deed you discover ze bodee, miss?"

"Jetzt! Yust now! I vass getting ze aspirin for ze Princess ant - here he voss!" she explained, in a reasonable attempt at a German accent.

"Ah, 'e is steel warm! Eez zere a Docteur in ze 'ouse?"

A man in a tweed suit and wild white hair came scurrying to the scene, this one affecting a Greek accent. Opening a doctor's bag, he whipped out a stethoscope, and applied it studiously to the recumbent and bloodied form.

"Dead! Deceased! Thith man ath been sthabbed repeatedly - frenziedly – a dozen times! And not ten minuth ago!" he announced grandly.

"ZEN!" declared Hercule, "ze killeur must steel be in zis building! All ze doors and windows are locked and so…let us enter ze dining carriage…and meet ze suspects!!"

The dining room had been impressively decorated to reproduce the dining car of the Orient Express, and Dot and Bella were escorted by Poirot to Table 5, where they were pleased to be sitting with a well-dressed couple who introduced themselves as Gavin and Lorraine and a very handsome actor in the uniform of a train valet, with the name 'Pierre' written on his label badge. When the guests were all seated, the chatter began and wine was ordered. The soup course arrived, carried by a gang of confused-looking teenagers supervised by an aggressive head waitress, who harried and chivvied her waiters and waitresses into action.

"Did you do it, love?" Bella asked Pierre as she slurped her courgette soup and set about the white wine, as did Dot.

"Non. Absolutement non. Ah 'ave no motive for keeling Mr.

THE HIDE

Ratchett."

Hercule appeared from nowhere, pulled up a seat and helped himself to a generous glass of wine, which he downed in one.

"NOT TRUE, PIERRE!" he exclaimed, wagging his index finger and waggling his waxed moustache. "I thheenk - you must explain 'ow you know Monsieur Ratchett!"

Staring with the utmost shame at his hands, Pierre went into a long and complex explanation of how he knew the mutilated man. The Princess and Mrs Hubbard made copious notes in a notebook that Bella had brought in her voluminous handbag.

"Well, what do you think of that then, Gavin?"

"I dunno. But I do think we should have another bottle of that white wine, Bella. Waiter!"

As soup was cleared away and some pork chops arrived, the actors circulated, and Pierre was replaced by a pious woman with a Swedish accent, whose name badge read 'Greta'.

"It's Ingrid Bergman!" hissed Bella to Lorraine. Through mouthfuls of pork washed down with a bottle of red, Greta, tightly clutching a bible, was duly interrogated by the table guests.

"Well, what do you think of that then, Gavin?"

"I dunno. But I do think we should have another bottle of that red wine, Bella. Waiter!"

Another guest actor arrived at their table, this time a nervous young man who apparently was Ratchett's secretary.

"It's Anthony Perkins!" hissed Bella to Lorraine. "OOOH! What's that crawling about under the table? There's a man in my carriage!" exclaimed Mrs. Hubbard/Bella, peering under the table cloth. Indeed there was a man in the carriage…Hercule crawled out from under the table, clutching a bloodied dagger and helped himself to another large

THE HIDE

glass of red, which he seemed to do at every table he visited.

"Zis…" he commenced, his eyes looking considerably deader than at the commencement of proceedings and his pomaded hair in semi-disarray "is…ze murder weapon! Ah…found it…under ZIS TABLE!"

"Yikes. Does that mean that the murderer could have dropped it whilst sitting here?" Gavin asked Poirot, enthusiastically. "That means Pierre, Greta, or McQueen!"

"PRECISELY MA THOUGHTS!" shouted Poirot, rising unsteadily to his feet and addressing the rest of the room. "I have in my 'and, a dagger. No, no, it iss not Shakespeare – eet is a clue! A dagger…itch a…ooh, the room's spinnin' - itch a…clue…or summink…" As he staggered into the middle of the room, his accent slipping badly into his native middle English, his waxed moustache fell off, much to the hilarity of the guests, whose behaviour was becoming rowdier with the drink. Bending to recover it, Poirot's legs gave way and he collapsed, spread-eagled on the carpet and his pomaded black wig slipped off his bald head.

"Bloimey, Porro's bin murdered!" shouted the man in the T-shirt in delight. However, judging from the reactions of his fellow actors, this was a highly unscripted 'death'. The other actors leapt from their table places and gathered anxiously around the stricken Belgian detective.

"What do we do now?" hissed a moustachioed colonel to a young Count.

"I keep telling Alan not to drink with the punters! He's fucking legless! He's out for the count!"

A tall butler took action. "Grab his legs, Tony. We'll have to cart him off. You'll have to take over as Poirot!"

"What?! I am Colonel Arbuthnot…I can't do Poirot!"

The argument continued as the cast left the dining room, some of the guests becoming rowdy, shouting catcalls and one unruly table, led by the man with the T-shirt, began throwing bread rolls. T-shirt's wife,

THE HIDE

Vest Top, emitted a continuous loud, horrible sound somewhere between screech and guttural cackle, which apparently was how she expressed laughter.

Table 5 were more orderly, but no less amused by Poirot's collapse.

"Hercule has drunk too much!" said Bella, stating the evident. "Well, what do you think of that then, Gavin?"

"I dunno. But I do think we should have another bottle of that red wine, Bella. Waiter!"

The cast, having hastily re-grouped in the 'Green Room', re-entered the dining room some minutes later, taking their seats and trying to carry on as before. Table 5 was joined by a young Countess in a white fur and ball gown, looking sheepish and not very talkative.

Then entered a new Poirot. The large fellow who had been playing the Colonel had somehow squeezed himself into the diminutive Poirot's evening suit, stuck on the waxed moustache and donned the pomaded wig.

"Mezdames ett mesewers. Zer is no need to worry. Porro is back. Now, this dagger is a cluuuuue." Unfortunately, Poirot II's accent was not much good – more an Inspector Clouseau of the *Pink Panther* films.

The catcalls began again.

"Ah weel seh zis only wance!" shouted the man in the T-shirt, in the manner of Officer Crabtree in *Allo 'Allo!*

"Ev you got a yyrrrrrooom? Ev you got a phun?" shouted his mate, doing Inspector Clouseau in *The Return of the Pink Panther.*

Vest Top wife surpassed her previous horrible laughter by simply shrieking at maximum volume, which apparently her husband and cronies welcomed as "her infectious laugh."

"Oh, sit down and give the man a chance, you ruffians!" threatened the

THE HIDE

young Count at their table, and a fight would have broken out had the butler not intervened and poured out more wine for the hecklers.

As puddings were served, Poirot II decided to try to curtail proceedings, by way of 'damage limitation'.

"Mezdames ett mesewers. Hildegarde ze maid will hand out your 'Whodunnit Cards' now - please write down who you think dunnit, your evidence and their motives. Thank you…I mean…sank you. Mursi."

"Boooooo!" We haven't met everyone yet!" yelled T-shirt. Surely there's more clues, Porro?"

Poirot II was about to attempt an explanation as more bread rolls were hurled his way, when there was a commotion in the hall involving raised voices and a tray of ten dishes containing swiss rolls in custard smashed to the ground.

A small bald man dressed only in vest, Y-fronts and long socks strode belligerently into the room, and began arguing loudly with Poirot II.

"How dare you schtrip me, Tony! Look at you - that's my bloody shuit you're wearing, my bloody mushtache! How DARE you think you can pull off Hercule? You are bloody hopeless as the Colonel, frankly!"

"Alan, Alan, stop this…" the Countess tried to escort the drunken Alan back to the Green Room, but he shrugged her off.

"Thish is MY bloody company, Erica! I AM 'Make Mine a Murder Theatre Company'! I was doing thish when you were in nappies. Now then…. MESDAMES ET MESSIEURS! Give me that wig and moustache and bugger off out of it, Tony. I will do this in me undies. The show MUSHT go on!"

"ATTEN-SION! Zer eez a vee-ery eemportan clue to give you, as you eat your Sweese yrolls. Conseeder zis…Zis 'ankerchief - I find eet on ze bodee – 'oo could 'ave dropped eet?!

THE HIDE

The rowdy table were in hysterics as Poirot II handed over the moustache and wig and stormed off, and some of the other actors followed suit. Poirot I circulated unconcerned in his socks, shaking the handkerchief clue above his head, and finally slumped down at Table 5.

Dot, Bella, Gavin and Lorraine were more than merry themselves, and found it hard to contain themselves. In fact, Gavin couldn't, and having poured Poirot the dregs of the latest wine bottle, which the drunken detective gratefully swigged down, Gavin collapsed in laughter and got the hiccups.

But Bella/Mrs Hubbard was determined to see it through, as she carefully compiled her 'Whodunnit Card', with far too much assistance from the slurring Hercule.

"Y'see, Hercule, if that handkerchief was dropped nearby the body - it must 'ave been a woman, cos that is a ladies hankie. And if the murder weapon was dropped at our table, and we only had Pierre, McQueen and Greta – it must be Greta!"

"It is, love, it is…" hissed Alan. "I like this table, not like that riff-raff over there. Eh, write this down, then let's go and 'ave one of yer fags. Greta's motive was that she was in love with Ratchett but he buggered off with the redhead one, Vanessa Redgrave, whatever. There was meant to be a love letter clue but that pillock Tony spoiled it - who the Hell does he think he is? I was only havin' one of me dizzy spells. That's it love, give us your paper. You'll win the mug, and I'll see your friend gets one too."

He rose from the table, determinedly. "MESDAMES ET MESSIEURS! I 'ope you 'ave enjoyed ze evening! As café is served, we weel collect your 'Oodunnit Cards, and zen announce ze winneur. Bon soir, et merci bien!"

And so it was that Bella and Dot clambered with difficulty into their taxi half an hour later, both clutching *Make Mine a Murder Theatre Company* tea mugs, and having promised Hercule they would certainly bring their husbands to the next event, which was to have a James Bond theme. As the taxi set off down the gravel drive of the hotel, in the gathering mist, a fist-fight had broken out between Poirot I and Poirot II, with the tall butler attempting to intervene.

"Well, that certainly wasn't dull!" offered Dot the Princess.

"Haha, well Dot, to quote Albert Finney in the film - *"but a farce, was it not, Linda Arden, to make a mockery of Poirot!"*

After a long and sound night's sleep and a quick perusal of the River Kent water meadows which yielded a yellow wagtail for the tick list, the birding trio were on their way to the M6, and were bang on time at 9am to meet Bullock's shooting party at Slaidburn in the Forest of Bowland. Outside the *Hark to Bounty* pub, Colonel Sykes sat on a bench with The General at his feet eating a bacon sandwich.

"Good morning to one and all! Ron, are you in good fettle? And Tom – are you sure you wont join us? Colin, good to meet you."

"How was the bird tour, Ron, come on in and meet the gang, are you sure you must be off directly, Tom? Well as you wish. Have a safe journey home. Right, come along then, Ron, we'll put your stuff in the old Volvo if you leave it here in the bar for now. Gentlemen, I'd like you all to meet Mr. Ron Bullock!"

Six gentlemen dressed in identical country garb welcomed Bullock to their circle in the bar snug.

Bullock was taken aback to be introduced to a round, ruddy-faced Lancastrian by the name of Sneddick, who so closely resembled Bullock as to present a mirror image, a fact not lost on the shooting party.

"Parted at birth, you two!" called one cloth-capped local, over a pint of mild.

THE HIDE

"I say, yes, there is a hit of the doppelganger!" remarked Sykes. The General found this amusing and grinned as he chomped on a porky scratching given to him by the barmaid Belinda, who was dispensing foaming pints of ale, despite the early hour.

"Oh no," groaned one of the men sitting at the table in the window. "One Snedders is enough for me!"

"Eh, Beefy, get a piccie of me and Ron together - the double-barrelled shotgun!"

As Bullock posed amiably for the photo, he was astonished to recognise the man behind the camera. It was Ian Botham. Sir Ian Botham! He feigned nonchalance, as if meeting one of his all-time cricketing heroes in a small Lancashire pub was all in a day's business.

"Right gentlemen," announced Sykes, "if we all have a glass in our hands, may I propose a toast to a wonderful day's shooting and to thank our marvellous gamekeeper Mr. Blacklock. Mr. Blacklock!"

"Blacklock!" rejoined the toast, as glasses were lifted in the direction of a feral-looking fellow in the corner, who tipped the peak of his cap deferentially, uncomfortable with the attention now being directed towards him. His weatherbeaten face, hooked nose and the yellow sclera of his eyes gave him the look of the cold-eyed predator, the sparrowhawk.

"Now, arrangements for the day, continued Sykes, "six guns - we shall put out shortly, the beaters are in place I believe, Blacklock?"

"Aye, sir."

"Jolly good, and may I remind you all that we are ONLY shooting the grouse today, please avoid all other birds, I expect there will be partridge and woodcock, but not today, gentlemen. This morning we will be in the butts for a driven shoot. Lunch will be served in the bothy, and following that, the afternoon shoot will consist of walking-up and shooting over dogs, following which we will return here to HQ."

THE HIDE

Bullock misheard "shooting over dogs" (a phrase with which he was not familiar) for "shooting dogs". He looked around the party nervously, wondering what sort of dogs they might shoot on the moor. Perhaps rabid strays, or some monster, like the Hound of the Baskervilles? He made a mental note to ask Colonel Sykes in private on that point, who in any case was continuing his address to the room.

"Now may I remind you of the rules. This is Mr. Bullock's first grouse shoot…"

"Uh-ho, duck or grouse then!" heckled Botham.

"Thank you, Sir Ian, sound advice," continued Sykes. "As I say, the rules…number one. Whilst competitiveness is fine on the sports field - and we have among us the pleasure of the company of one of the greatest contemporary sporting competitors - it is unnerving and dangerous when it comes to the fore on a grouse moor. Everyone would like to think they are a good shot. However, the most important thing is to be a SAFE shot and excessive aggression and competitiveness are not conducive to being a good neighbour, let alone a safe shot. I have noticed a tendency in recent years to hear that there is "no such thing as your neighbour's grouse". Now this is a nonsense and it simply won't stand here."

Blacklock and The General nodded in sage agreement.

"For your benefit, Ron, this means that some fools believe that every grouse in range is theirs to shoot at. This is nonsense and not cricket. The etiquette of not shooting your neighbour's birds is paramount, and I don't think I need to remind this particular party -for one very obvious reason."

Sykes nodded towards a tall and gaunt man, by the name of Pogson, who nodded grimly. To Bullock's horror, Pogson's right eye was opaque and scarred with blindness.

"Indeed, it is far easier to shoot your neighbour when you shoot at a covey of birds going towards him. The greatest likelihood of a dangerous shot occurring is when you shoot at incoming grouse too close to the line of butts. You have probably shot your first barrel too

THE HIDE

late and by the time you are ready to fire your second, the birds are too close to fire it safely. Some years ago, I remember a young nobleman shooting a retired ambassador in just this way, and of course Mr. Pogson suffered his horrific injury from a flagrant blasting from Lady Anstruther-Gough-Calthorpe. You all know my views on ladies shooting guns, and I warned you it was a mistake at the time. I am pleased that this shoot has heeded my advice and reverted to a gentleman-only club. I know it is unfashionable to say this in these absurd times we live in, with ladies boxing, playing rugby and even flying civil aircraft, but the grouse moor is no place for a lady, especially if she is armed."

There was a general murmur of approval from the misogynists in the room, of which there were several. Sykes cleared his throat, took a sip of beer, and continued.

"It is absolutely fundamental that one never swings through the line! Shooting in front, stopping the swing, lifting the gun over the butt line and then realigning it on birds flying away behind will ensure your neighbours don't feel vulnerable - there is nothing worse than looking down a pair of barrels, gentleman, I am sure you will agree!"

There was much raucous laughter on this point; Botham mimed a shotgun and aimed it at Sneddick, who responded by waving a white handkerchief in Botham's face.

"What's the matter, Snedders, it's not like you are an endangered species!" laughed Botham, pointing at Bullock, who was trying to work out what a butt line was.

"Ahem, if you please, gentlemen. Just in case there is a stray pellet - and it can happen to the best of us, I insist that we all wear these high-quality, shot-proof glasses with our ear defenders. And a word on our beaters. For those guns who insist on shooting at beaters when they are only 150 to 200 yards out, I would urge the guns to swap places. I can assure you that it is not much fun being shot at, at that distance."

"If ah could add a likkle word, on that, Colonel?" croaked up Gamekeeper Blacklock, in a Lancashire accent so thick as to be the stuff of Music Hall comedy. Botham couldn't help but shout out, "Eh up, it's Dervid Lllllloyd!" before being silenced by the descending palm of Sykes.

"Yes, do speak up, man. I am sure you have been on the wrong end of guns who consider you beyond range!"

"Aye, sir, many o' time. Ah would ask the gentlemen to consider me team o' beaters, I 'ad a good man riddled wi' shot only two week ago. The gun concerned reckoned 'e were beyond t'range, but we a good westerly a-blowin - it can carry! We don't mind a bit o' pepperin' now an' again, but we're not made o' leather, thee knows!"

Whilst Blacklock did look as though he were made of leather, he was able to proudly exhibit various blue dots about his face and arms in testament to having been shot whilst plodding about the moor with a horn and a flag.

"Ant, same for t' dogs – just luke at Dolly, if yer need further evidence!"

An aged English Setter, which looked as though she had been repeatedly blasted with a shotgun from point blank range, looked forlornly about the room. The General was very happy that Sykes would not allow him to be used as a beater's dog, but was compassionate to poor shot-blasted Dolly, and gave her nose an affectionate lick, noting that somehow she had retained her keen sight, despite her ears being full of tiny holes.

"Right, I think that is the rules made clear, gentlemen. May I suggest that Ron takes Butt 1 and One-eye Pogson number six? Sir Ian and I will take 2 and 5, they are the ones needing most care and experience. Sneddick at 3 and Barley-Waters at 4. Jolly good, twenty minutes please gentlemen and your carriage will await."

The shooting party was driven in a covered wagon towed by a Land Rover to the uplands, from whence they were escorted to a series of

THE HIDE

bunkers comprising dry stone wall topped with turf, each enclosed by a pair of metal hoops. Skyes took Bullock to the one at the end and issued him with the shotgun he had previously used in Sykes back garden. With a few words of encouragement and instruction, Sykes deposited a leather satchel of cartridges and left for his own butt.

Bullock nervously loaded up, Botham winking at him from the neighbouring butt. Through his binoculars, Bullock could see a line of men and dogs on the horizon, evidently preparing to move towards them. After a sign from Blacklock, a horn was blown and the beaters advanced with shouts and thrashing of sticks.

"Up they go!" shouted Sykes as some dots on the horizon took wing. As the beaters got nearer, there was much fluttering activity as the dots became birds, and the shooters began to open fire, the smell of cordite soon wafting from the butts.

In Butt 4, Barley-Waters, a chinless wonder with a permanent and stupid grin was blasting away merrily.

"Hold your fire, Barley-Waters!" commanded Sykes, reminding Bullock of Lieutenant John Chard leading the Company of the British Army's 24th Regiment of Foot facing thousands of Zulus at the Rorke's Drift. "Wait til they come within range, man!"

Something brown sped towards Butt 2, Bullock raised his gun, trying to remember Syke's instructions at the *Hark to Bounty* pub. "Not shooting your neighbour's birds is paramount!" he muttered to himself, and held his fire.

At fifty yards, two reports from Butt 2 brought the bird crashing to Earth.

"Good shooting, Beefy!" shouted Sneddick, as he took his own aim. Soon, the air was filled with birds and the guns opened up, birds dropping like stones to left and right.

Bullock was momentarily frozen, in fear of breaching etiquette and not entirely sure what he was doing. At that moment, a grouse speared directly towards him, the scarlet combs over its eye flashed vivid

THE HIDE

against the brown moor.

"Your shot, Ron!" roared Sir Beefy.

"Your Shot, Ron!"

Despite the rapidity of the bird, Bullock's perception went into slow motion. The unblinking bird whooshed its white wings and zoomed towards Bullock, who aimed both barrels. "Bloody Hell, it's flying right at me!" thought Bullock, and instinctively pulled the trigger once, then twice.

Hit with both barrels at ten yards, the grouse exploded and dropped at Bullock's feet in his butt, now no more than a bloody mop of feathers. He stared down at his victim, wondering if it was the same perfect creature that had hurtled towards him, or was some kind of nightmarish feather duster.

Ian Botham in the next butt was in stitches as he lit up a small cigar. "Crickey, Ron - there's not much left for the pot on that one! If you'd

THE HIDE

have left it any later, it would have smashed you in the face!"

As the beaters and dogs retreated for a second drive, The General, Dolly and a number of other dogs shot out to pick up under the instruction of Blackstock and his men, and the shooters clambered out of their butts for a break, lighting up pipes and swigging from hip flasks.

"Yes, try and take them a little earlier, Ron," frowned Sykes, picking up the feathery rag from Butt 1.

"Sorry, Colonel, I didn't realise they were so bloody fast!"

"Ah that's what makes the grouse special! Up to 80mph, they reckon, and they veer like peregrines. Oh, nice shooting Sir Ian, I see you've bagged a double brace – and Sneddick, excellent shot to take that one going across the line at a hundred yards! As for you, Barley-Waters, less is more, sir. It's not the O.K. Coral you know!"

"Great shooting yourself, Colonel," commended Beefy. "I think you may have beaten me on that drive. Five or six?"

"Oh, I think only five, Ian, and I did wing one - though The General won't let him suffer long." As the dogs zoomed back and forth, a pile of corpses was being stacked up by Blackstock. "Oh, I say, yes, good haul gentlemen! Pogson, you were rather quiet, I think you blanked, old man." Sykes inspected One-Eye quizzically.

Pogson rolled up a cigarette and scrunched his one good eye. "Not sure I 'ave the appetite for the killin' today, Colonel. I come over all funny during the blasting."

"Oh don't be so soft man! I don't think you will be saying that when you are roasting your brace! Right men, back to your positions!"

On the second drive, there were fewer birds, but nevertheless plenty to aim at. Bullock was determined to get things right this time. As the line of shooters fired ahead, another bird headed down his sightline between the metal hoops. "Right, Ronny, steady…"

THE HIDE

"BLAM…BLAM!!" The bird dropped fifty yards ahead.

"YEEESSS!" shouted Bullock, punching the air and beaming over at Botham, who fixed him with a frown.

"Shit!" thought Bullock. "Have I taken Botham's bird? He don't look very impressed!"

"Woops! You've taken down a woodie there, Ron! Couldn't you see its beak?"

During the next break, The General hurtled off and retrieved a number of birds, including Bullock's woodcock.

"Oh Bloody Hell, who has shot the woodcock, for God's sake? Didn't I make it clear, no partridge or woodcock today? Oh Christ, it's got a tracking device on its back. The bloody Greenies will be on to us now. Look, we may as well eat it - Blackstock, take this tracker and chuck it in the sea later on will you, there's a good chap."

"Hoho, Ronno…you are in trouble now! Don't worry mate, you are in good company. I shot a bloody peregrine the other week – it just zoomed into the pigeons I was bagging! Cant be 'elped sometimes. Take a swig o' this, good malt this one." Sneddick beamed at his "twin", his eyes crazed with killing.

Bullock was grateful of a nip of Old Pulteney before resuming for the final drive of the morning. This time, there were far fewer birds, and the beaters came closer. A bird took off from thirty yards and rose above Butt 3. From the corner of his eye, Bullock saw his doppelganger take aim – was he going to take the beater's head off? Indeed he did not, as he swung his gun over his head, and swivelled a hundred and eighty degrees, following the bird as it flew away behind him.

"BLAM!" With one barrel, the bird fell dead.

"Great work, Sneddick!" called Sykes.

At that instant, a bird took off right in front of Bullock and zoomed

THE HIDE

over his head.

"Yours, Ron!" shouted Botham.

Apeing Sneddick, Bullock swivelled around, catching his gun barrel on the metal frame, and seeing the bird disappearing into the distance, instinctively gave it both barrels.

One of the lads helping Blackstock, a wiry youth in an ill-fitting country shirt and tie under his baggy Barbour was idly standing behind Bullock's butt, next to a copse of hawthorn, his hands in his pockets and looking vaguely bored.

"JESUS!" he had time to shout, as the barrels of Bullock's gun blazed suddenly in his direction. Instinctively, he leapt athletically into the hawthorns, his arms covering his face. The grouse flew on into the distance, to live another day.

The lad was extracted from the hawthorn by Blackstock, as the shooting party rushed to see what had happened.

"Oh 'eck, I am sorry lad. Are tha' OK? 'Ave ah shot thee!" panted Bullock.

"If you 'ave it's 'is own silly fault, Mr. Bullock, it were perefckly reasonable, you're 'up and over'. WHAT WERE YER DOIN' STOOD THURE BOY??!!" thundered Blackstock in the lad's face, which, though scratched by the thorns, seemed not to have been peppered by shot, though there were a couple of holes in his cap, and the hem of his Barbour looked like a very effective colander sieve.

"Aye, ah'm reet sorry mister," stammered the lad.

"AH SHOULD THINK YOU BLOODY ARE!" continued Blackstock. "NOW GO AND PICK UP! Sorry about this gentlemen, the young 'uns are a bit slow to learn these days. It'll do 'im no arm ter feel a bit o' lead in 'is bonce. Might drive some sense into 'im."

Bullock was first relieved to see there was no serious injury to the boy, and then astounded to learn that he wasn't receiving any blame.

THE HIDE

"Yep, bit of a low shot, Ron," frowned Sykes, "but nevertheless a valid one. "Keep your men on lower ground, please, Blackstock. Now then gentlemen, a fine mornings shooting! We have twenty-three grouse and a, erm, ahem, woodcock. Time for luncheon!"

Lunch was served in a 'bothy' on the moor which also served as a bird hide. It reminded Bullock of the princely hide at Rutland Water. The shot grouse were hung on the decking of the balcony which afforded expansive views of the moor and the Bowl of Bowland. Rather to Bullock's surprise, lunch was supervised by a black West Indian man in full dinner suit, who was greeted expansively by Sir Ian, who grabbed Joseph in a bear hug and lifted him off the ground.

"Joseph, you old bugger, how are you, my friend!" Botham released Joseph and engaged in a complex series of high fives and obscure handshakes.

"Ah'm fine Sah Ian, jes' fiiine! How is Sah Viv, you seen 'im lately?"

"Yah, I saw Viv in Antigua last winter, be going out for the one day series – I expect we'll be hooking up at some point."

"Han smokin' some fiiiine sinsemilla together, I shouldn't doubt!" grinned Joseph, taking the lids of various silver salvers.

"Might 'ave a quick puff or two," winked Botham. "Hope you brought the Evil Sauce with you, mate?"

"Ho, yes sah…when ah knew you was comin', ha made a good fresh batch!

The party tucked into game pies, cold cuts, hunks of bread, pickle and cheese, and for those needing a warming, a vat of Lancashire hot pot. All this washed down with beer, red wine and whisky. Bullock could not help but notice and indeed participate in the vast amount of alcohol that seemed to be consumed during a shoot - he was wondering if this was entirely wise and if anyone could possibly shoot straight afterwards. Hugh Barley-Waters seemed especially keen on a tipple; his face turned crimson as he scoffed a game pie and washed it down

THE HIDE

with a whole bottle of a decent Chateau Margaux Bordeaux.

"I say, chaps do join me in a splosh of this stuff I brought up from the pile in Fwance. Rather dense with a velvet coating – just like me – hawhawhaw!"

"Don't mind if I do, Hugh! Though I am a Chardonnay man, meself. Here's a good bottle I brought with me – try this one, lads," boomed Botham. "Now Ron, have you tried Joseph's Evil Sauce, you absolutely have to – if you can stand it hot, of course!"

"Oh don't worry about that, Sir Ian," blustered Bullock, accepting a glass from Barley-Waters. "Hot? They can't make it hot enough fror me. Ah'm from Barnsley, lad, like Boycott – no constitution is as strong as ours!"

"Right then," responded Sir Ian, exchanging winks with Joseph out of Bullock's eyeline, "Joseph, bring Mr. Bullock some of that venison pie - honestly Ron, it goes well with that, it's so strong it's a jelly rather than a sauce, and it's got a bit of fruitiness too. I hope you're not as rude as Boycs by the way – to say we don't get on might be something of an understatement."

"Ladle it on, Joe, go on, ah can tek it! Do you know, Sir Ian, I made a cricketing comeback a couple o' years ago. Not bad for 62 as ah was then? Eh? Oh, thanks Joseph, right, let's give it a go…bit o' pie, bit o' sauce, that's it…"

Botham and Joseph watched Bullock conspiratorially as he munched and continued his tale.

"Yeah, me an' me mate Tom, I was cricketer o' the year, actually, and yeah, though he's Barnsley like me, I can't get on with Boycott on the radio – what a boring moaner he is. But who do you think presented me with me cricketer of the year trophy, then? It was none other than…HELL FIIIIRRRRRE!"

Bullock's tongue and palate felt like they had been ignited by a tiny petrol bomb. His face went puce, tears streamed down his face and he started to pant like a dog. Like wasabi, the heat rose up his nose and he

THE HIDE

spluttered copiously, wafting his hand in front of his mouth, and hopping about like he'd been suddenly blighted by St Vitus's Dance.

Botham and Joseph fell about with laughter in a very literal way - Botham tumbled to the floor holding his knees, and Joseph used the table for support lest he should do the same.

"I get you some milk, Mr. Bullock – we told you it was hot!" Joseph went to the fridge for a glass of milk, which Bullock gargled and spat violently out beyond the balcony.

"Ah, you pair of buggers!" gasped Bullock. "You laced that sauce up. That old gag!"

"What?" frowned Botham. "You big wuss, we did no such thing!"

"Right then, Beefy Boy - let's see you 'ave some then!" challenged Bullock.

"Joseph, pass me the jar." Eyeing Bullock up like a gun fighter, Botham took the jar (which Bullock noticed bore a likeness of Joseph's face on the label below '*Joseph's Evil Sauce*') and a tea spoon from the table. Not breaking eye contact with the Yorkshireman, he spooned a dollop into his mouth, swallowed it, then took another, and another. He then washed it all down with a glass of Chardonnay.

"Aaaah. I can eat that stuff all day, Joseph, I hope you've brought a jar to take with me?"

"Ah yes, Sah Ian, ah got a few."

Bullock wondered if they had switched jars on him – Botham didn't seem to break sweat or bat an eyelid. He sniffed the jar that Botham had eaten from - even the chilli vapour from the jar made his eyes water.

"Well Sir Ian, that's mighty impressive. You are a tough 'un alright! Right, I am gonna take a jar o' that Joseph's and test it out on me family. Anyway Sir Ian, I bet you get bored of bein' asked about the cricket - tell us about your football career at Scunthorpe. I used to be a

THE HIDE

player me, you know. Ronny the Rhino - centre forward."

Following further convivial chat and banter, the men smoked outside and drank black coffee, as Sykes prepared them for the afternoon ahead.

"Right, gentlemen, we'd better walk orf this splendid lunch. First, three cheers for Joseph…hip hip…"

"HOOORAYYY!"

After the third cheer and a smiling bow from Joseph, Sykes resumed his usual expression of deadly seriousness.

"Now, we shall be walking up initially and the when we get to the moor we will let the dogs orf and do some shooting over the dogs. Pointers and setters at the ready, Mr. Blackstock?"

"Aye, pointers and setters, sir, all good dogs. Trained 'em meself, ah did."

"Right, gentlemen, no silly shooting. Keep the line, no dawdlers or bolters. If one of the dogs points up, then we approach with caution. Forwards!"

Duly delivered to the adjoining moorland valley, the guns formed a line and marched slowly up the slope, looking much like Captain Mainwaring's platoon in the introduction to *Dad's Army*.

"SNIPE! NO SHOTS!" commanded Sykes as a small beaky bird shot up from the ground.

"Well done, Ron!" grinned Botham. "Commendable restraint!"

"GROUSE! Bag him!"

THE HIDE

A volley of shots rang out and the grouse was duly added to the bag. Before they reached the level ground of the moor top, three more grouse were taken, and the shooting party paused as the dog handlers readied the eager dogs, who began scurrying around with noses to the ground.

Bullock sat back on a shooting stick lent to him by Sykes and admired the dogs and their handlers, and scanned the moor for grouse or birds he might add to his birding list. To his excitement, he spied an upright grey bird with a yellow breast and black eye band perched on a rock, recognising it immediately as a wheatear.

"Haha, try and grip me off Tommy De'Ath with your little Siberian dunnock things - you been gripped boy!" he muttered to himself, reaching for his notebook. Then the bird suddenly flew off, disturbed by something approaching - many somethings, in fact.

A group of people were appearing on the plateau of the moor, as they walked up the escarpment opposite the shooting party. They seemed to be waving flags and blowing whistles, but they did not look like beaters.

"Erm, Colonel Sykes! It seems we may have company..."

"What's that, Bullock? Let me see, man. May I use your binoculars, they are stronger than mine?"

Sykes focussed where Bullock was pointing, and grimaced, the sinews of his jaw flexing.

"Bloody hunt sabs! They are carrying banners and chanting something. For God's sake! Right men, stand together, we will see this lot orf. Sneddick, when they get to two hundred yards, just send a volley their way and rain some shot on 'em. They are on private land on a registered shoot. I am not having this on my watch."

Sneddick's volley caused some shrieking and consternation among the group of forty or so protesters, but their pelting seemed to make them more determined - and they continued to march forward.

THE HIDE

"Er, I think they've got a film crew with them, Colonel," reported Bullock. "And I recognise their leader…who is…look this way… blimey, yep! It's Chris Packman!"

"Oh, no way," groaned Botham. "Not that pillock! I was arguing with him on Radio 4 the other day. He called us the 'Nasty Brigade'!

"Yeah, that's what it says on one of their banners, Sir Ian. "Kick Mr. Nasty Off the Moor. " "Save Our Sky Dancers". And what's that one? …"Stop Harrying Harriers Now".

"Pah!" Blacklock the gamekeeper spat bitterly to the moss. "These townies 'ave NO idea about harriers takin' the young grouse. 'Ave they seen it? No! Well I 'ave! And the foxes…talkin o' which, I put some fox snares out where those chumps are blunderin' n trespassin'. I 'ope they get caught in one!"

"Right chaps, though I would dearly love to order you to stand in rank and take these buggers down, I fear that discretion is the better part of valour on this occasion. Please break you guns and I will meet the leader of this useless rabble."

"GOOD AFTERNOON! Do you people understand that you are trespassing and interrupting a licensed shoot? Not only are you endangering yourselves, you are disturbing the livelihood of a commercial sporting activity here, which contributes to maintaining the moorland ecosystem."

"Wubbish. Yes, good afternoon everyone, we are fully aware that we are twespassing - in the name of wildlife pwotection."

"I see. What is your name, sir?"

"What? Are you being funny?"

"Not in the least. Your name, sir, if we are to continue this conversation before I have the local constabulary come up here to remove you. Frankly, they have better things to do."

"Well… I am Chris Packman, obviously…"

THE HIDE

"How are you spelling that?"

"Are you joking? You know full well who I am! I am *Springwatch*. Well, amongst many other things."

"I don't watch television, I am afraid."

"I know who you are, dickhead." Realising that cameras were running, Ian Botham had approached Packman and spoken quietly in the conservationist's ear.

"Good Lord! If it isn't Beefy, caught wed handed! You are weally on a sticky wicket now, Ian! I quite enjoyed our little sparring match on the wadio the other day!"

"I didn't. I want you fired off the BBC and off *Springwatch*. You are using your position of privilege to influence your wrong-headed claim about good people like ourselves, out enjoying ourselves and paying for the moorland to support a balanced ecosystem as well as supporting these guys earn a decent living doing what they love doing - and their fathers and grandfathers before them. Now, if you are filming this charade, you better bring the camera over here so we can give our side of the story."

"Well, that sounds a lot better than being shot at. Just look at my bwolly! It's got a hole shot right through it! Turn the cameras off boys - let's talk mano-y-mano, then."

"Pah, I'm not as stupid as Sam Allardyce, Packman!" snarled Botham. "You are probably all wired up! Anyway we've got nothing to hide, have we lads?!"

"Fucking Hell, it's you!" declared Packman, spotting Bullock. "You are the bloke that sent that nuthatch cwawling up my twousers at Birdfair! I've still got the scars! I might have guessed you were in the Nasty Brigade! Is that your twin brother with you?"

Bullock approached to join the conversation. "If I am Mr. Nasty, mate, you are Mr. Nonsense. Yep, I am enjoying doing a bit of shooting, just as I enjoy me birdwatching as well. And I will certainly enjoy eating

THE HIDE

the grouse I've shot. I suppose you are a vegan, are you?"

"Nope, and that's not the argument. If you're going to eat it, if you're culling an animal that is otherwise damaging the environment because it's too abundant, I have no pwoblem with killing animals. But we are here for the hen hawiers. I don't suppose your gamekeeper likes them much, does he?"

Blackstock was eager to shout out in response, "NO!!" but wisely held his tongue and gazed up at the heavens, which supplied interesting ammunition. "Look up yonder, Mr. Packman. 'En 'arrier!"

Botham looked up with glee. "It is too! So much for us destroying them, she is destroying your argument!"

"That one bird does not disguise the facts - the latest science says there should be 500 pairs of hen hawier nesting on gwouse moors in the UK – in wecent years there have been fewer than 20 pairs. The lack of hen hawiers is due almost entirely to systematic, illegal and unrelenting persecution by gwouse shooting interests such as yours. The Fowest of Bowland SPA was partly designated because it was the stronghold for hen hawiers nesting in England and has often held double figures of pairs raising 10-120 chicks – this year there were none at all! We are tracking these animals, we know where they are 24 hours a day and they are vanishing on the gwouse moors and it is that simple."

The crowd behind Packman cheered. "What do you say about that, Sir Ian?!" shouted one man, waving a banner.

"I tell you what I think, mate - in the last 15 years there's not been one prosecution for persecuting a hen harrier in England here or anywhere else! I think you extremists should clear off and do some rug weaving and tree hugging, and then give your crystal balls a good rub. And take a look at the *No Moor Myths* film - that'll give you some hard facts you won't much like! "

"Booo! Cover up! Dark satanic moors!" bayed the crowd.

Sykes took control once more. "Right, you've made your point, Mr. Packman, and I think it's time for you and your little army to clear orf.

THE HIDE

If it is any consolation to you, you have ruined our afternoon and there is little point in our continuing. You may wish to continue your little tirade in the *Hark to Bounty* pub in the village – I am sure the locals would be most pleased to have an opportunity to meet the man that is attempting to destroy their heritage and livelihood, and who is a wildlife extremist, to boot. Good day, sir. About face, men – return to HQ."

As the shooting party retreated, one member dithered, nervously glancing at Packman. Pogson, the one-eyed hunter, rolled up a cigarette and scrunched his one good eye. With a sudden decisiveness, he started marching towards the Harrier Brigade, but was brought up short by a sudden jolt to his buttocks. He stopped in his tracks and slowly looked around, to see Blackstock jabbing him with his gun barrel.

"Got summat to say to the 'ippies about 'arriers 'ave we, George? I notice you didn't shoot owt today. Turnin' traitor are we? Sir Botham is quite right – not been one single prosecution for persecuting a hen harrier in England - and that's the way it's gonna stay. Well, unless you want me to shoot yer bollocks off? I don't mind. And that would be just the start, cocker."

"Steady on, Henry. I was…just going to ask for an autograph, actually, the wife likes old Packman…"

"Does she now? Violet's siding with the extremist now, is she? Oh, that'll not do, George. Perhaps you both need a visit, one o' these dark nights? Or…we can both 'ave a nice quiet pint together in the *Hark*. That would be nicer, now, would it not?"

"Erm, yes, it would Henry. Sorry. I haven't been feelin' meself today - must be comin' down wi' summat. Yep, lets go an' ave a dram together."

The gamekeeper removed his gun from between Pogson's legs and broke it over his shoulder, now sporting a species of evil grin last seen on the face of Albert Steptoe.

"Aye, there's a good lad. Them townies can bugger off and leave us to

THE HIDE

look after the countryside the way it should be looked after. Eh, George?"

Pogson looked forlornly across the moor at the retreating protesters, his mouth a queasy wavy line. "Aye, 'enry. 'Appen yer right."

Sykes was still absolutely furious two hours later, as he drove Bullock and The General back down the M6 in his Volvo.

"I mean, the sheer impertinence of the man!" he fumed. "How dare he trespass our private land and interrupt perfectly legal, enjoyable camaraderie and sportsmanship, in the company of a former captain of the English Cricket Team. It beggars belief, Ron, it really does!"

"Well, we got most of the day in, and what a great day too! I still can't believe I 'ave shot grouse with Ian Botham. What a character that man is! Anyway, Colonel, I must owe you a few bob for that, mustn't I? And three brace o' grouse an'all. By gum, I will look forward to Bella doin' them as a Sunday roast - why don't you come round and have them with us? And The General of course! Basker would like that, he loves The General!"

"That would be most kind, Ron. Invitation accepted! As for today's fee, well, I can offer you a substantial discount as a friend. Shall we say 5? Is that OK?"

"Oh dear, Colonel, that's too generous. I didn't pay for a single drink or owt all day!"

Bullock was seriously relieved - it had been stupid and highly atypical of him to accept Sykes' invitation to the shoot without considering its cost - he had been told by Colin that a day's grouse shooting could cost thousands of pounds! Taking his wallet from his breast pocket, he took out a five pound note and folded it up, ready to pop it nonchalantly into the top pocket of the Colonel's Harris tweed pocket.

"Well, perhaps 6, then if you don't mind, Ron? Obviously we need to pay the beaters and pickers up, fuel, Joseph for lunch, drinks in the *Hark* - three brace of grouse, usually forty quid a bird...I usually tip Blackstock a fifty for coming along..."

Bullock began to sweat, and slowly slipped the fiver into his own breast pocket.

"Six...?" he ventured, feeling suddenly queasy.

"No, I insist. As we were, Ron. Let's say five hundred as it was your first trip. You can pay the proper price if you fancy coming again - and I certainly hope you will!"

"Five..." managed Bullock weakly. "Five...hundred..."

It took all the bravado that Bullock could muster to stay cool. "Yes, five hundred! Very generous of you, Colonel, for a very memorable day indeed. Five hundred. Just five hundred pounds. I will drop you a cheque in next week, if that's OK?" He stared ahead, hoping that Sykes would not catch the evident dismay writ large across his face. Bella was going to kill him - or more likely insist on five hundred quid to blow on a day's caprice of her own.

"Jolly good. Charged Beefy three grand! And that chump Barley-Waters four! Mind you, they can afford it, what?"

"Aye, I suppose they can." Bullock turned his bull neck to look around at the six floppy grouse and the woodcock in the rear compartment peering out of a plastic bag nestled next to a jar of *Joseph's Evil Sauce*, mentally calculating that each bird had cost him over seventy pounds apiece. Still, it had been quite an experience - and at that price, certainly one not to be soon
repeated. Bullock decided that his shooting days were over, and that it was better to concentrate on...The List!

- CHAPTER SIX -

Bittern Moon

Wherein Colin exchanges one inconvenient malady for another and is aided and abetted by his amanuenses. Bullock solves a bullying problem with the aid of a hedge. Here unfolds the dreadful tale of the squalid heron. There is a bad start to the New Year for Dirty Colin.

October provided Oldside with a splendid autumn of low rainfall, mild temperatures and little wind; the manifold shades of gold, ruby, orange, ochre and lingering green ornamented the trees and shrubs and the odour of fallen lime leaves and emerging autumn fungi perfumed the cool air.

Colin (no longer Dirty Colin), apparently cured of his Tourette's malady, was gripped by the return of another equally inconvenient one. After dropping off Tom De'Ath following their trip to the Lakes, he had returned home to feed his snakes, but could not get out of his head the Siberian accentor mega-rare migrant showing in East Yorkshire. Very early the following morning, he checked the bird alert app on his phone to see if the bird was still about, and with that confirmed, he made a 400 mile round day trip in order to witness the little brown bird and tick it off both his Life and Year List.

On his long and lonely drive home, he had calculated that his Year List was none too shabby; especially with his mentoring of Bullock and De'Ath, he was making frequent trips around the British Isles and on a service station pit stop, he worked out that he was already over 250 birds for the year, and that the milestone of 300, which he had only reached twice before, was again achievable. Even, he considered, he could push on from there - to break his personal best of 329 and possibly even surpass Sonny Robards for the most birds ticked during a year!

Regaining the road, one part of his brain was telling him that such a quest was meaningless and obsessive, that he had "been there and done it" and there was absolutely no need to do it again. But another part of his cerebellum was clamoring otherwise. He imagined himself strutting around next year's Birdfair, attracting admiring attention from the cognoscenti, as the very King of the Birders. The two voices competed with growing animosity, well after he returned home and turned in for the evening. But during the night, the battle continued to rage, and he woke blearily feeling that he had enjoyed little rest as he chomped a bowl of Cornflakes in the pre-dawn darkness of 6am. By the time the light broke, he found himself in the David Smith Hide at Clarendon, ticking off the early winter migrants that he had missed in the previous January. The next thing he knew he was visiting the Isles of Scilly for a day, and spending a night at the bird observatory at the island of Skokholm in west Pembrokeshire, ticking storm petrels and Manx shearwaters.

He kept his growing obsession quiet; his querulous and opposed brain-sides insisted that he should at least feel a little ashamed of his increasingly addictive behaviour, as if he had suddenly developed a taste for wearing women's stockings or incessantly playing *Candy Crush Saga*. The dualism inside made him anxious and morose; he turned off his Rare Bird Alert App and chucked his phone on the sofa, but twenty minutes later he turned it on again and desperately scanned the updates.

He cancelled a meeting with Bullock and De'Ath at Clarendon Marsh, thinking petulantly that they would want to watch everyday autumnal mundanities - De'Ath had even taken to photographing autumn fungi, and that was no use to him. Instead he drove alone to Cley in Norfolk to tick a western purple swamphen; the iridescent moorhen gave him no aesthetic pleasure at all, as he moodily stomped back to his car. Back at Oldside before the evening light had gone despite the clocks having gone back, he popped into Brocks for a mug of tea, where he sat hunched and alone with his back to the café, dismissive of the

THE HIDE

common birds clamoring at the feeders by the window, and making frenetic hieroglyphical pencil notes in his book as to where tick number 287 was coming from, conceiving in his spinning head a trip to the Shetland Isles. His malevolent reverie was broken by a familiar voice and a slam on his back of earthquake magnitude.

"Col! I thought you weren't 'ere today!"

"Hiya, Ron," replied Colin wearily, furtively pocketing his notebook and phone. "Yeah, sorry, I had some business, you know, family business to attend to. Alright, Tom. No, I won't join you, thanks, I've erm, just had a cuppa, I erm, should be off, really."

Bullock eyed his new friend and mentor, who was avoiding his beam-like eye contact as De'Ath went to fetch two teas and Kit-Kats.

"Eh, you shoulda been 'ere this morning, Col!" grinned Bullock. Colin's bad brainside suddenly whipped up into a fury, and he turned on Bullock, almost viciously.

"What? Why? Did I miss something? You didn't grip me Ron, did you? Not on me home patch?"

"Eh, calm down, son!" To Bullock's smiling face was added a frown. "You don't look well, Col. You need a shave, boy - that stubble don't suit you. Everythin' areet, lad?"

"I'm fine Ron - what did you see, this morning? Tell me!"

"Well, oh thanks, Tom. We was sittin' 'ere, weren't we, Tommo, just watchin' the birdies like…"

"Oh, fantatstic flock of goldfinches, one on every feeder hole - look at this photo I took with my phone, Colin…"

Colin greedily inspected the grainy image proffered to him by De'Ath of blurs of gold and red, trying to ascertain if some rarity was among the charm of goldfinches.

"Any 'ow," continued Bullock, "we was sittin' 'ere, and then this

THE HIDE

critter comes bolting out of that patch o' nettles over yonder and then scrambles up the table - I thought it was a squirrel at first...but Tom goes...it's a STOAT! There's a stoat on the bird table! And that's what it was Col - fancy that, a stoat!"

Colin managed a smile, more out of relief than amusement, and leaned back into his chair.

"I'm just off for a wee," announced De'Ath. "'Scuse me, chaps!"

When De'Ath was gone, Bullock took Colin's arm. "Col, I can see summat's up wi' yer. If yer don't wanna talk about it, fine by me, but if you want an ear, mate, as Mark Antony might say, you can be lending mine."

Colin looked away, with all the furtive tension of a secret alcoholic desperate to share his shame.

"I...I...I...ah Ron! I'm twitching again! I mean properly twitching!" Colin's voice was thick with emotion and self-pity, the opposite of the cocksure Colin that Bullock was getting to know.

"I mean, I stood you two mates up this morning. There weren't no family business! I stood you up to tick a bloody swamphen in the back end of Norfolk. Just a tarted up moorhen, Ron. I didn't see the sea, the beach, I didn't talk to anyone...I just put a tick in this fucking book!" Colin ripped the dog-earned journal from his Barbour pocket and tossed it onto the table. "Number 286 for the year! So what, eh!"

"Eh Col!" winked Bullock. "I reckon you are fully cured of the old Tourette's!"

"Why you say that, then?"

"You just said the f-word in an appropriate context at normal volume without leapin' about!"

"Did I?" smiled Colin, this time more genuinely. "That's good, ain't it, mate. But I won't push my luck with the old Gordon Ramsay word! But to be honest, Ron, it feels like I've got something worse. It's all I

THE HIDE

think about! Hey, don't tell Tom, I know he's just really diggin' the nature thing, and I wouldn't want to spoil that."

"Col, I get it! I do! I am the Barnsley twitcher! Not in your league, mind - I tell you what I want to do. I want to see all the birds in the *Observer's Book of Birds*. All two 'undred and fo'ty-three of 'em! "

"Hahaaa! Ron, you are priceless, mate. The Observer's Twitcher! Right then, yer on. Come on, get your little brown book out - let's see where you are with it!"

De'Ath returned from the toilet to find his buddies guffawing over the *Observer's* and making copious notes.

"Right, let's start at the beginning, Col. Magpie - done, common as muck. Jay, done. Carrion crow…RRRRAARK…done. Hooded crow?"

"Weeel, not likely that one, Ron. Isle of Man is your best bet."

"Isle of Man - I went on me honeymoon there yonks ago, so… therefore, de facto, I must 'ave seen one. Tick."

"Well," chuckled Colin, "that might be so, and in fact it's just a race of the carrion crow, so not really a different species. But up to you. Jackdaw, done. Ah, now then, chough. More difficult. A mate of mine has helped re-introduced them on Jersey, I reckon that's your best chance. Loads of other good stuff over there too."

"Ok, I will write that one down on me 'to do' list. Raven, done. Rook, done. Hawfinch, done. Greenfinch, done. Twite, done. Redpoll, goldfinch, linnet, crossbill, brambling, chaffinch, bullfinch, siskin, all done. Hmm, cirl bunting, nope, write that one down. Yellowhammer, yep, corn bunting, nope. Snow bunting, nope. Reed bunting, yep. What's this bugger…golden oriole?"

"Yeah, tough one, Ron, a proper twitch, that is. Lakenheath Reserve in Suffolk is best, but you'll have to wait 'til it comes back next summer."

"Right, there are no pictures of Ortolan and Lapland bunting, so they don't count. I only do the ones with pictures. House sparrer, yep, tree sparrer, yep. Eh, look at this fine feller. Waxwing?"

"Ah now, we will get these guys soon, I need 'em too for my Year List. Great birds, Ron. They are like little punk Cossack invaders, they swarm in, raiding all the berries, sometimes flocks 'o them - they call them 'irruptions' and they call like jingle bells. They are not shy either - they often bomb in to the PIHSIL car park and strip all the berries off. We will definitely see them - I just hope before the end of the year though. We need the cold weather to come early."

"It sounds like you are pushing on with your Year List again then, Colin?" De'Ath slurped through his tea.

"Er, yeah, Tom. I just spilled the beans to me father confessor here. I am sorry to say the bug has caught me again and I've gone a bit mad with the twitching."

"Tom, you might not be up for this lad, but I am gonna 'elp Col get 'is 300 and beyond before the year ends. And 'e is gonna help me be the Observer's Twitcher."

"No, no, I am up for it," replied De'Ath enthusiastically, munching a disappointingly small *Wagon Wheel*. "I am not as bothered as you two, but I like seeing the birds. That golden oriole looks magnificent!"

"Ok then, all for one and one for all - the Birding Musketeers!" toasted Bullock with his tea mug. "All for one…"

"And one for all!" came the chorus as they clinked mugs.

The study of the *Observer's* continued. There were gaps in the wagtails, pipits, warblers, owls, and several notables including nightingale, nightjar, shrike, wryneck and hoopoe.

"Oh, bloody 'ell…golden eagle! Not many o' them on me bird table. I've seen one at a zoo - does that count?"

"Fraid not, Ron, but if you fancy a trip to the Isle of Mull, you can be sure of a tick…and a capercaillie whilst we are at it?"

"Hmm, we'll 'ave to see about that. I might just stick to an England and Wales Observer's List. Spoonbill? Never 'eard o' that one. Eh up! The bittern. I knew he'd come up…come on, Tom…do yer silly dance, then!"

De'Ath was always game for a bit of bitterning and booming, and stood up to do so, alarming a posse of pensioners who had just come in for an over-stuffed corned beef bap.

"Yep, I am certainly gonna need old bittern, Ron. I hope he pops in here and saves me a trip to Dungeness. Nice bitterning, Tom. You are getting good at that!"

"Hey look, next one in the book, turtle dove. *Three French hens, two turtle doves, and a partridge in a pear tree!*" sang Bullock. "I remember them being common when me and Tich were lads. *Prrr prrr prrrr,* it went."

"Yeah! They are not so common these days, it was the sound o' summer, weren't it, back in the day! Eh, listen to me ring tone on me 'phone…"

"Eh, that's good that is, Col. Turtle dove ring tone. I'm gonna get one o' them. Woodpecker prob'ly. What do you do, just record it off the RSPB website?"

"Yeah, exactly. What about you, Tom?"

"Eh?"

"You know, what bird would you have as your ring tone?"

"Erm, well, a nightingale probably - not that I've ever heard one, I have to say."

"Do you know, I think that the nightingale song is totally over-rated," opined Bullock. "I listened to a recording of one, and it sound just like a blackbird to me. 'Ave you seen one, Col?"

THE HIDE

"Well, they are not easy to spy, Ron. You can hear them in Wyton Wood, but not easy to spot. But it's still a tick if you hear them, you know."

"Really? Well that means I can tick the tawny owl off then! Heard plenty o 'them twit-twoooooòing round our way!"

"Yeah, you can. 'Course it gets a bit controversial on the twitching circuit, so it's better if you can see 'em too. That's the thing about bittern. No problem hearing 'em but to see 'em creeping about in a reedbed - that's a different kettle o' worms! Anyway boys, I do feel so much better I shared me guilty secret with you, and if you are up for it, let's plan a few more trips, shall we?"

"Well, I can't promise 'owt, with 'er 'indoors like, but let's see. I tell yer, I wouldn't mind seein' an eagle in the wild, and that's for sure."

"Well, don't get too excited Ron, they are generally pretty high up. I know you, you'd be wanting one on yer arm, eating bits of meat! Anyway, I promise to give you a shout if anything local comes up."

As November turned cold in Oldside, the colour faded from the trees and they shed their leaves into the damp and trampled brownish mush. Many days of hazy rain dulled the skies to grey and the birdlife in the garden and the Marsh seemed to dwindle. But none of this could dampen Colin's twitching fervour - he sped about the country in his Land Rover now an unashamed mega-twitcher. Bullock declined to join him on his trip to Scotland, where he passed three hundred for his Year List. Hooking up with his old mate Neil Singleton on Jersey, he caught the last of the winter migrants and a couple of rarities, the Lapland bunting and Richard's pipit, both inconspicuous brown birds but twitching gold dust.

The dread of the twitcher - the dip - when a long journey was rewarded by no sighting of the hunted bird, was spared to Colin; everything he searched for - he found. He was on fire, and he sped past 300 with a pallid harrier in Somerset. And then - even better news.

Word came that the only other man with 300+ sightings for the year, the lugubrious Sonny Robards, had suffered an accident. Clambering on a drystone wall in Northumberland to catch a glimpse of a red-breasted flycatcher, he had been alarmed by the bellow of a shepherd aggressively waving a crook at him, to "get off me wall, you blattering prat!" Catching the toe of his walking boot in the crevasse of a topping stone, he had lost his balance and fell with a shriek to the sopping moss below, where he had landed badly. The muttering shepherd had been obliged to ferry him off the moor with his Yamaha quad bike and thereafter to Morpeth A & E, where he was diagnosed with a broken femur and plastered up. Having no friends, he was obliged to leave his car in a layby in Low Newton and take the train home to Leicester, where he was laid up and ordered to rest for a month.

Far from being sympathetic, the twitching community responded with unmitigated glee, one man posting on the *Twitchers Chat Site* that it was a shame that he hadn't fallen onto high voltage electricity wires or into a deep limestone gryke never to be seen again. Colin was elated, sending Robards a message to "get well late," as he sped off to Oare Marshes in Kent to tick a long-billed dowitcher.
November came to a freezing and frosty end as the Scandinavian migrants arrived, allowing Colin to keep his promise to show Bullock and De'Ath an irruption of waxwings. Colin telephoned Bullock to say that he was staying with an old bird watching friend of his in the West Country and that they had encountered the day before a huge flock of the punk-Cossacks at a nature reserve in Gloucestershire, shortly after ticking off a blue rock thrush at a cul-de-sac in Stow-on-the-Wold.

"Yeah, the usual rubbish from the armchair trolls saying the "rockie" was an escapee and didn't count on the list, Ron, but I can tell you it was a genuine vagrant. Anyway, pop over tomorrow morning - the wax-chappies will still be around and the forecast is for a bright day. And let's just say - you might have seen my mate on the telly."

"What, not another TV birding celebrity?"

THE HIDE

"No, not exactly. Anyway, come over, I think you'll like him. And if you don't like him, you will love these birds!"

Therefore, after an early start, Bullock and De'Ath found themselves bumping down the track of Robinswood Hill Country Park just outside of Gloucester in Bullock's Rover. They parked up and got into their gear. It was a perfect, cold, blue-skied morning with a rime of frost, the white edged grass crunching under their boots. All standing water had frozen - each pond they passed had thick glassy lids, and the larger water-bodies looked as though they would be safe for skating on.

They headed down the track to the first hide, which overlooked a large area of regenerating scrub, semi-woodland and a large pool, where Colin had told them to meet. Entering the hide, they were pleased to see Colin's bald head hunched over a ledge, next to him another bald fellow, save for a plume of long wispy hair growing from the back of his head.

"Eh up, Col! We made it!"

"Hiya, Ron! Hiya, Tom!" Colin rose and greeted them cheerfully. "What a great morning to see the wax-chappies! There's a big flock doing the rounds, they will be back here soon, I am sure of it."

Colin's friend didn't get up or look around – he seemed to be scrawling something in a notebook. Another semi-autistic celebrity, thought Bullock, getting ensconced at a bench with a series of grunts, then carefully cleaned the lenses of his binoculars.

"Hey lads, this is my mate Bill! Well, Mark actually, but I think you'd know him as Bill?"

Bill stopped his scrawling and looked round at the new visitors with slightly crazed blue eyes. He stroked his grey goatee beard and fiddled with a silver ring in his left ear, before extending his hand to them both. "Alright, lads."

"It's Bill Bailey!" yelped De'Ath immediately.

"It is, Tom!" grinned Colin. "I know all the stars, don't I?"

THE HIDE

"Bill…?" Bullock looked hard at Bill Bailey, and wracked his recognition. "Oh! Are you one of the *Hairy Bikers*, lad? I can't think which one though?"

Bill, Colin and De'Ath laughed heartily.

"No you daft prat, Ron! Bill Bailey - haven't you seen him on TV?"

"Erm…no…?"

"I have!" exclaimed De'Ath excitedly. "*Black Books*! Brilliant that was, I am a big fan of *Black Books*! And he's on *Have I Got News for You*…and *QI*!"

"Oh thanks, buddy," replied Bailey in a London accent faintly flavoured in West Country , "glad you enjoyed the progs. Erm, your mate evidently doesn't watch those shows, does he?"

"I don't, lad! So, what are you then, like an anchor man or summat, like that Steven Fry, or what's 'is name?...Bella likes him…Carr, that's it, Jimmy Carr?"

"Well, not really. I'm a stand-up comedian when it comes down to it."

"Really! What like Frank Carson? Or Ken Dodd? Eh, we are in for some fun this mornin' then!"

"Well, like a lot of comedians, Bill isn't very funny when he's in normal life, are you Bill," explained Colin, sitting down and rooting a flask out of his pack.

"No, I'm not," agreed Bill. "Though I'm not as bad as Russell Brand when he's off duty - bloody miserable he is. And old 'Sir' Steven Fry - you don't want to get him on a bad day, I can tell you!"

"Are you a celebrity birdwatcher as well then…like Bill Oddie or Packman? We met them at the Birdfair."

"Nah, I done some nature shows like, but this is my hobby. Been

THE HIDE

doing it since I was a kid in the West Country, ticking the birds off in me little *Observer's Book of Birds*."

"Nowt wrong wi' the *Observer's Book of Birds*, Bill. Me and Col got off on the wrong foot about that, didn't we, lad?" observed Bullock.

"Aye, we did. These are the lads that cured me of me Tourette's, Bill. Shock therapy!"

"Well, I am pleased for you, Col, but I used to love your Tourette's. Especially when somebody came in the hide whilst we were birdwatching. They never stayed long, eh! Oh, thanks, mate, a drop of coffee would be grand. My mug's on here somewhere...here you go."

Bill extended his mug, which read "I love TITS" above small doodles of bearded, blue, great, crested and other tit species, into which Colin poured coffee from his flask.

"Do you think that mug is funny, Bill?" frowned Bullock.

"Yes. Yes, I do. Don't you?"

"In a word, Bill, no. You would probably enjoy Chris Packman's underpants, I reckon. Are you an artist, as well? I see you are sketching a bird in yer notebook."

"Yeah, actually I've got a little publishing deal happening. It's going to be called '*Bill Bailey's Remarkable Guide to British Birds*'. It's sort of a humorous and personal guide to my favourite British birds, with drawings, notes and cartoons. Sort of a quirky guide."

"I don't want to be rude, Bill, but if this is the standard of yer drawing, I should get yourself an illustrator to work with. My daughter-in-law Surinda may be able to 'elp yer - she's a good drawer, she is. What is this meant to be?"

"Ah that one, yeah, that's a crow."

Bullock laughed out loud. "You'll never get that published, lad! Even if you are a celebrity. It's rubbish, is that!"

THE HIDE

Bailey narrowed his eyes and took back his notebook. There was an icy silence for a while.

"Here they come!" announced Colin. "The wax-chappies are back! Bill, keep your eyes out for a cedar waxwing - not been one in the UK since 1996, when I found one in Nottingham. White undertail instead of orange, and bit thinner and sleeker - you never know with birding! "

In a violent trilling flurry, a large gang of Bohemian waxwings came crashing into a rowan tree and like a group of vandals smashing up a shop, they grabbed and gobbled every berry on the tree.

"WOW!" enthused Bullock. "Look at these guys go - I love these wax-chappies!"

"They reckon old *Bombycilla garrulous* is called the waxwing 'cos it looks like the wings have been dipped in sealing wax," noted Bailey. "Can you see? And the name 'Bohemian' is in reference to their nomadic behaviour during the winter, when they are continually on the move in search of fruit and berries. And 'garralous' 'cos they don't fucking shut up."

"Eh, put that in yer book, Bill!" guffawed Bullock. "'Ang on, I'll do a little doodle for yer…" De'Ath looked forlornly on as Bullock scrawled rapidly on his notepad, annotated it with arrows and squiggles, tore it off his pad and handed it to Bailey.

THE HIDE

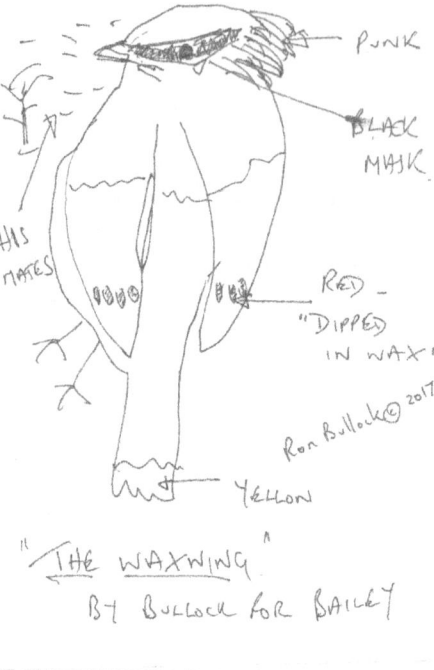

De'Ath rather feared that Bullock's introduction to the celeb wasn't going very well.

"Er, thanks, Ron. Yeah, may use that. Very, erm, expressionist, isn't it."

"You want to get in touch with Fred Hopple at Seahouses. He paints crap pictures of birds an' all. Tom's got one of his gannets aint yer, lad? Did you ever put it up?"

"Er, no. Dot took one look at it and put it in the pantry," replied De'Ath with a watery smile.

Just then, a small white object bounded onto the frozen pool before them - it was a golf ball.

"What the…where did that come from?" exclaimed Bullock.

THE HIDE

"Oh there's a golf course adjacent to the reserve," explained Colin, matter-of-factly. "You can always be sure of finding a few golf balls here. The crows pick 'em up sometimes, thinking they are missing eggs."

"Eh, you should add that to your drawing, Bill," suggested Bullock. "It'll give it some interest."

"Hey, that's a good idea that, Ron. I will add it right now!" responded Bailey enthusiastically. Bullock rolled his eyes at De'Ath, and focused his optics on the ice-stranded golf ball.

"Eh up, that's a Titleist Pro V1 ball, that is! Must be Tony Jacklin playin' over there. Oh 'eck! It ain't Tony Jacklin, but whoever it is - he is coming on the ice to get 'is ball!"

The birders observed with interest a portly brown-skinned man in extremely expensive modern golf wear, warily stepping across the ice, using his pitching wedge to test the thickness in front.

"I think I know that bloke," murmured Bailey. "I reckon…that is Naughty Boy!"

"Well he certainly is a naughty boy," returned Bullock, "walking about on a bird reserve on thin ice. What's he up to?"

"No, not *a* naughty boy, Ron, Naughty Boy. He's a record producer and DJ. Works with all the top musicians - Emeli Sandé, Leona Lewis, Cheryl Cole, Ed Sheeran, Gabrielle, you name 'em. I didn't know he was a golfer though! OI! NAUGHTY BOY! IT'S BILL BAILEY! OVER HERE!" Bailey leaned out of the hide and waved at the celebrity record producer, who had arrived at his ball. He squinted, shading his eyes from the low sun.

"Hello, Bill! What are you doing in that shed?"

"Bird watching. I didn't know you were a golfer?"

"Yeah, getting pretty good. I never hit one off ice before though…

watch this!"

"He can't play that…it's out of bounds!" remarked Bullock indignantly. But that is just what Naughty Boy was preparing to do. He took up a stance over the ball and looked over the pool and trees to the green beyond.

"This'll be interesting, he certainly won't be able to take a divot!" Bullock focused his binoculars on the ball as Naughty Boy took a backswing.

"Sounds like you know your golf a bit then, Ronno," remarked Colin, also watching carefully.

"Oh aye, played a bit. Not seriously like, but I can hit a good long drive, me…CHRIST ALMIGHTY!"

Naughty Boy's swing, due to him raising his head too early, resulted in what golfers call a 'fat shot' or 'duff'. Had he been on grass, the club head would have stubbed into the turf well before the ball which would then dribble off a few yards. However, on the ice, the duff shot had a more catastrophic impact. Naughty Boy's pitching wedge clattered into the ice, and his planted feet immediately lost their grip, whereupon he pitched backwards. His considerable posterior slammed down with a force sufficient to smash a large hole, into which he immediately disappeared, with a yowl.

"JESUS!" yelled Bailey, joining the others in rushing for the door of the hide. "Naughty Boy has gone through the ice!"

Fortunately for the celebrity music producer, the pool was not deep, and he was able to scramble like a seal out of the hole, and propel himself across the ice towards the alarmed rescuers. Bullock braved the ice and hauled the slithering mammal to the safety of the bank; Naughty Boy staggered gasping into the hide with aid of Colin and Bullock, and sat sopping and dripping on one of the benches.

"That was a daft thing to do," opined Bullock as he removed a pair of Nike Lunar Control 4 golf shoes from the DJ's feet. "Do I call you Boy or Naughty by the way?"

THE HIDE

"You can call me Shahid, mate. Yeah, 'specially as me mate was videoing it. That'll be going viral that will, even as we speak. How you doing, Bill, we met a Knebworth didn't we?"

"That's right, I was playing the Sonisphere Festival, erm…2011?"

"A musician as well, Bill?" asked a simpering De'Ath, wrapping the shivering Naughty Boy in his Barbour coat.

"Well, you know Tom, bit o' this, bit o' that. Not much of a golfer though. Unlike old Shahid Shackleton McIlroy here!"

Colin had a change of clothes in his car, and it wasn't long before Naughty Boy had assumed the garb of a birdwatcher. His panting and anxious golf partner joined him in the hide by the more conventional route of the footpath. Grateful of hot coffee, the DJ was able to laugh as much as any of them at the I-Phone video, which was duly posted to YouTube, quickly becoming the sensation of the day's internet.

"Well lads, I'd better get home for a hot bath and international internet ignominy. Come on DJ Fat Rascal, let's split. Thanks lads, I might give this bird watching thing a go – looks like a bit of good fun!"

As the light in the hide began to fade and the birds flocked in to roost, the birders decided to call it a day and headed back up the track.

"Eh Bill, there was no need for you to do yer stand-up comedy today was there, mate? That was one o' the funniest things I've ever seen, old Naughty Boy crashing through the ice!"

"Yeah, I'm gonna do a doodle of that for me book, Ron. Unless you'd care to do one for me, of course? Hey, and any time you want to come and give me a right royal heckling at one of my shows, just give Colin a call. I'm touring next year so come and see me. If we don't see each other again on the birding circuit, that is. See yer Col, even without your Tourette's that was the best fun I've had with me clothes on for a long time. Waxwings and Shahid Shackleton McIlroy in one day - what a hoot!"

After Bailey had gone, De'Ath was anxious to press Colin for some Bill Bailey show tickets, but thought he'd leave it a while. Bullock was more interested in Colin's twitching progress.

"With the blue rock thrush this morning – and that's a bloody counter, that is - that's 317 for the year, Ron. Nowhere near the British record of 386, of course, but there's more clear water between me and Robards than between Oxford and Cambridge in recent Boat Races. Some decent spots next month and I should be home and dry by New Year's Eve!"

Bella's eleven-year old grandson Tanaga was becoming difficult. As an only child to a giant Fijian father and statuesque British mother, his already elongated stature was the cause of teasing and even bullying at his new secondary school, where much shorter older boys, intimidated by Tanaga's height, decided to harry him like rooks after a buzzard. His slow-witted father didn't notice his son turning introspective and forlorn, and his mother was too exhausted after her shift as a recruitment consultant to do much else than make him a meal and see that he did his homework. Retreating to his bedroom, he blared out agrressive rap music, and stalked the streets playing solitary *Pokemon Go*.

Tana had always been Bella's unashamed favourite of her six grand-children; she didn't see a lot of the three 'French boys' who lived with their divorced mother in Montpelier and the 'Indian twins' Petula and Jitendra who lived in Kettering were very sweet but only holiday visitors. Tana lived down the road and often just walked into Bella's kitchen with his school rucksack and wordlessly turned on the TV, where he would indulgently be served tea and buttered crumpets.

"What's up, love?" sighed Bella, lighting up an Embassy and eyeing the sullen form of the long-legged boy, his head shaggy with embryonic dreadlocks, expressionlessly staring at *Adventure Time with Finn & Jake*.

"Nothing, Nana…" he replied in an irritated whine.

"I don't believe you. Come on, you can tell your old Nana. I know when my boy's not right!"

Tana shot his nana an irritated glance. "It's nothing, Nana. It's…" And then he did something that Bella had never seen before in her happy-go-lucky, slightly mischievous and life-loving grandson. He burst into a welter of sobbing tears, which ran down his dusky cheeks and flattened nose like the waterfalls of Tavoro.

Bella sprang up and took him protectively into her arms, perching on the arm of his chair and ruffling his locks, compressing him in the hug of a matriarchal grizzly bear.

"Ah, sorry, Nana," he sobbed. "Er, I can't breathe and your fag ash is going in me hair."

"Right, let's get to the bottom of this," Bella boomed, releasing her cub and stubbing out her cigarette in a nearby ash tray. "First job, get your coat on - we are going to the sweet shop for some strawberry bonbons." She tore off her apron and went out into the hall for her coat.

"But it's raining, Nana. And I'm too old for strawberry bonbons."

"You are never too old for strawberry bonbons. And look - here comes Grandpa! He will cheer you up."

"Oh no! Don't tell him I cried, Nana!" Tana shot up the stairs to wash his face and blow his nose.

"Areet love?" puffed Bullock, emerging from the porch and starting to take his coat off.

"I am, but summat's up with Tana. Keep your coat on, we are going down the parade. Summat's up at school, I reckon. He won't say but he's upset."

"Hey, how's me big feller! Give us your best punch!"

A slightly restored Tana swung his bony little fist into his grandad's massive fleshy hand as he ran downstairs.

"Eh? Call that a punch? Give me another! THAT'S more like it. Come on, let's all go down the sweetie shop, I wouldn't mind some sherbet lemons. And you can tell me how your new school is goin'".

Rather reluctantly, Tana slouched down The Nook between his grandparents in the drizzle, Bella holding her brolly emblazoned with *Gala Bingo* protectively over his head. Turning into the main road towards a parade of shops, Tana stopped dead. At the bus stop, three youths of about fourteen were messing about with their mobiles and passing round a cigarette.

"Oh no!" yelped Tana. "It's them! It's the Enemy Posse!"

Bullock narrowed his eyes, as the youths caught site of their quarry. One of them flicked the cigarette at them.

"Oh look, it's Mowgli! Is that your Mum and Dad? What gimmers! I bet they adopted you after the wolf pack chucked you out!"

"Let's go back, Grandpa. They are the bullies. Let's just go back, shall we?"
"Bullies yer say! Well, they are not keeping me from me sherbets! Proceed, my boy."

The three youths stared insouciantly as they approached. One of the lads, a real badass nicknamed Pug, made a grab for Bella's voluminous handbag, not meaning to steal it, but to cause alarm and offence. He had picked the wrong victim. Bella swung around in fury, and furled up the *Gala* umbrella.

"Oh no," groaned Bullock. "He is gonna get it now!"

THE HIDE

Bella set about Pug with ferocity, pulverizing him with the brolly. He cringed over, receiving hefty blows to his back and head. "OW! You mad woman! Get off me! Lads…get her!"

But Pug's henchman weren't fancying tackling the whirling dervish with the Gala Bingo brolly, as she span around, applying slicing blows to Pug's legs.

"NOW DO THAT AGAIN!" shouted Bella. "GO ON! Try and steal me bag again, I dare you!"

"You silly old woman! Just wait til we get Mowgli on his own. He'll pay for this!" Pug straightened himself up, and spat at Bella, narrowly missing her. That was an even bigger mistake. An outraged Bullock simply picked the lad up by pinning his arms to his sides, carted him to an adjacent privet hedge, and threw him into it. Apart from his two splayed legs, Pug simply disappeared from view.

"Go on, Tana," whispered Bullock in his grandson's ear. "Give him a good kick in the goolies."

Tana needed no further encouragement. With all the pent up fury that had built up during his harassment, he let out a roar and swung his right leg between Pug's legs, who squealed in anguish.

"Now then, what about you two pillocks? Do I need to throw you in the 'edge as well?" Bullock glowered menacingly at the boys, who looked shiftily at each other and the waving legs of their stricken leader.

"Or do you prefer a bit of brolly?" grimaced Bella, raising the weapon in threat. One of the lads decided enough was enough, and ran off. The other one seemed too scared to move.

"Stephen's alright," said Tana, approaching the lad. "He just does what Pug tells him."

"Well, I'll tell you what, shall we get Pug out of the hedge, and he can tell Stephen here to stop being a coward? Yes, let's do that, shall we?"

THE HIDE

Bullock yanked Pug roughly out of the hedge, which left him looking like...he'd been dragged through a hedge. His gelled hair was in disarray, his glasses comically wonky and his clothes ripped and ruined. As he staggered to his feet he looked so ludicrous that Tanaga and Stephen started laughing at him.

"I'll be getting my Dad onto you mister. He'll sort you out. And you two are dead. Where's Podger gone?"

"Yeah, I'll be ready to meet your father and tell him what a rotten job he's doing with you, son. And bear in mind - I am Tanaga's GRANDAD. His DAD is seven foot tall and will rip the arms off you *and* your Dad's if he gets wind of you bullying his boy! Now bugger off out of it before I kick your sorry arse all the way down Gilmorton Road."

"Yeah, gitoutofit!!" growled Bella, shaking the bingo brolly at him in fury.

"Come on Steve, let's leave these losers. This is war, this is!" Pug wailed in wounded bravado, but there were too many leaves in his hair to take him seriously.

"Er, nah, I'm going this way, Pug, see you tomorrow," grinned Stephen feebly.

Pug trudged off alone, realizing that being thrown into a hedge by Tana's granddad and then being kicked solidly in the nuts by his victim would be tomorrow's school news. And since he didn't know where his Dad was these days, his was a very hollow threat of revenge. And his drunken mother wouldn't be much use either - or her latest rat-faced boyfriend.

"Do you want to come to Madden's with us, Stephen?" offered Bella, sparking up an Embassy, "Ron's buying. And I won't offer you a fag - it stunts yer growth - as you can see from me!"

They all had a chuckle at this. "Hey," grinned Tana. "Pug is the Hedgepug now! HEDGEPUG!"

THE HIDE

"Yeah, Hedgepug! Haha!" Stephen joined in. "Hey, shall we go to the Pokestop, Tana, it's just over there? I need a Snorlax. "

"Yeah, I want a Blastoise. Nana, Grandpa, see you in the sweetshop! Come on Steve!"

The lads tore off up the road, Bullock and Bella watching fondly as their grandson seemed restored to his former energetic self. The two sextenarian warriors walked arm in arm, soon to become schoolyard legends at Oldside Academy Trust.

Clarendon Marsh Nature Reserve was a busy and popular place - never a day in the calendar passed without visitors to the hides and tea shop, and schoolchildren thronged the Education Centre and dipping ponds in term time. But by night, the woods and pools belonged to the other myriad species - human visits were rare. Rare, but not unknown. Jack Ward would often leave his caravan to prowl around, recognizing nocturnal calls and shapes, occasionally bumping into fellow mortals up to no good or no harm, perhaps spotting owls or vandalising the Iron Age round house.

However on the evening of the full super-moon on December 14th, more human forms than were usual were gathering at the visitors' car park as the light faded well before 4pm, the winter solstice only a week away. The reason for the gathering was the recent sighting of bitterns in the reedbeds, and not just the great bittern, either. Two days previously, the local birding community had been alerted to a not uncommon concern; the owner of *Boptics* and fiddle player for the *Hurdy Grinders*, Arthur Lostweathiel, had gone missing. Usually, he was found wandering around somewhere or sleeping in a tree, and when found was simply taken home, sometimes unwillingly, as he would protest he had "gone walkabout", or in his preferred Cornish dialect, had gone for "a fair old stank."

Bullock and De'Ath had been party to the "gone missing" alerts, and now regular visitors to the marsh, they were taking a stroll during a bright December morning. As they approached the Newlands reedbed, they had been suddenly startled by a violent rustling in the tall *Phragmites* before them. Their reaction had been one of mild alarm.

"Bloody Hell, what's that coming toward us?! If it's an otter, it's a bloody big one!"

"It must be a deer, Ron. Maybe bigger than a muntjac though - do they get the other ones here?"

"Well, whatever it is, I wish I 'ad me gun, Tom. Could be that big black cat that some folk 'as seen? Perhaps summat 'as escaped from Tredley Zoo? That's not uncommon, is it, not with old Hughie Whale still in charge!"

Now wary of a possible escaped gorilla or motley tiger, the men stepped back and crouched as the rustling came nearer and nearer. What emerged onto the path however, was neither ape nor big cat – it was the missing Cornishman.

"Mr. Lostweasel! Everybody's been worried about you, son! Where on Earth have you been, lad?"

It was evident from Lostweathiel's dishevelment that he had been out in the reedbed some considerable time - he was caked in mud onto which many reeds and panicles had adhered.

"Wurgle. I been 'avin a mooch around in the reeds, 'aven't I. Bit cold last night, it was."

De'Ath was incredulous. "What? You have been walking about in the reedbeds? Wasn't the water deep out there?"

"Well, I 'ad a couple o'plunges. Over me 'ead in places. But it were worth it," grinned the addled Cornishman. "I seen a squalous bittern last night. Came and sat on me for a bit, actwally."

"Blimey, a bittern sat on you," said Bullock, impressed. "Did it boom?"

"No, you pilchard! Weren't a reg'lar bittern, though there's a couple o' them out there. I just said, it wa-as the squalid bittern. *Botaurus squalidus.* Them don't boom. They'm make a croakin' noise - like a rusty frog."

De'Ath consulted his *Collins.* "Ah, you must mean the squacco heron - *Ardeola ralloides*, Mr. Lostweathiel. A rare vagrant to Britain, it says here."

"Don't be a daft 'un!" scoffed Lostweathiel. "I done said it. The squalid bittern. *Botaurus squalidus.* First for Britain, I reckon. He is livin' mainly in the wadis of Yemen. And rare even there, 'e be. By God, 'e is an ugly bastard. One o' the ugliest birds on God's Earth. Uglier than the marabou stork. Even uglier than the shoe bill. 'E got a frazzled pink neck, evil eyes, and 'e be as brown as a dog shit."

Bullock thought that Lostweathiel was probably suffering from exposure-driven hallucinations, and ushered the old man up the track.

"I think we'd better be getting you home, Mr. Lostweasel. Er, do you mind sitting on some newspaper in me car - you are a bit on the muddy side."

"Yeah, I best be gettin' 'ome fer a bath I s'pose. But I better be tellin' Mr. Stern about the squalid bittern. He'd be interested, no doubt."

The muddied explorer insisted on being taken to *Boptics*, where after a change of clothes, a quick wash and a mug of tea, he picked up the telephone to call Aldous Stern to report his rare sighting. However, as Bullock and De'Ath were preparing to leave, they noted that the Cornishman had fallen into a sudden slumber, just as Stern had answered the call. They could hear him bellowing, and Bullock picked up the receiver from the sleeping Cornishman's hand.

"Hello? Hello? Who is this, dammit? If this is a sales call from Bombay, then do not call this number again. You are a blessed nuisance and I can't understand what you are trying to say. Hello?"

"Ah, hello, Mr. Stern, this is Ron Bullock, we…"

"Bullock! What do you want? I am at luncheon!"

"Ah, apologies, but actually - we are at *Boptics* with Arthur Lostweasel. He was telephoning you in fact, but he, well, he has just gone to sleep. Me and Tom found 'im on t'Marsh this morning and brought him home."

"Ah, jolly good, well done. He is a worry at times, but he generally turns up. At Clarendon Marsh, you say?"

"Yep, he had been there a couple of days. In the reedbed. He says he saw something called a squalid heron, but I think he…"

"A SQUALID HERON?? It can't be! Impossible! Put Arthur on - immediately!"

Bullock tried to rouse the snoring explorer, but with no success.

"Mr. Stern? No, I can't wake him, I'm afraid. Mr. Stern…? Bloody 'ell, 'e's rung off!"

"I expect he is on his way, Ron. I just looked this squalid heron up on the internet on me phone. It's never been seen in Britain before. Til now. Looks like Clarendon Marsh has a mega-twitch on its hands. I suppose we should wait until Mr. Stern arrives. Let's have a brew, shall we? I think I will go and get some fresh milk though - this stuff in the 'fridge has blue fungus floating about in it."

Aldous Stern had been incredulous to learn from the finally roused Lostweathiel that there was a confirmed squalid heron on Clarendon Marsh. He had firmly instructed all present at *Boptics* to "keep schtumm" until another sighting could be confirmed as he did not want "my reserve to be crawling unnecessarily with bally twitchers". He agreed to Bullock's request to add Colin and Prof. Ball to a "select band" who would study the Marsh in strict confidence and secrecy, and since a bright full super-moon was predicted during the week, they made due and hasty plans.

And so it was that on December 14th, gathered Bullock, De'Ath, Arthur Lostweathiel, Dirty Colin, Professor Ball, David Smith and Jack Ward to receive a breezy briefing from Aldous Stern.

"Right men, I don't trust these mobile telephones, so I am issuing these walkie-talkies so that we can keep in touch. I have fully charged them myself. Ron, Tom, and Colin to the David Smith Hide. Arthur, Ward and Professor Ball to the Christine Thomas Hide. And David and I shall take position in the Andrew Tasker Hide. Any sightings, immediately inform the other teams. And I don't want a word of this out until we have another confirmed sighting of the beast in question. Understood?"

As the light faded and the super-moon began to rise, the party set off into the gloaming. A huge murmuration of starlings swooped over the reedbed, a shape-shifting cloud of wheeling and twisting life energy, at which all marveled as they headed down the darkening path onto the Marsh.

"Right, David and I in here," growled Stern, as they approached the Andrew Tasker Hide. "Just a moment…what the Devil is going on in there?"

A commotion of the intimate kind between man and woman was emanating from within; there was a low continuous grunting sound interspersed by female moans and whelps, and the whole hide was rocking slightly.

Apoplectic, Stern banged fiercely on the door. "This is a nature reserve, not a knocking shop! This hide is being requisitioned for survey purposes so please desist and evacuate with immediate effect!"

From within came giggling and the sound of hurried dressing. Emerging into the twilight came a very tall, gaunt man, his crimped hair held back in a black Alice band, theatrically zipping up his skinny jeans as he descended the wooden steps and beaming broadly. Behind him, hastily wrapping herself into a fake leopard skin fur coat and adjusting her cleavage into a scarlet bra, came a much younger

THE HIDE

woman, her face a well-blushed pink and her red hair in fetching disarray.

"Andi Fox! And Lorna!" squealed Ball. "You were at Tom's bonfire party last year!"

"We were indeed, sir! And Tom, how are you? I didn't know you had taken up birdwatching!"

"I wouldn't mind watching that bird!" Ward whispered laddishly into Bullock's ear as he ran his eyes lasciviously down Lorna's bare milk white legs.

"Ah, Andi, yes, erm…this is our next door neighbour, everyone," replied De'Ath, staring at the ground.

"Well, I don't care who you are, man, and I certainly don't care to know what you two were up to in the Andrew Tasker Hide, but whatever you were doing, I don't wish to hear of its repeat. Are you a member here, sir?"

"Well, erm… not in the strict sense of the word that I pay an annual subscription, but I do take part in the annual census of the glow-worm here and I am something of an expert in amphibians. As well as a highly respected bird watcher, of course."

"And sex-god," added Lorna, shamelessly.

"Ah yes, of course that as well," confirmed Fox with a debauched grin, feigning mortifying embarrassment. "Anyway, what's going on - it looks like you guys are here for some sort of night survey. Can I be of help in any way?"

"No you damned well can't," responded Stern venomously. "And if you are not a fee-paying member of the Trust, you can bugger off and buy your lady friend some decent winter attire. We don't want freeloaders at Clarendon Marsh, Mr. Fox, so clear off!"

Insouciantly, Lorna took Fox's arm and they sauntered off up the path, waving back at the group and giggling.

THE HIDE

Dave Smith had the foresight to inspect the hide before Stern took office, and it was wise that he did so. Discovering a pair of black and pink lacy pants draped over one of the benches, he had little choice but to stuff them in his Barbour pocket. Finding no further evidence of licentious hide-based activity, he settled down to watch for night herons.

The others were dispatched to their hides by Stern and, smoking and joking, they set off for their respective vantage points. Once in position, the three teams checked their walkie-talkie devices.

"This is Mobile 3, over. Dredge calling from the Smith Hide, over. Are you receiving Mobile 1 and 2? Over…" broadcasted Colin, proficiently.

"This is Stern on Mobile 1, over. Receiving you loud and clear, Colin. Over. Mobile 2 are you receiving. Over."

There was a pause over the shortwave airways, awaiting a contribution from Mobile 2.

"Mobile 2 are your receiving. Over?" repeated Stern.

Mobile 2! ARE YOUR RECEIVING!? Over!" shouted Stern.

Finally, there was a crackling sound, apparently emanating from the trio at the Christine Thomas Hide.

"Oooh, does anyone know how to work this? I thought you were meant to press this one? Wurgle. Dunno, John. Wurgle. Oooh, let's try pressing this one. Hello?"

"John, it's Colin, on Mobile 3, over. You need to press the green button to talk. Can you hear me, the green button? Over."

There was a hissing sound from Mobile 2, followed by intermittent contributions from Ball. "Roger, Colin…I….green…doesn't seem to….can…me?"

THE HIDE

"John, you need to keep your finger on the fucking green button! Er, over."

"Mobile 1, Stern here. Less of the language Colin, I thought you had given up that Tourette's nonsense. Over. But yes, John, keep your finger…

"Mobile 2, Mobile 2, John Ball here. Over? Are you receiving Mobile 1 and Mobile 3?"

"Yes, we can hear you Mobile 2. Over," responded Stern and Colin simultaneously.

"Mobile 2, John…….ssssssssssssssss…...in posit… ssssssss…o…."

"FUUUUUUUCK'S SAKE!" bellowed Colin, his finger off the green button. "Sorry, Ron, you are going to have to take over this gadget before me Tourette's *does* come back. I wanna see that squalid heron - that's a big bloomin' lifer that is. Let's get set up. Got some night vision bins which should help us, lads. "

All was silence for a while, as the walkie-talkies hushed and the sky turned deep blue. A voluminous silver moon rose into the sky, silhouetting the bare branches of black poplar and oak.

"Bittern!" called Colin suddenly. "In the sky – look, boys!"

The three followed the silhouette of a short-winged, long necked bird as it flew through the moon before plunging into distant reeds.

"Get in! Did you get him, guys?" exalted Colin. "Oh yeah! That's saved me a nerve-wracking trip to Dungeness next week! Great bittern ticked! You too, Ronno?"

"Aye, got 'im, Col! In the book with 'im!"

"Was that the squalid heron, then, Colin? Is that what we are looking for?" asked De'Ath looking confused.

"No, Tom, that wasn't the squalid, just a great. You won't hear him booming til the spring of course, but we might see him creeping about later on…"

"Mobile 1, Stern, over. Any news?" Bullock responded on behalf of Mobile 3.

"Mobile 3 at The Dave Smith Hide, Bullock here. Over. Just sighted flying overhead a great bittern. No squalid bittern as yet, over."

"Mobile 1, splendid to hear, over. Nothing here. Over."

"sssss….Mob….2…Oooooooh!….boooom….ssssss…."

"For God's sake," groaned Colin, slapping his forehead. "God help us if Bally spots the squalid."

After a few more minutes, the sky turned from navy to velvety black, but the rising moon provided a ghostly light over the windless marsh. All was calm, all was bright.

"Jesus." Colin, peering intently with his night-sight binoculars, began to tremble. "I don't believe it. It's there! It's the squalid. Right on the edge of the reedbed. Jesus. What a beast."

"Christ, that is an ugly bird. Do you have him, Tom?" Bullock nudged De'Ath in the ribs, but the bearded one, wearing an expression of mild terror, evidently had a clear view of the black and foreboding shape creeping slowly across the moonlit shallows.

"Er, yep. I rather wish I didn't. He is the stuff of pure nightmare."

THE HIDE

The Squalid Comes Forth

"Mobile 3, Bullock. Over." whispered Bullock, his finger on the green button. "We have the squalid. Repeat. We have the squalid. Over."

"Mobile 1, Stern. Extraordinary, Ron. We are on our way, over."

"Ssssssss….Oooooooh….Mob…John Ball…squal…."

"John, just get over here, never mind the walkie-talkie. Over and out," sighed Bullock.

Five minutes later, a highly flustered Stern accompanied by the grinning calm of Dave Smith quietly entered The Hide.

THE HIDE

"Where is it?" whispered Stern, getting seated.

"There, Aldous," returned Colin still trembling, as he shakily handed over the night-sights. "Follow my finger…"

"Keep it still man…oh, I have him. Good Lord. It is. It's the squalid. Do you have him, David?"

"Yep, that's the squalid alright. Look at that horrible bill. Even the way it moves is revolting. Giving me the shivers, it is."

Ball then burst into The Hide, followed by Ward. Lostweathiel was apparently some way behind.

"Oooh, where's the birdy, where's the birdy!" Ball exclaimed in great and palpable excitement.

"Hush, man, for Heaven's sake!" hissed Stern. "He's over there - silhouetted against the moon. You can't miss him!"

"Oh ye-es! He is absolutely horrible, isn't he!"

For some minutes, the men watched in silent awe, as the terrible bird mauled along the edge of the reedbed, getting ever closer to The Hide. Behind them, the door squealed slowly open; assuming it was Lostweathiel, nobody turned around.

"Congratulations, Arthur. The first UK sighting of *Botaurus squalidus* is yours and confirmed," whispered Stern, still trained on the bird, which was now only 20 yards from The Hide. But it wasn't Lostweathiel that took a place at the trestle benches and trained his binoculars on the wading heron. It was Andi Fox.

"Well, well, well, gentlemen. A squalid heron, as I live and breathe. What an abomination of a bird it is. Uglier than the marabou stork and shoe bill spliced together in some horrible mutation." Fox put down his field glasses and tapped a message into a device on his lap.

"What the Devil are you doing here, man!" thundered Stern and rising to his feet. "You have a nerve following us…this is top secret

THE HIDE

intelligence work!"

"Why?" protested Fox. "Is it spying for the Russians or something?"

"As you may know, this is a very considerable rarity, sir. We are here to validate Mr. Lostweathiel's sighting of two days ago, before the place is besieged by ruffian twitchers - like you! I want to be quite prepared for that influx, so this news will not be broadcast until AFTER I have convened an emergency meeting tomorrow morning both with the Oldnact directors and the Volunteer Group Committee. We will need to be providing wardening and patrol facilities and..."

"Erm, oh, ah...silly old me," grinned Fox, slightly nervously. "I erm, just posted on Bird Alert...er..."

"YOU HAVE WHAT!" bellowed Stern. The squalid bittern looked up with its evil eyes at the slots above it and stopped ripping frogs limb from limb, listening intently as it tilted its hideous head.

"You have what?" repeated Stern, this time in an aggressive whisper.

"Yeah, I erm, sorry, haha, didn't realise that there was any secrecy, I mean usually when you see a rare bird you want to alert the country... well, it's sort of a duty really. And of course something of a coup to be the person that does so. Little old me, in this case!"

"Oh cobblers, Andi, you know what this means don't you?" moaned Colin. "If it's on Alert you can bet that Sonny Robards will be straight in his car and on his way, even if he is on crutches. He only lives in Leicester...I thought just for once I could grip him off with this 'un, at least til the end of the year. There's only a couple of ticks between us for the Year List!"

"Ah, OK Colin, I get that, but it doesn't seem right to keep it a secret..."

"Oh shut up, boy, and bugger off out of it! You are not even a blessed member. And your hair is ridiculous."

"Right, erm well...I will be on my way, got a Christmas gig to get to, ah…well, as George Michael would say, ahem…" Mr. Fox broke into a whispering falsetto warble: "*Once <u>bittern</u> and twice shy, I keep my distance but you still catch my eye*! Merry Christmas, everyone!"

With that, he bounded off into the night, tossing his crimpy fringe and grinning maniacally.

"The cheek of the man!" growled an outraged Stern. "But where is Arthur? I thought that was him coming in, not that…fop!"

"Oooh, I thought he was behind us!" exclaimed Ball in concern. Wasn't he with you, Jack?"

"Nah, he stopped for a jimmy riddle…"

"Well, we'd better go and find him. Oh, confound it all, damn that non-fee paying popinjay letting the cat out of the bag, as it were. We'll have to draw up emergency plans, gentlemen, someone will have to stay through the night and after that there will be round-the-clock shift duty. Right, David, come with me to find Arthur, the rest of you stay here and keep your eyes glued on the squalid."

The bittern was still eyeing up The Hide, suspicious of the movement and clumping noises coming from within. It began to feel that it might be wise to move into some cover, and

swaggered off into the reeds to find some ducks to spike with its lethal bill.

"Ah, it's moved into the reeds just over there," noted Colin following the menacing steps of the retreating heron. "Can't see it now. I bet you that Robards will be here within the hour. Sounds crap of me, I know, but I 'ope he don't see it."

Bullock had an idea enter his head, a mischievous one. What if he scared the rare heron away - just as Robards had been known to do at other twitches! Why not? Robards deserved to be gripped off by Colin, and for that matter, by himself and Tom. And Arthur had already seen it - at extremely close quarters.

THE HIDE

"Erm, just popping out to watter the marsh, lads. All this excitement has gone to me bladder."

Once outside, Bullock collected a few stones and circled around the back of The Hide to the patch of reed where the squalid bittern had taken refuge. He lobbed a few stones, hearing them plop into the water. He watched and listened. Nothing seemed to move. Nestling in the reed fringe, half buried in mud, was a half brick - he decided to use heavier artillery.

Inside The Hide, Ball was chattering merrily, and decided that Humphrey needed an outing, much to Ward's chagrin.

"Don't touch me, Humphrey, or I'll feed you to the squalid. Looks like he could swallow you down in one!"

"Oh, nasty Jack! Humphrey doesn't want to be fed to the squalid!"

"Well, find him somewhere to hibernate then, and then we'll all be happy!"

"Will you two shut up, I think I saw the squalid move again." Colin trained his night-sites into the reeds, and Ball and Ward joined him in his search. De'Ath saw a mallard peeping out of the reeds on the other side of the scrape, and thinking that rather cuter than the squalid, decided to shift his attention. There was something about the sight of *Botaurus squalidus* that had made him feel queasy and his beard itch.

Outside, Bullock noticed a slight rustle in the reeds in front of him, and lobbed the half-brick in an arc in its general direction. Instead of the sploosh of water he had expected, there was a sickening crunching sound, followed by a dreadful, guttural, agonised croak.

Bullock knew immediately what he had done. He rushed in panic back into The Hide, to find his four comrades staring at the black moonlit water in collective consternation.

"What the Hell was that noise?!" uttered Colin in alarm. "I knew they croaked, but my God, I can see why they call them the Devil's heron in Yemen!"

THE HIDE

"Er, I think I hit the squalid with a brick, lads!" confessed Bullock, his face perspiring despite the cold of the evening.

"What?! You chucked a brick at the squalid? Was it attacking you?" Colin turned around to see if Bullock was playing one of his jokes, and had made the noise himself, somehow. It was immediately evident from Bullock's shocked face, that it wasn't a prank.

"Oooh. Something is floating out of the reeds! It looks like the squalid! Poor squalid!"

Professor Ball was pointing to a bedraggled object which floated hideously in front of The Hide, glinting darkly in the moonlight, like a huge lump of anthracite coal. The open eyes of the dead heron stared up at them in menacing accusation.

"Ahhh nooooo!" Bullock coverered his face in anguish. "I am the Ancient Mariner! I killed the squalid bittern! I was trying to flush it out - so Sonny Robards couldn't twitch it, Col!"

Colin was moved that anyone would support his cause in such a brotherly (yet violent) manner.

"Ron! I never…well…this is all my fault for being an obsessive twitcher! It's karma! It's payback time! I killed that bird, not you. I am the Ancient Mariner!" He rose to pat the slumped back of Bullock, who held his large head in his bucket hands, much as he had after scoring a duck in his recent cricketing comeback.

De'Ath also rose to his feet, assuming a noble pose. "My friends, we are the birding musketeers. All for one…and one for all," he said solemnly. "I am also the Ancient Mariner. Je Suis Charlie."

Jack Ward rolled up a cigarette and popped it in his mouth.

"Well, I'll be d'Artagnan, then. Bugger it, I am the Ancient Mariner too. But not Charlie."

All eyes turned to Professor Ball, the remaining man in The Hide, who was fiddling about with Humphrey again, clearing his throat noisily several times before he spoke.

"Yes, poor squalid. The first one ever to visit these islands. Smacked on the head with a brick. Well now, The Wildlife and Countryside Act of 1981 is the primary legislation which protects birds, and the key word is to 'intentionally kill' and Ron wasn't doing that were you, Ron?"

"No Prof, certainly not. But it was a bloody stupid thing to do. Really, bloody…stupid."

"Ah then," continued Ball, in his studious mode. "Then we come to "recklessly disturb any wild bird", which you probably did - BUT that only refers to birds building or actually on a nest, which poor squalid wasn't. So…I don't see that you could be charged and fined £5,000, and/or be given six months' imprisonment, Ron."

"Just now, Prof, that is of little consolation to me. I think they *should* bang me up for six months!"

"Well, here is another way of looking at it," said Jack thoughtfully, lighting up his cigarette and blowing a blue plume of smoke out of the window flap before him and into the night. "Suppose that Ron lobbed that brick, and just as he 'intentionally' meant to do, old squalid was so pissed off that he flew off straight back to Yemen? Come to think of it, I think I did see old squalid flying off south, if I am not mistaken? And I reckon I could drag that there corpse out of the water and see to it that it ain't discovered? Well, there's five good men in the Dave Smith Hide that know that story ain't exactly true – and those good five fellers would need to keep their mouths shut. But I would say, in my own judgment, that little white lie saves everyone a great deal of trouble. You might call it "honourable secrecy" as they used to say in British intelligence circles. What say you, gentlemen? We have little time to decide. Are you joining the musketeers, Prof?"

"Erm…do you mind if I ask Humphrey first?"

THE HIDE

"Asking Humphrey"

Perhaps because of the tension and the absurdity of their situation, laughter broke out among them all.

"Erm, if I said no…I suppose that you could also kill me and Humphrey, hide our bodies in the swamp, and tell everyone we'd gone to Yemen too! Heehee!"

"Well, tempting though that is, John," responded Ward with a grin, "I think we would all come quietly. I reckon if we told old Aldous, he wouldn't want the story out so he'd just have to give us all a massive ticking off. In a way, we'd be doing Aldous a favour too by keeping quiet about the erm, murder. Well, birdslaughter, not murder. "

"Yep, I think in this case, you are right, Jack. OK. I will join the conspiracy. But only on two conditions. One, that Ron never chucks bricks at birdies again, even to flush them out. And two. On every evening on of December 14th - we five return here to commemorate - The Squalid Bittern Plot!"

"Agreed!" was the call of the four. "All for one…and one for all!"

"Shit, I can hear voices - it's Aldous and the guys!" hissed Ward. "OK, I just have time to nip out and drag that bird out, but you'll have to close all the flaps and cover for me. Buy me some time - scramble!"

Jack Ward darted out of The Hide and as fast as he could, fetched the punting pole from the boat in which he had rescued Colin after the near-destruction of The Hide earlier in the year, and found an old sack from the bottom of the boat. Colin and De'Ath slammed shut the window flaps, and they took their positions centre-stage, all suddenly assiduously studying by Colin's torchlight a thick tome entitled *Herons, Egrets and Bitterns of Arabia* by FR Spoon.

Aldous had returned with the vagrant Cornishman and Dave Smith, eager to see the horrible heron again. He was immediately surprised that no watchmen were at their posts, and furthermore that the windows of The Hide were closed up! The four appeared to be in loud debate about the taxonomy of bitterns, especially Professor Ball, who was at full volume.

"Yes, I am with you Colin. The American bittern is hardly a separate species to *Botaurus stellaris,* to my mind it must be a sub-species, because…ah Arthur, we wondered where you had got to! David, you look frozen, erm, what do you think about the American bittern? Aldous, how nice to see you again!"

Aldous narrowed his eyes, suspiciously. "Who has been smoking in here? And why are the windows closed?"

From beyond the closed flaps came a sloshing sound and Stern leaned over to open one of the flaps to investigate. Thinking that he was now probably on stage in an amateur production of a farce by Brian Rix, and he had to prevent a returning wife from looking in the wardrobe to discover his lover, Bullock leapt like a salmon to bar Stern's way.

"Oh, you don't want to do that, Mr. Stern. It got terrible cold in 'ere after you left, so we thought we'd generate a bit o' body heat like, just for a bit, you know."

"What? Close the windows? What about your vigil on the squalid? Have you deserted your posts?!"

"Oh, the squalid flew off, Aldous," Colin said matter-of-factly, inspecting his grubby nails. "Just after you left. Must've been the sound of you arguing with Andi Fox, I reckon."

"Flew off? It was showing clearly when we left!"

"Yep, just flew off south, Mr. Stern. Looked like it was leaving the reserve to me. We followed it until it was a dot in the sky!" added De'Ath lying unconvincingly, and causing Stern's eyes to narrow yet further.

"I shall scan for myself. Get out of my way, Bullock. I am surprised at a tough like you, fearing a little cold." Bullock retreated from the window flaps as slowly as does a substituted football player called from the pitch when his team is leading in

the dying minutes of a game. Stern sat down and reached up to open up one of the flaps.

"Ooooh, let me and Humphrey help you with that, Aldous! Humphrey is good at opening flaps, aren't you, Humphrey! " Ball and Humphrey sprang into action, blocking the window and Stern's attempt to open it. Then Humphrey jumped onto Stern's head, and ran down his back.

"Professor, unhand me with that puppet, what in God's name is going on?! I think you men have gone doolally tap out here! Get out of my way, confound you all!"

Finally, a ruffled Aldous Stern managed to open up a window flap, and then another, and another. Ahead of him, a smooth black pool reflecting the white disc of the moon. Nothing more.

Relieved that Part 1 of the plot was complete, the conspirators joined Stern and Smith in silently scanning the ever-darkening fringes of the

THE HIDE

pool, the moon casting long reedy shadows which rippled slightly in a northerly breeze. Eventually, Stern spoke again.

"Arthur, I am so sorry you haven't seen the squalid again! Really, it was showing so well - and so close to the Hide!"

"Not bothered, Ald. You wanna 'ave one sit on yer chest, boy! 'Tis a spectacle terr-bule to be-old! Wurgle." With that, Lostweathel slumped over on the ledge and went to sleep, his head upon his arms.

Dave Smith offered everyone coffee from his flask which all gratefully accepted, along with a shared packet of *HobNobs*.

"Do you know, Dave, these were the very biscuits that led us to take up bird watching!" chomped De'Ath. "Ron's dog ate practically a whole packet, was banished to the garden, and brought us back a baby song thrush!"

"Well in that case, *HobNobs* have a lot to answer for!" responded Stern, with a hint of good humoured irony.

Just then, the door of The Hide burst open. A desperate-looking fellow stomped in on crutches, wearing a leg plaster underneath a pair of voluminous striped pyjama bottoms. Under his black ulster overcoat he wore a white vest from which sprouted copious black chest hair, in which nestled a large golden medallion formed into the initials 'SR'.

"Sonny Robards. Well, well, well." Colin stood up to size up his opponent, like a boxer at a press conference.

"Where is it? Where is the squalid?" Robards demanded.

"Sorry, Robards. It was showing brilliantly not 30 minutes ago. Then it flew off. Headed south."

"You what? Don't give me that shit, Dredge. I busted three red lights and two speed cameras to get here! It was only posted on Bird Alert an hour ago! You've gone and chased it off, you greedy sod!"

"What - like you would have done? Sorry, I wouldn't stoop so low.

THE HIDE

HobNob?"

"No I don't want a fucking HobNob, I want the squalid!" screeched Robards like a spoiled child, waking Lostweathiel from his slumbers. The Cornishman got up, and simply kicked Robards on his plastered leg with his ancient leather walking boot, the toe of which had aged as hard as iron.

"AAAAAEEEIIIII! Me leg!! What you do that for, you Cornish mentalist?!"

"You 'ad that comin' ye morgee dogfish! And you know plain well why. Now pish off. Squalid ain't 'ere. Gorn it 'as."

"I will do no such thing! I don't believe any of you. 'Specially not you, Dredge. I will sit here until dawn, if I need to! I am not passing up a lifer and getting gripped off by you lot!"

"Suit yourself!" barked Stern, "but I shall be placing a sign in the car park to say that the squalid heron has very likely left the stage. And Colin, you'd better do the same on that dratted Bird Alert thing. And then, I am going home to my wife and my bed!"

Perhaps if it hadn't been Sonny Robards, the Squalid Four might have felt guilty about abandoning him to a fruitless night of gazing at nothing in the clammy cold – but for him, it seemed their shame made an exception, and all the party exited The Hide, leaving Robards resolutely staring into space with his infra-red binoculars.

Having put up a sign in the car park reading "SQUALID HERON DEPARTED SOUTH", Stern, Lostweathiel and Smith drove away into the night. When their headlights had reached the main road, emerging from the shadows of the car park came Ward, a damp sack upon his back.

"Care for a nightcap, gentlemen?"

Cramped into Ward's caravan, and fortified by tumblers of Laphroaig, the conspirators watched on grimly as Jack stoked up his wood burner, until the flames illuminated the faces of Bullock, De'Ath, Ball and

Dredge in dancing yellow. They all watched in solemn silence as the flames rose.

When Jack considered the burner hot enough, he opened up the door of the burner, and rose to his feet with the dreadful damp sack.

"I dunno abayt this, lads," he frowned. "Don't seem right. Chucking the first UK recorded squalid bittern on the fire. Let's 'ave a look at 'im at least, before 'e goes on."
He tipped the contents of the sack onto the floor and with a dull thud, the bedraggled heron emerged in a crumpled mess of greasy feathers. The gathering gasped as Jack splayed out the wings and frazzled pink neck, and the squalid once more fixed them with an accusing stare from its hateful black eyes which froze all five men to their very marrow.

"Christ, I wish you hadn't done that Jack," muttered Colin, taking down a strong draught of whisky, "I feel like the damned thing is cursing me!"

"It's me it's cursing, Colin - the man who killed the squalidus," quavered the usually fearless Bullock.

"Oh, it's eeeeeeevil!" grinned Ball. "Just look at its hooked talon – and bill – sharp as a dagger!"

Jack sat down again and they sat once more in silence, gazes forlornly fixed on the terrible form at their feet. At length, Jack spoke again.

"I got another idea, guys. How about this. Tomorrow, as it were, I was doing my usual rounds on the reserve and I was to find a dead bird in the reeds. It wouldn't be very unusual, would it? It's just that the dead bird in question would be a super-rarity to these shores. This dark feller, in fact. And I might say to meself, "I will take this to the man who first witnessed it, Arthur Lostweathiel. And Arthur, no doubt, would take it straight to Leonard Bristow to be stuffed. Then, the squalid could gaze down from the walls of *Boptics* for all to see. What think you, musketeers?"

"Ooooh! Yes, it would be a bit like the 'Hastings Rarities Affair' that

Leonard's great grand-father was involved in! Except *this* one is a genuine UK visitor!" grinned Ball gleefully.

"I'm not so sure, Jack," frowned Bullock. "The evidence would still be there, wouldn't it - Bally told me they copped onto the Hastings business after they analysed one o' the stuffed birds years later and found the skin 'ad been cured in China, or somewhere. What if some forensic expert of the future examines the bird and links it all back to me? Shame on the family name forever!"

"Well, they mount the skin and feathers, Ron, there'd be no trace of 'is bashed in skull." Ward put his hand onto the birds head, feeling the crushed skull under the undamaged feathers. "Anyway, who's to say how it died. I might 'ave put me boot on it's skull before I saw it was there. No, the only way this gets out is if one of us blabs it."

"I say give it to Arthur." De'Ath spoke with conviction. "We five will keep our secret, and Arthur will get his reward. He has been generous enough to us with his opticals."

"I am with you, Tom," said Colin. "At least we'd always be able to see the bird again. There may never be another!"

"Then that's three of us," grunted Ward. "Ron?"

Bullock thought for a while, wondering if he could stand to see the squalid staring down at him from the walls of *Boptics*. But perhaps, after all, it is precisely what I deserve, he mused.

"Aye. I'm in. Stuff it!"

"Bally?" asked Ward. "Do you want to consult Sir Humphrey again?"

With a broad grin, Sir Humphrey was produced from Ball's pocket. The hedgehog began to slowly and solemnly nod. This broke the tension, laughter abounded and glasses were re-filled.

And so it was agreed. The Clarendon Five drank a final toast to conspiratorial solidarity, and with the hour approaching eleven, Ward's visitors took their leave and returned to the cheery Christmas lights of

THE HIDE

Oldside.

The following day, Ward took the corpse to *Boptics*. It was difficult to know when Arthur Lostweathiel was delighted, since his features were long weathered and salted into a permanent quizzical grimace, but the upward movement on one eyebrow and the corner of his mouth suggested that he might not be displeased. Ward obstinately refused the large wad of cash offered to him from the till, telling the Cornishman that a good bottle of malt would be repayment enough. Lostweathiel took the bird the same day to the taxidermist's shop on the edge of town, and Leonard Bristow promised that he would have it mounted and cased by the end of the month, as he only allowed himself holiday on Christmas Day, just like the Victorian clerk he resembled.

Spurred on by gripping off the hapless Sonny Robards, whose fruitless and freezing night in The Hide left him with a severe cold and even further incapacitated, Colin roared on with his twitching in the final two weeks of the year as Christmas approached.

He was rarely to be seen in Oldside and at Clarendon Marsh, but when his mobile rang one morning just as he was once more heading for the East coast, he saw that it was Bullock, and answered.

"Colin, a marvelous thing is happening in my back garden! You must come over! The redwings have come!"

"How splendid, Ron! OK, I'll drop over for a coffee. I can't stay long though!"

Pulling up at The Nook, Bella greeted Colin at the rattling iron door of the porch.

"Come in, love, they are in the back. There's a load of thrushes with red wings eating all the berries. The poor blackbirds don't know what's hit them!"

THE HIDE

"I see! I won't stop long, Bella…but let's see what is going on out there!"

Seated in warm clothing with mugs of coffee at the patio table, Bullock and De'Ath were glued to the frantic activity taking place at a rowan tree heavy with red berries. A flock of twenty thrushes with distinctive red patches under their wings were busy stripping every single berry from the tree. De'Ath was unsuccessfully attempting to photograph the birds with a camera which lacked a long enough lens, and he had taken lots of photos consisting of brown and red blurs.

"Alright lads, you've got a good flock o' redwings going on there – they probably come to your garden every year, though you didn't notice 'em before you became birders. Eh up, you've got a fieldfare up there as well, look! Look the grey-headed fat one at the back of the tree..."

"Oh yeah! Well done, Col, another *Observer's* tick for me! It was worth you comin' round, we should've spotted that farefielder, Tom."

"Well, I feel sorry for the blackbirds," said Bella. "These robbers swooping in and stealin' their berries."

"Ah don't worry about them, they'll be alright Bella. These red fellers have flown all the way from the frozen north so you can't begrudge 'em a berry or ten. You might even get the waxwings, Ron, if you are lucky!"

"Oh that would be good, I love them waxy boys, I do. Anyway, which unremarkable brown bird are you off to tick off today then, Col?"

"Haha, little bunting, Ron, and an outside chance of isabelline wheatear. And yeah, they are pretty brown - the isabelline isn't as pretty as your regular wheatear, actually. Still, two more ticks in the box eh? With old Robards laid up, I should be home and dry by New Year's Eve. Right, enjoy the thrushes, chaps and thanks for the coffee, Bella. The house looks very festive, lovely, it is. Are you expecting many for Christmas lunch?"

THE HIDE

"Oh yeah, full house as always, Colin. You be careful on the road, it will get icy this next few days."

"Eh, Col," said Bullock, "why don't you join us on New Year's Eve? We are 'avin a little supper 'ere with Tom and Dot and our mate Colonel Sykes – we are roastin' the game I shot up north in the autumn."

"Well that's kind of you, Ron, and I must say it would be nice to celebrate with you if I do end up topping the List this year. I will let you know - I am twitching up to the wire so I wouldn't be surprised if I am away that day, but if I can get back, I will join you! Oh, by the way, there's otters to be seen at the Carlton Hide at Clarendon if you are interested. Showing well in the day, they are."

"Otters! Right, I will take my Dot to see them," beamed De'Ath. "She loves otters! What about you, Ron?"

"Don't be daft, Tom. There's no ticks for a bloody otter. See you soon, Col, let me know how you get on."

With that, Colin took his leave, and as Bella had threatened, it was time for her and Bullock to go into battle and undertake the Christmas shopping.

Christmas came and Christmas went, the Bullock family enjoying a rumbustious family affair, whilst Dot and Tom dined happily and peacefully alone.

On the last day of the year of birding, Bella was scurrying around her kitchen roasting game birds, preparing for a New Year's Eve supper with the De'Aths and Colonel Sykes. Bullock had announced that evening attire was expected, and as Bella struggled to attach his bow tie round his wing collar, she still in her dressing gown and curlers, the doorbell rang, much to her muttering annoyance.

THE HIDE

"It'll be Dot and Tom – why are they always early? Did you not tell them eight o' clock, Ron?"

"Yep. But don't matter, love, I will look after 'em whilst you get your frock on. By gum, I look good in a dinner jacket. I am James Bond."

Bullock plodded downstairs, where Basker too had made an effort and was wearing a bow-tie round his collar. He was unable to stop continuously drooling however, due to the delicious smells wafting from the oven.

"Evening all! Great to see you, Dot, you look lovely - ooh a tiara, we weren't expecting royalty!"

"Hello Ron, well it was left over from our nice Murder Mystery Evening so I thought I would give it another airing. And you do look smart! Gosh, it suits you that bow tie. You look like an extremely formidable doorman. Are we on the guest list?"

"Doorman?" laughed Bullock. "I am James Bond, I am, Dot. Oh, bloody Hell, Tom. What the Devil is that you are wearing, I told you to dress up!"

De'Ath, much to his own merriment and apparently that of his wife as well, was wearing a black dinner jacket T-shirt featuring a screen-printed bow tie and breast-pocket handkerchief.

"Isn't it a hoot, Ron," laughed Dot gaily, slipping out of her coat and throwing Bullock her black boa.

"Bloody hilarious," grimaced Ron, rolling his eyes at his mate, who responded by punching the air in glee.

"My, something smells absolutely delicious in the kitchen, and OOOH! Basky, look at you with your bow tie. How smart you look!"

"At least the dog made an effort, Dot. Wait 'til The General arrives – he'll probably be wearing a cravat or summat! Now, what can I get you both to drink?"

THE HIDE

At eight sharp, Colonel Sykes arrived, looking immaculate in a fawn cashmere overcoat over his cummerbunded dinner suit. The General wore a sleek bow-tie and gave everyone his toothy grin and a furious tail-wag before settling into his usual composure. Basker was as ever delighted to receive his company, and gave him a drooling lick on his nose.

"Good grub tonight, General. There's giblets a-plenty for us!"

"Splendid! I hope the New Year fireworks won't upset you, old thing. Shouldn't be as bad as Bonfire Night."

Bella descend the stairs regally in a chrysanthemum print black dress, and greeted her guests warmly.

"Oh, love that dress, Bella! Where did you get it?"

"Marks - twenty quid, not bad, eh? Now I hope you all have a drink, please all be seated whilst I finish off the dinner. Ron, get the red wine open and dogs - come with me to the kitchen!"

The dogs were not disappointed with their gravy-laden bowls of offal and off-cuts and neither less were the human guests, who supped royally on woodcock and grouse served with several bottles of Châteauneuf-du-Pape.

Slurring slightly, Sykes declared it the best meal he had ever eaten, and regaled the company with faintly salacious army songs, which The General was able to embroider with chorus howls.

As midnight approached, the telephone rang.

"Is that Geoffrey calling from Italy?" enquired Bella, half way through an *After Eight* mint. "Bit early to wish us Happy New Year isn't it? Ron, you get it, love. Tell him he's too early - ooh hang on, it's an hour later there, isn't it?"

"Hello? Oh, it's not Geoffrey! It's Colin! Where are you lad? You are where? At Leicester Forest Service Station? Oh, you'll not make it for

THE HIDE

midnight then? Have you? 333? Oh that's brilliant, mate well done, you! 'Ang on, I'll just tell Tom...it's Colin Tom! He's done it - 333 birds for the year finishing with a girtled snipe in Hereford. Birder of the Year, he is! Eh, Col, we are all gonna raise a toast to you here..listen...raise your glasses everyone – "To King Col, The Champion!" KING COL! Did y'ear that mate? Yes, you go 'ome and 'ave a good rest. That's it, give them snakes an extra rat, or whatever they like to eat. Aye mate. Aye. No, it's been our pleasure, really. It has. It has. Reet, well, I'd best get ready to do me first-footing. Aye, I go out the back and come in the front wi' a loaf o'bread and a bit o'coal. All the best to you, son. You are The Man! Aye, 'appy New Year, Col. Happy New Year. Tek care, aye. Same to you, lad. Aye. See you next year!"

"Well done, Colin, he watches 'em and I shoot 'em! Eh Ron?" guffawed Sykes. "I say, FOR HE'S A JOLLY GOOD FELLOW? FOR HE'S A JOLLY GOOD FELLOW...come on, everyone join in..."

"THAT NOBODY CAN DENYYYYYYYYY!!!"

After Ron had performed his first-footing duties, a bottle of champagne was cracked open, and *Auld Lang Syne* enthusiastically rendered by the hand-holding ring which included the two dogs. After another toast to "Colin - the King of the Birders", followed a game of Monopoly, which Skyes won handsomely, largely due to his ownership of all four railway stations and astute housing development on the Orange ones.

At 2am, the party ended, The General leading a wobbly Sykes down the path accompanied by Dot and De'Ath. Bella, a happy hostess, clambered heavily up the stairs, leaving Bullock as ever to lock up and switch off the lights.

As he grinned at the glimmering Christmas tree and tossed down a final brandy, he reflected on an adventure-packed year. Patting the *Observers Book of Birds*, he mounted the familiar stairs for the last time that year, brushed his teeth, put on his pyjamas and snuggled up to Bella, who was already snoring like a warthog.

THE HIDE

Postscript

Opening his bedroom curtains on the first grey morning of the New Year, Bullock was feeling rather worse for wear. He burped repeatedly as he inspected his bleary, glowing face in the dressing table mirror. Addressing the crumpled form of his wife as she lay groaning and wrapped like a chrysalis in a *Tony the Tiger* duvet, he pulled on a pair of tracksuit pants.

"Happy New Year, my sweetness! Good night last night, weren't it!"

"Bugger off and make us a cuppa. And feed the dog."

With a shrug, Bullock went downstairs, carelessly tugged open the living room curtains and yanked open the kitchen door to find Basker in his basket lying on his back with his legs splayed comically in the air.

"Morning Basky, lad! Happy New Year!" He footled the dog's long ears affectionately, and poured some kibbles into a metal bowl. Basker decided he wasn't ready for getting up yet and went back to sleep with a loud "Haruummph!" through his jowly muzzle.

Bullock filled the kettle and turned on the transistor radio, then went out of the back door onto the patio in his vest for a breath of New Year air and a good stretch. He noted with satisfaction the long-tailed, blue and great tits swooping around the bird table, and a robin nodded its greetings.

In the kitchen, the sound of the boiling kettle obscured the 9am news bulletin on Radio Oldside.

"An Oldshire man has been found dead at his home early this morning after making a 999 call to report that he had been bitten by a deadly green mamba snake that he was apparently keeping as a pet in his vivarium. Medics arriving at the scene with anti-venom were too late to save the man, named as Colin Dredge, a well-known local

THE HIDE

ornithologist. Experts say the bite of the green mamba can be fatal in as little as thirty minutes. And now the weather for New Year's Day; after a cloudy start it will brighten up in most places, with the threat of the occasional shower of rain or sleet in the east of the county. That's the weather, now back to Zany Ed!

Thanks Miranda, and now a hit from 1981, made it to number 2 in the Hit Parade, it's The Tweets aaaaaaaand...The Birdie Song!..."

Returning from the chilly back garden, Ron was delighted to make the tea in time to *The Birdie Song,* variously holding his hands in his armpits waving his wings; opening and closing his fingers in a beak shape, and wiggling his voluminous bottom as he carousel-ed around the kitchen.

"Come on Basky, get up - it's a brand new year, boy! *"It's a little bit of this, and a little bit of that, der-der-der-der- da-da-da-da*!"

Mounting the stairs with two over-filled tea mugs and feeling far from coordinated, he caught his slipper in a loose stair rod and hot tea sloshed down the front of his jogging pants.

"Oh, damn and blast it! There's a good way to start the New Year off… scalded meat and two veg…Bella!…come and tek these bloody cups off me!"

His disheveled wife leaned over the banister, bearing a telephone receiver and a grim face.

"Never mind yer soggy bottoms - it's Tom on the 'phone. Colin's green mamba has got out of its tank and bit 'im to death! I told 'im, didn't I?! Keeping deadly snakes in the house - it's playin' with fire, that's what it is!"

"What?! Col's dead?!! I cannot believe it! Really! The daft auld prat. Who will tek me to see the golden oriole now, then?!"

Bullock sat down in a tea puddle on the stair carpet in shock, feeling an unpleasant warmth soaking into his Y-fronts, whilst contemplating the dreadful vicissitudes of human life. His thoughts turned

THE HIDE

uncharacteristically gothic - perhaps, after all, the curse of the squalid heron was upon them?

But his guilty brooding was summarily interrupted - Bella had lit up an Embassy and was determinedly squirting both stairs and husband with *Dr. Beckmann Carpet Stain Remover*.

At precisely the same time, across town in *Boptics,* Arthur Lostweathiel was mounting a rickety step-ladder in his carpet slippers, armed with a hammer and a rusty nail. Huffing and puffing as the ladder squeaked and rattled, the Cornishman gingerly tapped the nail into the loose and crumbling plaster above his desk.

He descended, to regard with satisfaction the large glass case delivered to him by Leonard Bristow the previous day. Bristow had done a magnificent job. The squalid heron, as if revived, stalked a swathe of reeds with a mutilated eel in its talons; the eyes bright with evil intent, the sharp bill slightly open to lend an expression of malign cruelty. Lifting the weighty case, Lostweathiel staggered and wobbled up the ladder and after much effort, located the nail into the brass D-ring on the back of the display cabinet. He descended to gaze up at the squalid, a veritable horror to behold. Satisfied with his work, he packed up the ladder, made a cup of tea, and sat down at his desk, directly beneath his nightmarish display.

An articulated lorry, its driver furious to be working on New Year's Day, thundered down the High Street, rumbling and vibrating the walls and floors of the buildings and shops near to the road, including *Boptics*. The single nail carrying the considerable weight of the squalid heron's case directly above Arthur Lostweathiel's fluffy head juddered and shifted. Flakes of soft plaster fluttered down, like snow on a January marsh.

www.ingramcontent.com/pod-product-compliance
Lightning Source LLC
Chambersburg PA
CBHW071649090426
42738CB00009B/1471